CONFIRMED
KILL

CONFIRMED KILL

Heroic Sniper Stories
from the Jungles of Vietnam
to the Mountains of Afghanistan

Nigel Cawthorne

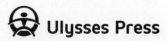 Ulysses Press

Published in the United States by
ULYSSES PRESS
P.O. Box 3440
Berkeley, CA 94703
www.ulyssespress.com

ISBN13: 978-1-61243-023-2
Library of Congress Catalog Number: 2011934775

Printed in the United States by Bang Printing

10 9 8 7 6 5 4 3 2 1

Acquisitions: Keith Riegert
Managing Editor: Claire Chun
Editors: Richard Harris, Lauren Harrison
Proofreader: Barbara Schultz
Production: Abigail Reser, Judith Metzener
Cover design: what!design @ whatweb.com
Front cover photo: © vesilvio/istockphoto.com
Back cover photos: left U.S. Army photo by SSgt. Gary A. Witte *(U.S.
Army Pfc. Claudio J. Wilson of the 327th Infantry Regiment scans a ridge-
line in Afghanistan's Kunar Province as mortar shells rain down against an
enemy sniper)*; right U.S. Army photo by Sgt. Michael J. MacLeod
*(U.S. Army Pvt. 1st Class Justin Vandersanden and Staff Sgt. Waylon
Coats of the 82nd Airborne Division provide added security for a combined
U.S. Iraqi medical engagement in Kubaysah, Iraq.)*

Distributed by Publishers Group West

Contents

Introduction

Not all those who fall to snipers' bullets are considered confirmed kills. To get a confirmed kill, the body must be examined to make sure the enemy is dead, then it is searched for weapons, maps, and other documents. Traditionally, the sniper had to fill out a "kill sheet." This carried the name of the sniper and his spotter, if he had one with him; the date and time of the kill; the number of the rifle and the scope the sniper used; the map coordinates of the incident or where the body or bodies were left; and the number of enemy engaged during the incident, their direction of travel, and details of the weapons they were carrying. Details of the deceased were also included, giving their sex and approximate age. The skin, eyes, teeth, and fingernails were checked for signs of malnutrition or disease. The state of their uniform and equipment was noted, along with any food they may have been carrying. The sheet then had to be signed by the highest ranking officer present. It was rare for the bodies to be brought back to an American base for burial. Usually they were left where they lay. If there was no time to complete the paperwork in the field, snipers were trained to develop their powers of observation so that the kill sheet could be filled out when they returned to a secure area. No kill sheet, no confirmed kill. If it is not possible to reach the body due to the intensity of fire, the fatality is listed as a "probable."

All soldiers are trained to destroy an opponent, but snipers have honed the art of killing to a fine edge. Even before 9/11 intensified the nation's fight against terrorism, US Army leaders had recognized that traditional sniper techniques would not work well in a world where terrorists hit and ran from city buildings and busy streets. The army began teaching urban sniper techniques in a five-week course at Fort Benning, Georgia, where these elite warriors learn to stalk their prey, conceal their movements, spot telltale signs of an enemy shooter, and take down a target with a single shot. To be considered for the school, a soldier must qualify as an expert marksman, pass a physical examination, and undergo a psychological screening. The rigorous course fails more than half its students.

The US Marine Corps Sniper School offers what is widely regarded in the military as the finest sniper training program. However, it is open to candidates from all branches of the US armed services. They must have a rank between lance corporal and captain, and be infantry trained. Recruits need 20/20 vision in both eyes, though glasses and contact lenses are allowed. Color blindness is a problem though. They have to be going on to a posting as a scout-sniper and have completed at least 12 months of service, unless they are a reservist. No one with a court martial need apply and recruits must have stayed out of trouble for at least six months. They must be a volunteer with no history of mental illness. Otherwise they must be physically fit and be able to swim. It is also recommended that they have attended courses in most scout-sniper skills, including land navigation, patrolling, reconnaissance, and calling in supporting armament. Candidate must be currently rated as rifle experts, though they do not need to be dead shots. That can be taught.

The course begins with range shooting at 300, 500, 600, 700, 800, 900, and 1,000 yards. At ranges up to 800 yards, students will be expected to hit moving targets. Using binoculars and a spotting scope, they must be able to pick out hidden objects at long distances and to produce a detailed field sketch of any area of operation. The student will then move on to stalking and shooting targets at unknown distances, before being taught advanced field skills and mission employment.

The failure rate from the Marine Corps Sniper School is usually around 60 percent, though it can be much higher. But the skill and dedication of the sharpshooters who graduate is unmatched, and they know what it takes to be a top marksman—deadly aim, iron nerve, killer instincts, and unwavering courage. The military do not want their snipers to be hotheads or mindless killers. They want scout-snipers who are independently minded and self-reliant. After all, they will often be called on to risk their lives on their own in hostile territory, far beyond friendly lines.

Snipers must also be deeply committed to their country, their cause, and their service. On their shoulders lies the life or death of the other men, the ordinary grunts, who follow behind. If a sniper can take out key personnel and throw the enemy into confusion, they can make the difference between a battle lost or won.

In this book are stories of men who have attempted to live up to these high ideals. Many have excelled. Some have shown human failings. The question for every reader is, Could I have performed as well under the circumstances? I know that I, the author, certainly could not.

Nigel Cawthorne
Bloomsbury, UK, October 2011

PART ONE
VIETNAM

CHAPTER ONE

First Blood to the Marines

When lead elements of the 3rd Marine Regiment, 3rd Marine Division first landed in force in Vietnam in March 1965, they found they had a problem. The Communist insurgents—the Vietcong—found that they could move around with relative impunity. They were safe from the marines' small-arms fire, especially at long range. What was needed to fight them were snipers.

In September 1965, Captain Robert A. Russell was tasked with setting up a sniper team and began recruiting scout-snipers for the 3rd Division in Da Nang. One of those seconded into the team was Corporal Gary "Hillbilly" Edwards from Tennessee. At boot camp he had qualified as an "expert" in marksmanship, scoring 228 out of 250. There were 20 men on the course. After five days' training, they were each given a Winchester Model 70 .30-06 bolt-action sniper rifle with a box of Camp Perry match ammunition.

"Twenty rounds each," Gunnery Sergeant George Hurt told them. "I want 20 kills. One shot, one kill."

But having trained snipers in the division was still a new departure for the marines, and they had yet to learn how to use them. At first the snipers were put on sentry duty. Then when they complained, they were sent out on patrol with regular grunts. Next came rather more aggressive patrolling. Even then they would be escorted by men carrying M14s, M60 machine guns, and M79 grenade launchers. Eventually, the snipers were let loose on their own and were sent out into enemy territory where, under the rules of engagement, they could kill anyone they saw, provided the targets were carrying weapons.

On their first mission, Corporal Edwards, Sergeant Brown, and a lance corporal known as Kentucky—also graduates of Russell's sniper course—were put on a Sikorsky H-34 Choctaw helicopter and flown out to a post manned by South Vietnamese soldiers. The following morning, a lieutenant with the Army of the Republic of Vietnam (ARVN) led them out to a jungle track which, he said, was used by the Vietcong at about 0930 hours each morning.

Edwards, Brown, and Kentucky set up on a hillside overlooking the track where it emerged into a clearing. The rest of the ARVN patrol hid themselves in case they were needed to provide covering fire.

At 0905 hours, five Vietcong appeared. Dressed in black pajamas, they looked happy and relaxed. Edwards was to take the first one; Brown and Kentucky, the two that followed. They were around 1,000 yards (914 meters) away. As he looked though his scope, Edwards could see that the lead man was young—but then, so was he. With the crosshairs on the target, he followed his training to the letter. First he breathed in, then slowly out halfway and stopped, then he squeezed the trigger gently, as his instructor had told him, as if it were a woman's nipple. The lead man fell, followed by the two behind him. The other two VC ran back toward the jungle. The ARVN patrol fired on them with an M60, but they escaped. Nevertheless, the platoon commander was happy with the body count.

The marines called in a helicopter to carry the snipers and the bodies back to the marine base at Phu Bai where they became confirmed kills and were buried. Once the marines' paperwork was done, *Stars and Stripes* carried Edwards's story as the first recorded kill by a sniper unit in Vietnam. Edwards later said he never forgot the first man he shot: He had a gold tooth and a bag of rice tied around his waist. Along with his black pajamas, he was wearing Ho Chi Minh sandals cut from old car tires. And, just before he died, he was laughing.

Even though Edwards and his buddies had proved themselves as snipers, they were sent out on regular patrols again. But then a communications post requested their services. It was on the top of a hill and surrounded by barbed wire and mines. Each morning at around 0900, a VC would emerge from the jungle and send a few bursts of fire up in their direction. Apart from putting a few holes in the marines' tents, he rarely hit anything. But he was an annoyance.

Edwards, Brown, and Kentucky were flown out to the hill with a spotter scope and set up on top of the ridge. The first day, the VC emerged with a Chinese-made PPSh submachine gun, loosed off a few rounds, then disappeared back into the bush. He was young, about 18 years old. The next day when he emerged, he was hit in the throat by a bullet from Brown. It was a shot of about 250 yards (230 meters).

The three men were used on other sniper missions, but it was Edwards's first kill as a sniper that stuck with him—even though he witnessed many more terrible things when sent out with an M14 as an ordinary grunt.

Marine Lance Corporal Craig Roberts was a rifleman with the 2nd Battalion of the 9th Marines when he landed in Vietnam in July 1965. After taking a sniper course, he would go out at night with his spotter, Sal Rodriguez, a Chicano from Los Angeles. They would set up in a hide and wait until dawn when the VC guerrillas would be going home after their night's work. Most of those he killed were no older than 16, but as Roberts was only 19 at the time, this did not bother him too much.

He recalled that one night a marine patrol dropped them off by a large rock. Roberts and Sal scaled the rock and set themselves up in the grass on the top of it, while their security rifleman hid himself at the bottom. Roberts clamped an M14 bipod to the barrel of his Winchester and extended the legs. Silently he cut some grass to put over the gun and disguise its silhouette. Then he rolled over on his back and looked up at the stars, trying hard not to think of what his girlfriend, Rita, was doing at home in the States.

As dawn broke, he looked down on the paddy fields, which were broken up into squares by long dikes. It was a hot morning, and Sal wiped sweat from his eyes as he scanned the landscape with his binoculars looking for VC guerrillas making their way back to their daytime hiding holes. Then he said: "Seven hundred meters at two o'clock."

Roberts looked through his scope and saw seven VC walking single-file along a dike. They were carrying weapons, so they were legitimate targets and Roberts could engage them. He had read a book about World War II snipers. Back then a sniper would take out the last man in a patrol, then the next, then the next, working his way up from the back. If he was firing from far enough away, the targets would not hear the shots or notice that those behind had fallen by the wayside.

He put the crosshairs on the top of the last man's head, anticipating that the bullet would drop at that range. He could still see the face of the man he was about to kill and the SKS Soviet semi-automatic rifle on his shoulder. Roberts pulled his head back slightly so the scope would not strike his eyebrow when the rifle recoiled. Then he squeezed the trigger.

Roberts was out of luck though. The bullet knocked the man off the dike, but it had not killed him. He splashed around wounded in the rice paddy, alerting the others. Two of the VC jumped into the paddy to rescue him, while the others raced along the dike toward the trees.

As Roberts took aim again, Sal warned him to watch his breathing as he could see the muzzle rise and fall. He held his breath and fired again. A spout of water erupted ahead of the fleeing men. He could not understand why did they did not drop like their fallen comrade and make off. Through the scope, Roberts could see them getting away. But the Winchester's light barrel made it hard to get back on target once a shot had been loosed off. He squeezed off another shot. One of the men stumbled but kept on going.

Sal started firing with his M14. The rifleman then joined them, but their M14s were not accurate enough at that distance, and there was no way they could prevent the enemy escaping. The only thing they could do was get the hell out of there now that they had given away their position. They slid off the rock and headed down the escape route they had already picked out. Soon the VC would surround the rock. Then the hunters would become the hunted.

For Roberts, sniping made the killing personal—unlike in a firefight, where it was difficult to tell who had shot whom. When you looked through a scope, you would see the face of the person you were about to kill, though he would not see you. But this did not bother Roberts. He was avenging all those marines who had been killed or maimed by booby traps, mines, and enemy snipers. And he was taking the fight to the enemy, not waiting until they came to him. During his 10 months in-country, he made 18 confirmed kills and 35 probables.

However, Roberts was badly wounded at Da Nang, and, after 11 months in-country, he was sent home. In 1969, he joined the Tulsa Police Department and was later seconded into their TAC squad (SWAT team) because of his experience as a sniper. He went on to become an author whose books include *The Walking Dead: A Marine's Story of Vietnam, Doorway to Hell: Disaster in Somalia, One Shot, One Kill: American Combat Snipers, World War II, Korea, Vietnam, Beirut,* and *Crosshairs on the Kill Zone: American Combat Snipers, Vietnam through Operation Iraqi Freedom.*

Master Sergeant William D. Abbot, a marksman on the US Olympic team in 1965, became platoon commander of the 3rd Marines Scout-Snipers in 1966. When he was appointed, regimental commander Colonel John Lanigan told him that the snipers' skills were going to waste. They were being used on guard duty, mess duty, even disposing of the latrine waste. Abbot was told to round up the snipers, retrain them, and meld them into a unit. While his men went back to shooting from dawn to dusk, Sergeant Abbot took 15 days' rations and covered their entire area of operation looking for the best places to interdict North Vietnamese Army (NVA) infiltration across the demilitarized zone into South Vietnam.

The Communists were regularly sniping at convoys along Route 9, the supply route to the marine base at Khe Sanh. Abbot set up 10 scout-sniper teams that could reach any place along Route 9 within half an hour when convoys were fired on.

CHAPTER TWO

The White Feather

US Marine Sergeant Carlos Hathcock became a legend in Vietnam with 93 confirmed kills and over 200 unconfirmed to his name. The Vietcong and the soldiers of the NVA called him *Long Tr'ang*—the "White Feather"—for the plume he stuck in the side of his bush hat for luck. The Hanoi government offered three years' pay to any soldier who took that feather from his hatband. To do that, of course, they would also have to remove his head from his neck. To make things more difficult, when a platoon of Vietnamese snipers was sent to track him down, other marine snipers began wearing white feathers to confuse the enemy.

Born in Little Rock, Arkansas, in 1942, Hathcock went hunting in the woods as a youth to help feed his family. As a boy, he went out pretending he was hunting Nazis, carrying an old Mauser rifle his father had brought back from Europe at the end of World War II. At the age of 15, Hathcock joined the marines and, before being sent overseas, he won a number of shooting competitions, including the Wimbledon Cup at Camp Perry with a 1,000-yard (914-meter) shot.

After Captain Russell started a sniper course for the 3rd Marine Division, Captain Edward J. Land began training snipers for the 1st Division at the marine firebase on Hill 55 south of Da Nang. He selected recruits not because they were tougher or meaner than other grunts but because they were good marines with strong moral values and a desire to preserve life rather than take it. At the beginning of the course, Land would give volunteers his set-piece speech:

> When you go on a mission there is no crowd to applaud you—no one for whom you can flex your muscles or show how tough you are. When you go on a mission you are alone.
>
> You have to be strong enough to endure physically lying in weeds day after day, letting the bugs crawl over you and bite you. Shitting and pissing in your pants but lying there. Lying there because you know Charlie's coming and you're gonna kill him.
>
> You don't select the first gooner that comes into your field of fire either. You select your target carefully, making sure that the gooner you kill is Charlie, so you can waste the bastard with no doubts or remorse... I know that as grunts it was easy for you to feel justified in killing the enemy when he attacked you—he was trying to kill you. If you attacked him he also had a choice to fight or surrender—you did not murder him because he died trying to kill you. That's self-defense.
>
> As a sniper you do not have that luxury. You will be killing the enemy when he is unaware of your presence. You will be assassinating him without giving him the option to run or fight, surrender or die. You will be, in a sense, committing murder on him—premeditated.
>
> To deal with this successfully you must be mentally strong. You must believe in what you are doing—that these efforts are

defeating our enemy and that your selected kills of their leaders and key personnel are preventing death and carnage that this enemy would otherwise bring upon your brothers.

As winner of the Wimbledon Cup, Hathcock was one of Land's prize recruits. He had made his first kill in 1966 while still a marine military policeman. Keeping watch for enemy action, a flash of movement caught his eye. He then made out a figure crouched in the distance. The man was in civilian clothes, but he had the rifle slung over his back. Clearly he was a Vietcong guerrilla. Hathcock was armed with a standard M14, not the finely fitted National Match M1 he had used in competition. But the range was between 300 and 400 yards (275 and 365 meters)—a cinch for Hathcock. As he brought his weapon to bear, he checked his target. The man was armed and he had hostile intent. He appeared to be placing a booby trap.

Hathcock let the front sight settle naturally, centered on the crouching soldier. He was nervous. He felt his heart race and his chest tighten. While he was a world-class marksman, he had yet to kill a man. Silently he eased the safety forward and his right hand settled into place on the small of the stock. He got into what he called the "bubble," a state of "utter, complete, absolute concentration." As he slowly breathed out, he could see the target in sharp focus in the front sight and centered in the rear aperture. He held the rifle absolutely still and took up the slack in the two-stage trigger. Then he squeezed. The rifle jolted against his shoulder. He was so deep in concentration he hardly felt it. The bolt cycled. The empty case hit the ground to his right. Then the M14 settled back into position. It was cocked and ready for a second shot. But the Vietcong guerrilla lay dead. Hathcock had made his first kill, though it was officially unconfirmed. It was the first of 14 unconfirmed kills he was to make before being assigned as a marine sniper. But the status of the kill did not concern him.

The guerilla had been mining a trail that fellow marines would be patrolling that day. He had taken the life of one enemy and saved those of several other grunts. While Hathcock made 93 confirmed kills, he estimated that he had probably killed half again as many. While most snipers were young and single, by the time he became a sniper in Vietnam, Hathcock was already 24 and had a wife and child back in the States. An unassuming man, he dedicated his life to the Marine Corps. Land singled him out for special praise for his psychological strength, saying:

> The sniper does not hate the enemy, he respects him or her as a quarry. Psychologically, the only motive that will sustain the sniper is the knowledge that he is doing a necessary job and the confidence that he is the best person to do it. On the battlefield hate will destroy any man—and the sniper quicker than most.
>
> The sniper is the big-game hunter of the battlefield and he needs all the skills of a woodsman, marksman, hunter, and poacher. He must possess the field craft to be able to position himself for a killing shot, and he must be able to effectively place a single bullet into his intended target. Gunnery Sergeant Hathcock was all of these things with a full measure of silent courage and quiet optimism of a true champion.

Having been trained in concealment and field craft, Hathcock felt a lot safer in the jungle than behind the wire on Hill 55, where he felt like a sitting duck. Like other military snipers, Hathcock took no pleasure in killing. But he figured that for every enemy he killed, one more American would be going home alive.

"Hell, anybody would be crazy to like to go out and kill folks," he once told a fellow marine. "I never did enjoy killing anybody. It's my job. If I don't get those bastards, then they're going to kill a lot of these kids. That's the way I look at it."

Nevertheless, for Hathcock, sniping was a uniquely personal experience. Through your scope you could see the face of your enemy and were only too aware that he was human, he said. You had complete, godlike control over his life. When you pulled the trigger, you ended it and for the rest of your life you carried that last picture of him you saw through the sight.

Nevertheless, Hathcock took on missions that were akin to assassination. On one occasion, he shot a Frenchman who had helped the North Vietnamese interrogate prisoners, and he went after a Vietcong woman who tortured young GIs to death. Her tactic was to kill them slowly and painfully so that others could hear their screams. He killed her with one long-range shot that hit while she was trying to make her escape. A second bullet to her body on the ground ensured that she was dead. Hathcock pounded the earth in triumph. It was one of the few occasions he showed emotion in his work.

Hathcock liked to get on higher ground to reach what is known as the "triangle of opportunity." While most snipers go for a head shot if they can, as it is almost always lethal, Hathcock would shoot from an elevated position so if the head shot failed to give a clean kill, the bullet would travel on down the neck and go through the heart before emerging from the lower back, vastly increasing the chances of hitting a major organ.

A true professional, he constantly analyzed his kills and checked any tendency to fall into a routine. He was all too well aware that in Vietnam he was in a competition where the second prize was a body bag. He also liked to operate on his own initiative. On one occasion, Hathcock and his spotter, Corporal Johnny Burke, thought it might be a good idea to stake out Elephant Valley. This was the Cade River Valley that the NVA was using to infiltrate into South Vietnam. One night in June 1965, men from the 3rd Marine Regiment had deployed out there when, to their surprise, they heard the trumpeting of elephants. They called the artillery and asked them to light up the valley with illumination rounds. Sure enough, there were elephants there. The Vietcong were using them to carry ammunition and artillery. The marines called in an artillery barrage, which killed the elephants in what became the Battle of Elephant Valley.

As always, Hathcock and Burke traveled light. Hathcock had a Winchester Model 70 .30–06 caliber sniper rifle with a standard x8 Unertl scope; Burke had an M14. Strung across Hathcock's chest was a canvas bandoleer carrying 84 rounds of match-grade .30-06 full metal jacket ammunition. He also carried a .45 pistol, a KA-BAR combat knife, a map and compass, two canteens, and C ration cans of jelly, peanut butter, cheese, and crackers. They also had a radio, a high-powered spotting scope, and a pair of binoculars.

The two snipers hitched a ride on a helicopter to join a patrol that would escort them into Elephant Valley. As soon as they entered the valley, the sniper team peeled off. Watching their back trail to make sure they were not being followed, they headed for the jungle-covered ridge of Dong Den. After scouting possible escape routes, they set up their hide there. It overlooked a large paddy field, and about 770 yards (705 meters) in front of them was a dike. As the sun set, they bedded down—without a word, as sound carries, especially at night. They wanted to be rested and ready for the Vietcong who would be heading back to their lairs along the dike at dawn.

As the sun rose, instead of seeing a handful of VC creeping home, they saw a whole company of NVA, some 80 men, heading toward their position. Hathcock and Burke could see that they were fresh, young recruits with new uniforms and boots. Their officers were little more experienced. Rather than sticking to the tree line, they led the column toward the paddy field. Then, when it reached the narrow dike, the column spread out, single file. It was the perfect target. Hathcock and Burke could not believe their eyes.

Normally they would not have taken on such a large formation and would not even have considered it in this case if they had been seasoned troops. But even these rookies were capable of killing a marine, so it was necessary to take them on. They could have called in a rapid reaction force, but they might have lost men in the ensuing action. And artillery would have scattered them, leaving many alive to fight again another day. So Hathcock and Burke decided to take them on by themselves.

It was easy shooting. There was no wind, no mist, and, in the cool of the morning, no shimmering heat mirage. Hathcock dropped the officer at the head of the column. At the rear was an NCO armed with a pistol. Burke wasted him before the sound of Hathcock's shot echoed from the ridge. The troops panicked. Hathcock managed to drop another before they dived for the only cover available to them—the filthy stagnant water behind the dike.

The raw recruits had made a fatal mistake. If they had made a run for it along the dike, Hathcock and Burke would have picked off a few more. But most of them would have reached the trees beyond and escaped. Now, as the two snipers scanned the top of the dike through their sights, the Vietcong were trapped. Every now and then, one of them put his head up—and Hathcock blew it off. For the two snipers, it was like a shooting gallery. The one surviving officer was so frightened that he tried to make a run for it across the paddy field. He took no more than a few steps through the churning water before Hathcock took him out.

The two snipers had observed the NVA column as it marched down the trail toward the paddy field, so they already knew that they had no machine guns to give them covering fire in a rush on the ridge. Nor did they have a radio to call in support. All Hathcock and Burke had to do was keep them pinned down. And the best way to do that was to crawl along the ridge, under cover, to new firing positions to give the impression that there were a large number of men strung out along the ridge.

It was a hot day. Even in the shade, the snipers were sweating. The trapped troops were out in the full sun. They would soon be running short of water. The Vietnamese used human excrement as fertilizer, so they dared not drink the water from the paddy field. Their strength and morale would be sapping. All Hathcock and Burke needed do was keep an eye out for reinforcements.

When Hathcock radioed in their situation report, the rapid reaction force on Hill 55 made preparations to chopper in. But Hathcock could see no reason for them to risk their lives and advised against it.

As the afternoon drew on, one of the NVA put his head above the dike. He scanned the ridge. Hathcock watched him through his scope but did not fire. He could see the man talking to the others and hoped that they, too, would be foolish enough to raise their heads above the parapet. When none of them were, Hathcock squeezed the trigger. The bullet hit the soldier in the throat. He fell back in a haze of blood. After that, no one moved. Plainly they were waiting for nightfall.

But when night came, Hathcock robbed them of the cover of darkness by radioing the artillery that kept Elephant Valley bathed in light from 105-mm flares. The two snipers took turns sleeping and, every so often, fired a round just to let the NVA know they were still there.

The following day was even hotter. It was already 100°F at 1000 hours when Hathcock spotted some movement behind the dike. Eight NVA jumped up, flung themselves over the dike, and charged the ridge. But it was nearly half a mile to the tree line across a paddy field where the water and mud made it difficult to run. They aimed their AK-47s at the patch of jungle where the snipers had had their first hide. No one was there now. Hathcock dropped six, one after the other. The other two turned and ran back toward the dike. One fell as he reached it. The other leaped over to safety.

The two snipers changed position again, taking two hours to move 300 yards (275 meters). By then, the temperature had reached 120°F, and flies were swarming around the bloated corpses in the paddy field below. Tomorrow they would be full of maggots.

On the second night, the sky was filled with flares again. No one in the rice field below moved. On the third morning, five NVA soldiers tried making a frontal assault on the tree line again. But Hathcock and Burke had moved to the flanks.

"We killed them so casually, I was almost ashamed of it," Hathcock said.

The day grew hotter. Then, in the distance, they spotted some rain clouds that might offer some relief. These brought with them a breeze that wafted the sickening reek of rotting corpses up to the snipers on the ridge. What it was like for the men in the paddy field below who had no choice but to piss and shit in their pants, they could hardly imagine. Patrols as far away as five miles could smell the stench. A few raindrops fell, but not the downpour that the NVA needed to cloak their escape.

That night, the snipers toyed with their prey. Instead of keeping up the constant illumination of flares, they briefly allowed it to fall dark. This allowed the NVA recruits false hope. In the darkness, they tried to escape, only to be caught in the open when the next flare went up. Each time, Hathcock and Burke took out the leaders, forcing the rest to flee back to the cover of the dike.

Eventually, the trapped soldiers got themselves organized. Next time it fell dark, about half of them made a run for it. They were a decoy. When the flares caught them out in the open, the others fired at the snipers' muzzle flashes. But the AK-47 only has an effective range of 440 yards (400 meters). Burke suggested withdrawing, but Hathcock kept firing and said he would only consider retreating if the NVA charged their position directly. As it was, a few more shots sent the survivors scurrying back behind the dike.

By then, the two snipers were tired and haggard. But they knew the NVA were much worse off. They took turns to sleep and moved yet again. In the morning, two or three enemy soldiers attacked their old hide, giving the snipers the opportunity to pick them off.

On the afternoon of the fourth day, a soldier gingerly peeked over the dike. Hathcock told a skeptical Burke that if he did that again, he would drop him. The soldier did, and Hathcock took him out. Later, 10 young soldiers tried to make a break for the river. Some did not even carry their weapons. All 10 died.

That evening, the sky was full of flares again. By then the NVA had spotted where the snipers were and opened up in their direction. Again Hathcock and Burke moved. Hathcock set up about 50 feet (15 meters) away, sitting cross-legged with his Winchester resting on a fallen tree trunk. Burke took cover in a sinkhole with his M14 resting on a mound of earth in front of him.

As the NVA charged, Hathcock shot the first man, who fell back screaming into the water. When a second man knelt to tend him, Hathcock put a bullet in his chest. More bullets took their toll, and few soldiers made it back to the dike. By then, there can have only been 10 or 12 left.

That night a light drizzle began to fall. At daybreak, Hathcock and Burke knew they had had enough—never mind the poor bastards in the paddy field below. The snipers radioed the artillery, asking for a few minutes to withdraw before they rained high explosives down onto Elephant Valley. Hathcock and Burke were back on Hill 55 when they heard the roar of shells coming over. Only one man in the NVA column survived. He was found later by the rapid reaction force, quaking with fear, fatigue, and hunger. He could not believe his entire company had been wiped out by two snipers.

The NVA, of course, were bent on revenge. A wounded Vietnamese woman told American intelligence that a North Vietnamese sniper platoon had sworn a blood oath not to return without Hathcock's white feather. Circulars had already been handed out in villages with Hathcock's picture on them. But Hathcock was determined not to let this psyche him out.

"I don't care how hard them hamburgers think they are," he told the company gunnery sergeant. "There ain't none of them hard enough to get me."

But the woman had also said there was one enemy sniper whose reputation even outshone Hathcock's. He spent his entire time living in the jungle, eating worms, rats, and snakes, claiming that it gave him the edge.

"The woman said this guy catches cobras with his bare hands and eats them raw," Hathcock was told. He began to think of his adversary as the "Cobra."

At the time, Hathcock was cooped up behind the wire. He was already afraid that one of the incoming rockets or mortars would have his name on it. Now, he noted, a sniper was at work on the low knolls 765 yards (700 meters) across the valley from Hill 55. At that range, he could pick off marines at will. And Hathcock knew he was good. He never fired more than one shot from the same place. Nor did he fire twice at the same time of day. Once he hit a sergeant outside Hathcock's hootch, and Hathcock became convinced that the bullet had been intended for him. He was sure that the sniper was the man he thought of as the Cobra. The next time he fired on the marines, Hathcock was determined to get him.

A few days later, as dusk approached, another marine fell to the sniper. Hathcock grabbed his Winchester and headed out with

Johnny Burke. After about an hour, they came across a faint trail. There were slight indentations in the soil, a broken twig, flattened grass. The trail only led them to an overgrown ditch filled with scummy water. They slipped quietly into the ditch and followed it downstream.

Soon they spotted broken weeds along the bank where someone had gotten out. The trail led them up to a wooded ridge. But the monsoon clouds were moving in, and Hathcock and Burke hid in the undergrowth under their ponchos and waited until morning.

The next day they were back on the sniper's trail. Soon they came upon a clearing. A small shelter had been dug in the middle. It was filled with dried grass where someone had been sleeping. But there was only one way in and out. Hathcock suspected it was a trap.

The clearing was overlooked by a ridge on the far side, the perfect place for a sniper to take a shot. Avoiding the clearing, Hathcock and Burke crawled around through the undergrowth and headed for the ridge. At the bottom there was a gully filled with birds. The Cobra had sprinkled rice there to attract them, giving him an early warning in case his pursuers had avoided his trap in the clearing.

Hathcock threw a branch into the gully to scare off the birds. This, he felt, would make the Cobra abandon his hide. Sure enough, they heard someone scrambling down the other end of the ridge. Slowly, Hathcock and Burke edged their way up onto the higher ground. Below they could see thick undergrowth where they felt certain the Cobra was hiding.

It was midafternoon, and the sun was high. Hathcock crawled forward to the shade of a tree. As Burke followed, there was a shot. Then Hathcock heard the Cobra crashing though the undergrowth to change position. Burke, Hathcock was sure, was dead. But then he appeared behind the tree.

"The bastard shot me in the ass," he said.

Hathcock took a look but found no blood. Only water. The Cobra had put a hole in Burke's canteen. The pursuit continued. Hathcock was sure the Cobra was still in the area. For that bounty of three years' pay, the Cobra was bound to take chances.

They waited motionless in a standoff. The sun moved around behind Hathcock and Burke's backs, giving them the advantage. But not for long. The monsoon clouds were rolling in again. Then they spotted a flash in the gully below. Hathcock locked onto it with his scope. Burke scanned the area with his binoculars but could not clearly identify the target.

Hathcock was not a man to take a potshot. He liked to wait until he was sure of his target before squeezing off a shot. In a duel with another sniper, you only got one chance. An ill-considered shot would give his position away, putting him at a fatal disadvantage. But he knew if he did not shoot now, he might not get another chance. He kept his crosshairs on the tiny patch of reflected light and pulled the trigger. There was a commotion in the bushes. Hathcock had noted before that a man shot through the head flaps around like a decapitated chicken. All the nerves fire one last time, sending the arms and legs flailing. Suddenly, a headless body emerged through the undergrowth before falling back among the blood-soaked bushes.

When they reached the dead sniper, they found both the front and back lenses of his scope had been shattered. Hathcock's bullet had passed down it, into the Cobra's right eye. That meant the rifle had been trained on Hathcock. But Hathcock had been lucky enough to get his shot off first. Given the traveling time, they could easily have shot each other.

Hathcock did not always use a Winchester. He also used a Browning .50-caliber machine gun with an x10 scope as a sniper weapon, which had first been done in the Korean War. With this unusual combination, he made the then-longest known single-shot kill, taking out a VC arms runner at 2,500 yards (2,286 meters)—nearly a mile and a half.

Hathcock did not wear his famous white feather on his most famous exploit. A few days before he was about to be rotated home, a marine captain came to see him. He said he had a very risky job, one that he thought only Hathcock could pull off. Although Hathcock was not ordered to take the mission, because of the short time before he was due to go home, he realized that if he did not take it, some other less experienced sniper would be sent and might well not survive. There was a superstition among short-timers that if they went on one last mission, they were doomed to die. But Hathcock volunteered for the mission even before he knew what it was.

The job was to shoot an NVA general in his own headquarters. Hathcock would only get one shot. To be sure of success, the range would have to be 800 yards (about 730 meters) or less. Hathcock examined the layout of the general's headquarters. It was separated from the surrounding forest by a broad clearing. To get within range, he would have to cover 1,500 yards (about 1,375 meters) of open ground without being detected.

Although Land's snipers were trained to operate with a spotter in two-man teams, this time Hathcock would be going alone. For the mission he stripped himself of all his personal items, even his watch. Then he pulled the lucky white feather from his bush hat, put it between the pages of his Marine Corps–issue New Testament and locked it in his footlocker. At 0605, he walked down Hill 55 to meet the patrol that would escort him to the dropping-off point. All he was carrying was his rifle, his KA-BAR knife, some camouflage greasepaint, and a canteen hooked to his belt. Hathcock freely admitted he was scared.

They walked to the landing zone, got on a helicopter, and flew due west into the high karst mountains that border Laos. After being dropped in a clearing, the patrol moved quickly toward his dropping-off point. By noon, Hathcock was sitting alone, leaning on a tree. Then he set off through the dense vegetation, arriving at the tree line at dusk. He decked the straps and button holes on his uniform with local vegetation. Every inch of exposed skin was smeared with light and dark green camouflage paint.

Across the open ground in front of him, he could see the heavily guarded NVA building with its gun emplacements. He had little idea of where he was. The maps and aerial reconnaissance photographs he had been given had no names on them, and from the flight time, he could as well be in Laos as Vietnam.

He retouched his camouflage, covering the jungle green with a tinge of yellow to match the straw-colored grass he was about to cross. As he came out of the tree line onto the open ground, he turned on his side so that he would leave a narrower trail. He inched forward slowly, aiming not to move the foot-high grass that grew from the ground or make it crackle. He prayed for rain. That would soften the grass and obscure the enemy's vision.

He had only traveled 30 feet (9 meters) from the tree line when he heard a patrol approach. It was a moonless night, and he could not see them, but he lay still and held his breath. He could feel the sweat that was covering his skin and was afraid that they would be able to smell him. Behind him he could see the narrow trail of broken grass. It could easily give him away. He saw legs flashing past him. The men spoke quietly in Vietnamese. Then he realized they were goofing off. They were not even looking for intruders and would hardly be expecting a one-man assault on their headquarters. Once he was sure they were safely out of earshot, he inched forward again.

As dawn approached, Hathcock began to feel tired. But falling asleep would be fatal. He had trained for this eventuality. Over the past few months, he had taught himself to take a nap with his eyes open. He remained wide awake for all intents and purposes, but he always felt rested afterward.

Once the sun was up, Hathcock saw the general's white car pull away from the house. It was a colonial residence that Hathcock assumed had once belonged to a French planter. The general then drove off along the track that led out to the trees. Hathcock was relieved. With the general away, his men were sure to be less attentive. There was still a way to go. He wormed past the two twin .51s to his left. Another two lay to his right. These were set up for an air attack, and he doubted that they could be depressed far enough to engage him on the ground. Beside them, the gun crews were cooking their breakfast. He could smell it. Hathcock was hungry and thirsty but put it out of his mind. He had a job to do and had to remain inside his bubble.

By dusk he had put 500 yards (460 meters) between him and the tree line. Then the white sedan returned, and Hathcock saw its passenger re-enter the house. The evening security patrol began. Ten men toured the perimeter, but by the time they approached Hathcock, darkness had fallen. They had spread out into a line with 20- or 30-yard gaps between them. He could only see three of them. The other seven were on his blind side. But they all seemed to be looking out toward the tree line and walked straight past him.

He had now been lying on the ground for 24 hours. Hundreds of ants had crawled inside his uniform and were dining on his sweaty flesh. His body ached from their bites, and he wondered how many ant bites it would take to kill a man.

By morning, Hathcock was still 1,200 yards (about 1,000 meters) from the headquarters building. He could see the sentries being changed. During the day, he could see couriers coming and going as he inched relentlessly onward. He had also spotted a possible escape route. To the right of his firing position, he could see a shallow gully that ran almost out to the tree line. He figured that after he had taken his shot, he could make his way down it, all the way back to the undergrowth, without being spotted.

If the danger of being seen by an NVA sentry were not bad enough, he then came face-to-face with a bamboo viper. One bite, one scratch from its fangs and he would be dead in minutes. He could see the viper's forked tongue flicking in and out just six inches in front of his eyes. But there was nothing he could do. It raised its body as if testing the air, then slithered away through the grass.

It took a long time for Hathcock's pounding heartbeat to subside, and the surge of adrenaline the confrontation with the snake had given him intensified his hunger and thirst. Slowly he reached for his canteen and carefully unscrewed the top. He could not risk any rapid movements, and it was almost half an hour before he felt the water soothe his swollen tongue.

By now blisters covered his arm, hip, and knee, where they had been pushed and dragged along the ground. Every movement was racked with pain. He was now just 1,000 yards (915 meters) from his goal. All his best shots—both in competition and in action— had been taken from that range. But none were as important as this one. He would stick to his original plan and push on another 200 yards (180 meters).

Eventually he reached a slight depression at the end of the gully, which he knew was just 800 yards (730 meters) from the building. Hathcock spent the night assessing the humidity, wind speed, and direction—anything that might affect the flight of his bullet. Another patrol walked past him. Hathcock was no longer worried. He had come to believe that the NVA were far more worried about an air strike than they were about any one-man attack along the ground.

Before dawn of the fourth day, he spread out a cloth on the ground. This would prevent the exhaust gases from his rifle kicking up dust and giving away his position. By the time the sun was up, he had his eye clamped to his scope, searching for his target. From that range, he would need his target to be standing still, either full-face or with his back to him. Hathcock also listened for the rustling of leaves and watched the billow of the smoke from the cooking fires and the waving of the grass to get an estimate of the wind speed between him and the target. Estimating the wind speed, he multiplied it by eight for the distance in hundreds of yards, then divided by four to give the number of half-minutes of angle, or clicks on his scope, he should allow to compensate for windage.

As the sun rose higher in the sky, it beat down on the back of his neck, and he was once more bathed in sweat. Then he heard the sound of a car's engine, and the white sedan appeared from a bunker. As the general emerged from the door of the plantation house, Hathcock centered the crosshairs on his profile, but before the general turned face-on, his aide-de-camp stepped in front of him, blocking Hathcock's shot.

Hathcock's brain was still making last-minute calculations. He would have to aim slightly to the right in case the bullet was blown to the left. He would also aim low, as the heat would make the powder burn faster, propelling the bullet faster through the air and flattening the trajectory. And the hot air rising from the ground would raise the bullet slightly. For the moment, though, the general was surrounded by his officers. Then they moved away, leaving the general alone with his aide. The young officer took his place beside his commanding officer as they walked toward the car. Then, miraculously, they stopped. Hathcock's crosshairs were on the general's heart. He held his breath and squeezed the trigger.

As the rifle recoiled, he blinked. When he opened his eyes, the general was flat on his back with blood gushing from his chest. His aide-de-camp dived behind some sandbags. The other officers ran for cover. Meanwhile Hathcock slipped into the gully and, flat on his belly, used both arms and both legs to propel himself forward.

It took him just five hours to cover the ground it had taken three days to cross on the way in. No patrols came out after him. Plainly no one had seen his muzzle flash. He had not expected them to in full daylight at 800 yards (730 meters). He did hear men far to his left, but they had acres to search. If they came close, however, he would be all too easy to locate as he stank of urine. During his time flat on the ground he had had no choice but to relieve himself in his pants.

By nightfall he had reached the tree line. Then finally, after four days lying down, he could get to his feet. The pain was excruciating, the sensation exhilarating. But he had not reached safety yet. It was dark, and he was in a forest that would be full of mines and booby traps. But in a few hours he had traveled the one and three-quarters miles (three kilometers) to the rendezvous point. He hid in the bushes, aware that the NVA might be hunting the forest for him. Then he heard men coming up the ridge.

He heard a voice say: "Sergeant Hathcock." It was the marine who had led the patrol that had brought him there four days earlier. He had news from intelligence that there had been a rapid increase in radio traffic, indicating that the general had been killed. Hathcock was certain of it.

He took a swig from a canteen and headed for the LZ, where the helicopter picked him up and carried him back to Hill 55. Afterward, though, Hathcock had second thoughts about the killing. In the weeks that followed, American casualties soared as if the NVA were taking their revenge, and he began to feel that taking out the general might have been a mistake.

Hathcock's sniper career came to a sudden end on his second tour in 1969 when an Amtrac he was riding on hit an antitank mine. He pulled seven marines from the flaming vehicle before jumping to safety. But in the conflagration, he suffered burns over 43 percent of his body. When he recovered, he helped establish the

Marine Corps Scout Sniper School in Quantico, Virginia, where he taught snipers the tricks of the trade.

After the war, a friend showed Hathcock a passage written by Ernest Hemingway that read, "Certainly there is no hunting like the hunting of man, and those who have hunted armed men long enough and like it, never really care for anything else thereafter."

"He got that right," Hathcock said. "It was the hunt, not the killing."

CHAPTER THREE

Sniper Discipline

When Hathcock returned to Vietnam on his second tour of duty and was made sniper platoon leader, he became very particular about whom he took on as trainee snipers. Once, while out in the field, one of his pupils had suggested they shoot some Vietnamese farmers. Hathcock had sent him back to his line unit, saying, "He just wanted to shoot somebody—anybody. Snipers aren't trained that way."

According to Hathcock, a sniper had to train his mind to control every emotion. As well as being knowledgable about weapons and field craft, he had to be intelligent, quiet, malleable, and observant, with the ability to get his observations down in writing. And he had to have patience. Hathcock himself had lain in one spot for three days, just observing. During that time, his concentration had to be absolute. It was what Hathcock called "getting in his bubble."

Gunnery Sergeant Mark Limpic—at one time the squad leader of another marine legend from the Vietnam War, the notoriously diffident Chuck Mawhinney—told a story about how hard it was to instill the virtue of patience into new snipers and train them to sit still for hours until they got the right shot.

On one occasion he had taken two scout-snipers from Hill 65 down to the Bon Son River, where they set up. After a while, some NVA soldiers came for a swim. The young snipers wanted to fire off a couple of shots at them, but Limpic told them to wait. He figured that more swimmers would come, and those that were already there were in no hurry to leave. In fact, they would venture out to deeper water, where it would be hard to run away when the shooting started. They waited, and more swimmers did turn up. When they started shooting, they lost count of how many they killed.

Trained as a sniper by Carlos Hathcock, Thomas D. Ferran was assigned to M Company of the 3rd Battalion, 7th Marines, who did not really know what to do with him. When he reported for duty at a hilltop base near Chu Lai, the first sergeant assigned him to be his bodyguard. As the base was surrounded by NVA preparing to attack, this was a waste of his talents, so Ferran persuaded him to let him join a weapons platoon.

They were sent to a hill south of Chu Lai. Ferran spotted an enemy soldier digging a spider hole about 1,420 yards (1,300 meters) away, beyond the range of the marines' machine guns and mortars. Ferran had been trained to take a shot up to 1,200 yards (1,100 meters). At that range, he could put a bullet in a 10-inch (25-centimeter) circle 8 out of 10 times. He asked his partner, Pee-Wee, to spot for him and told him that he was going to put his first shot high and right, over the man's head. Pee-Wee defocused his binoculars by half a turn so he could read the wind and still see where the bullet hit. He reported that the round fell low and to the left. Ferran made the necessary correction.

The enemy soldier could hardly believe that he had been shot at from such a range. But still he took cover. After a few minutes, he resumed working on his spider hole. Ferran's next shot hit him.

The marines looking on burst into applause. Ferran had proved the worth of a sniper to the unit.

Snipers usually worked in pairs, and Ferran was particular about his partner. He did not like married men with children, whom he considered "baggage." They were in Vietnam to kill the enemy, not talk about family life. He was single and would remain that way as long as he was making a contribution to the war.

One partner left him one foggy night to check on the adjacent infantry lines, even though he had been told not to. He said that he would be away for just a few minutes, but after 45 minutes he still had not returned. Ferran then heard some movement nearby. The elephant grass in front of him started to move. Ferran called out, "Halt!" There was no reply. He repeated the challenge twice more, then flicked the safety off and put his rifle on full automatic. He put four pounds of pressure on the trigger, which needed only five pounds to fire. Suddenly the elephant grass parted and his partner appeared, calling out Ferran's nickname.

Ferran took his finger off the trigger and hit him in the face with the butt.

"You son of a bitch, I almost just killed you," he said.

After that, he got a new partner. And he continued changing them. He did not like getting too comfortable, preferring to keep his edge and rely on himself.

Not that he did not make mistakes. Once he forgot to put the lens cap on his rifle's scope when he left it leaning against a tree. When he came to check his weapon, he found that the vernier scale used to determine distance had melted.

As a sniper, Ferran was taught how to kill from a distance, usually safely out of the range of normal infantry fire. But all snipers come face-to-face with the enemy sometime. On one occasion, his two-man sniper team, accompanied by a four-man backup, was traveling with an infantry unit on a search-and-destroy mission.

Their role was intelligence gathering, and after a short rest break they were to crawl away from the rest of the outfit to convince any enemy scout that may have been tracking them that the infantry unit had deployed its reconnaissance element.

They took up a position in the undergrowth on a riverbank to wait for darkness. If no one had followed them, they would infiltrate the nearby village to find out what they could discover about enemy activity. On the other side of the river was an NVA unit. Having seen the marine infantry unit move off, they readied themselves to cross the river. Ferran had been asleep until his partner awakened him. Across the river, they could hear the sounds of AK-47s being prepared for action. One NVA soldier was preparing to cross. It seemed certain that he would land at the sniper team's position. As point man, his job was to secure the bridgehead so the rest could cross in safety.

Using hand signals, the sniper team put together a hastily prepared ambush. They allowed the first man to cross the river. The sniper team was well camouflaged in the undergrowth, and he did not see them, though they were only about 11 yards (10 meters) away. Training had taught the sniper team to wait for the most effective moment before hitting the enemy.

After surveying the area with field glasses, the NVA point man signaled for the rest of the unit to cross. The sniper team then moved into position, and Ferran put the NVA point man in his sights. The scope on his M40 was turned to 9x magnification, and the man was so close he could only see his eyes. The tension of the situation made Ferran's heart pound, and the sights jumped up and down, so he adjusted the magnification to three.

As the first of the rest of the unit reached the bank, one of the other marines flipped the selector on his M16 from "safe" to "auto." The click alerted the NVA. As his scope's magnification settled, Ferran could see the point man turn in the direction of the sniper team. His finger was on the trigger of his AK-47, ready to spray their position. Ferran jerked the trigger on his M40. Nevertheless, his 173-grain match round hit the NVA point man square in the forehead, killing him instantly. The other marines opened up. But in a close-quarters firefight, an M40—or any other bolt-action sniper rifle—is of little use, so Ferran ran forward to the dead NVA point and grabbed his AK-47.

By the time someone yelled "cease fire," there were 12 NVA dead on the battlefield. Others many have been killed in the water and been carried downstream, and some of the wounded may have escaped. As the Americans regrouped and moved position in case of a counterattack, they examined the documents they had captured. The troops they had ambushed were a reconnaissance unit. Papers listed the names of 42 Communist spies in the ARVN and the positions of their 82mm mortars and recoilless rifles. The result was a battalion-size operation against those positions.

Back at Hill 55, Ferran had to hand in the AK-47, as marines were not allowed to use foreign weapons. He protested, pointing out that his M40 was no use in those types of situations. He was told that snipers were not supposed to get themselves into those types of situations. Nevertheless, he asked to carry a .45 pistol for his protection. A marine veteran told him that when he needed a .45, he would wish he had had a rifle. From then on, Ferran carried an M16 along with his M40.

Five years later, he saw that AK-47 again. It hung on a wall at Camp Pendleton, alongside a plaque explaining how it had been captured.

With Hathcock out of action, three snipers were sent to replace him. One of them was Marine Steve Suttles. In October 1969, fighting in Arizona Territory, which lay across the Tinh Yen River from Hill 55, snipers Suttles and Jackson were threatened with court-martial when they disobeyed orders and joined an M60 machine gun crew that went out to rescue a patrol that had been ambushed.

Later, Suttles and Jackson were on the tower with an officer when he saw a gun-toting, pajama-clad VC walking along the other side of the river. What the VC did not know was that he had wandered into the KD—know-distance—range. The snipers had drawn up range cards showing the distance to various features. The VC was by a tree that was 1,250 yards (1,140 meters) away.

Suttles asked permission to engage. The officer did not seem to believe he could make the shot, but gave his permission anyway. Suttles downed the man with one shot.

Corporal Jeffrey Clifford, a scout-sniper with C Company, 1st Battalion, 1st Marine Regiment, also made his first kill from Hill 55. A small patrol of VC appeared from behind some trees. Clifford took aim at the tail-end Charlie from around 600 yards (550 meters). The bullet hit the human target, who was carrying an M1, in the lower back and came out the front. When the body was recovered, it was discovered to be an 18-year-old girl—and she was pregnant. The marines joked that it was a double kill.

At Hue during the Tet Offensive in 1968, Clifford made a shot of over 1,400 yards (1,280 meters). He had made the same shot 10 times up a boulevard on the other side of the river without hitting anything, estimating it at 1,000 yards (915 meters). Then he borrowed a range finder from a lieutenant with a tank group and discovered that his estimate of the distance to the NVA troops on the other side of the river was 400 yards (365 meters) short.

The NVA were beside a pagoda approximately 20 feet (6 meters) high. Clifford put the crosshairs several feet above the pagoda roof and fired, but his spotter, Lance Corporal Regas, could not see the strike. Clifford told him to get some tracer. Through binoculars it was possible to see the tracer's high arc. It hit an NVA soldier in the upper chest. It was such an astonishing shot that the lieutenant called in his captain to confirm the kill.

After that, they decided they needed a little relaxation. Lance Corporal Regas said he had found a convent where there was bound to be food and running water. Although it was in "Indian territory," they decided to make use of the facilities and eat and bathe. After they had cleaned up, Clifford set up on the second floor while Regas went to see if he could find where the communion wine was stored. A well-trained sniper, Clifford took up position some 8 feet (2.4 meters) back from the window in a darkened room. He could see an enemy tracer coming from a second-floor window about 300 yards (275 meters) down the boulevard. They were aimed at marines in the courtyard below. He took aim and waited for the enemy to loose off another burst. Then he put a 7.62 round just above the muzzle flash.

While the machine gun fell quiet, a few minutes later a rocket-propelled grenade (RPG) came through the window. It blew out the floor, and Clifford and his gun tumbled into the ground-floor room below. He was bleeding, torn by fragments, and covered in plaster but otherwise unhurt. He would need another bath, though.

CHAPTER FOUR

Mawhinney's Heirs

Joseph T. Ward arrived at the 5th Marines Combat Base at An Hoa in April 1969, where he was to serve as a scout-sniper. His first task was to go to the clearing snipers use to sight their rifles and find an M14 he was comfortable with. At sniper school in Camp Pendleton, California, he was used to firing a bolt-action rifle with telescopic sights and found it difficult to get used to iron sights again. In Vietnam, the bolt-action weapon was only issued to team leaders. The M14 was still used by spotters. It used the same .308 ammunition as the Remington Model 700, which replaced the Winchester as a sniper rifle, so in an emergency they could exchange ammunition. The 5.56-mm ammunition used by the newly introduced M16 fit neither rifle. In a pinch, the M14 could even use rounds from an M60 machine gun, but they were much too inaccurate to be used in the Remington.

After a week, Ward was sent out to Delta Company of the 1st Battalion, 5th Marines, where he met Chuck Mawhinney. After 11 months in-country, Mawhinney already had a reputation as the best sniper in the Marine Corps. Before dawn the following morning, Ward and Mawhinney left camp with a routine patrol. Mawhinney left his usual spotter, Dan Collier, behind, saying he wanted to see how Ward could handle himself in the field. After about an hour, the man on point spotted some enemy soldiers moving through a clearing 900 yards (820 meters) away. The patrol took cover while the snipers were called up.

Mawhinney and Ward raced across a small paddy field to a rise 75 yards (70 meters) away while the platoon leader yelled after them to slow down and watch out for booby traps. Mawhinney dropped to a kneeling position behind the rise. Ward took up his position to the left and two feet to the rear as he had been trained. He focused his binoculars. He checked that the men in the clearing had weapons, making them a legitimate target. Mawhinney was already on them. He checked his breath and squeezed off a shot. One enemy soldier dropped, and the rest ran for the tree line. Mawhinney fired again. A second man fell. Ward watched as another man ran the wrong way and got separated from the rest of his unit. He made the mistake of trying to rejoin the others. A third bullet from Mawhinney took him down. In barely 30 seconds, he had killed three of the enemy.

The bodies remained in hostile territory, but Mawhinney was nearing the end of his tour. He already had 100 confirmed kills to his credit, but he wanted to add these three. The commanding lieutenant would not let the sniper team go out and check the bodies unless they could get enough volunteers to make up a fire party.

Mawhinney was already a legend among marines, so it was not difficult to get the numbers, even though they had to cross 900 yards of open terrain knowing that the enemy was in the area. They reached the first man without incident. Half his skull was gone, but he was still, miraculously, alive—though he was dying. This did not interest Mawhinney. They had a job to do. So they began going through his pockets, looking for documents. Mawhinney found a wad of money, while Ward found maps, documents, and a small photograph of a young Vietnamese woman. He wondered whether this was the man's wife, girlfriend, or even his sister. Mawhinney pointed to the wedding ring on his finger.

Ward found himself fighting against the wish to give the dead man an identity. Mawhinney, though, had long since closed himself off from any such feelings.

"Once I had a Charlie in my scope, it was my job to kill him before he killed me," he said in a January 2000 interview with the *Los Angeles Times Saturday Journal*. "I never looked in their eyes, I never stopped to think about whether the guy had a wife or kids."

As Mawhinney always told the snipers he trained in the field, "That wasn't a man you just killed; it was an enemy. This is our job. This is what war is all about. You screw up, you die."

He had been told the same words after he had made his first kill.

They finished searching the body quickly, as they were out in the open in an exposed position. Mawhinney left a match round on the dying man's chest so the Vietcong would know that a sniper was responsible. As they set off back to the platoon, Ward heard a marine behind him say, "This one ain't dead yet." Then there was the sound of a shot from an M16. Later Ward saw the man's wedding ring being used as a stake in a poker game.

Again Mawhinney was unmoved. He admitted to "mercy killings" himself.

"Sometimes, depending on where they're hit, they'll just drop and not move," he said. "Nobody dies the same, and I've seen it all. I did a lot of mercy-shooting. I wounded people and then cranked another round into them. I didn't want them crawling around out there."

Mawhinney's outing with Ward was his last patrol. When the lieutenant signed his "kill sheet," Mawhinney said for him the war was over. He flew back to An Hoa, where he served as central squad leader, then rotated back to the United States. By then, he had 103 confirmed kills to his name and 216 probables. He was just 20 years old.

The son of a marine veteran from World War II, Mawhinney was born in 1949 and raised Lakeview, Oregon. When he was six, his father taught him to shoot "the marine way." With his BB gun, he shot at anything that crawled or flew, and he particularly enjoyed shooting flies that landed on the fence. Later he went deer hunting with his father, carrying a .270 Winchester with a Redfield 4x scope.

After graduating from high school in 1967, he joined the Marine Corps, though he delayed his entry until mid-October after the deer season. After five weeks at boot camp, he was sent to Camp Pendleton for rifle training. He qualified as expert on the M14 and was offered a place at the new scout-sniper school. There he was taught about camouflage, stalking, night navigation, and field craft and spent long hours on the shooting range.

He was sent to Vietnam after the Tet Offensive in January 1968, when 105 towns and cities across South Vietnam—including the capital, Saigon—were hit simultaneously by the enemy. He was sent to Lima Company of the 3rd Battalion, 5th Marines. The company was down to half strength, and Mawhinney was told that they did not need a sniper. With just 65 men, what they needed were regular riflemen. So for the first three months of his tour, he was an ordinary grunt.

There were advantages to this. He began to learn his way around the jungle and paddy fields. He knew what equipment to carry with him and what to leave behind, and he learned how to get along in an infantry company. But he grew frustrated and was eager to put his special skills to good use. To get reassigned he had to get to the 5th Marine Regiment Combat Base at An Hoa. So he faked a toothache and was sent to An Hoa to see a dentist. But he also took the time to see the head of the scout-sniper platoon, Master Gunnery Sergeant Mark Limpic. After three days, Mawhinney was assigned to partner Corporal Cliff Albury.

Soon Mawhinney graduated from his M14 to an M40A1. Then he got his own Remington Model 700 bolt-action sniper rifle, serial number 221552. It was chambered for the 7.62-mm NATO cartridge and carried a Redfield 3-9x variable scope. He took great care of it, cleaning and lubricating it after shooting. He said he treated it "like a mother with a newborn baby," and would even "tuck it in at night."

He was particularly annoyed when the armorers made adjustments to his rifle while he was away on R&R, though he had given explicit instructions that it should be left alone. One occasion bothered him particularly. Mawhinney had just returned from leave to An Hoa, where the armorer swore that he had not allowed any adjustments to the rifle in Mawhinney's absence. Nevertheless, Mawhinney decided to test-fire the weapon with some sighting-in shots. He took up a cross-legged position near the perimeter wire. By chance, Mawhinney spotted a peasant in pajamas walking across a rice paddy about 300 yards (275 meters) away. He took a closer look to see if the man had a weapon. When the man stepped up onto a dike, the muzzle of a rifle he had slung by his side swung out. He was a legitimate target.

"I squeezed off a shot, and I missed," Mawhinney said. "You talk about eyes—he turned around and looked directly at me in total disbelief. I'm thinking: Why is this SOB still alive? Then I realized that the armorer had fucked around with my scope, there's no doubt."

But he did not have a spotter with him and he did not see where the bullet had fallen, so he did not know what adjustment to make.

The target then began to run. To Mawhinney this was a challenge. He had a motto: "Don't bother to run, you'll just die tired."

In this case, it plainly did not apply. He shot to the left, he shot to the right, he shot high, he shot low. Finally the man disappeared completely unscathed.

"I'll never forget that look he gave me," Mawhinney told a *Los Angeles Times* reporter 30 years later "It's one of the few things that bother me about Vietnam. I can't help thinking about how many people that he may have killed later, how many of my friends, how many marines. He fucked up and he deserved to die. That still bothers me."

When he caught up with the armorer, Mawhinney discovered that he had removed the scope to tighten the base mounting screws. As a result, the rifle was shooting 5 feet (1.5 meters) high and to the right.

Mawhinney carried just 40 rounds when out on a mission, but his spotter with an M14 carried five or six 20-round magazines. The M14 was also useful for sniping, particularly at night when fitted with a Starlight scope that amplified the ambient lights 60,000 times. Mawhinney used the Starlight scope to make around 35 percent of his kills.

He kept the sight on his Remington Model 700 zeroed at 500 yards (460 meters) for distances up to 700 yards (640 meters). Beyond that he would set the dial to a thousand yards (910 meters), then raise or lower his aim if the distance was longer or shorter. Usually he confined himself to shots out to 800 yards (730 meters) where he was confident that he could kill anyone he shot at.

Mawhinney estimated the range by guessing how many 100-yard (91-meter) football fields would fit between him and the target. He and his spotter would hone this skill constantly when out on patrol. They would pick a distant object, estimate the distance, then count out the number of paces they took to reach it.

As soon as he could get off the base and into the field, he went. He said he felt much safer in a hide than in camp as he was not being watched there. There were other dangers, though. On one occasion, he had to lay stock still while a large snake slithered across his body. But lying motionless for hour after hour was par for the course for a sniper.

"Normally I would shoot and run, but if I had them at a long distance, I wasn't worried," said Mawhinney. "I would shoot and then lay there and wait and wait and wait and pretty soon somebody else would start moving toward the body. Then I would shoot again."

Mawhinney achieved some remarkable feats of marksmanship. Once he was in a hilltop staging area near the Liberty Bridge, which Americans had built to give the marines an easy route to move men and materiel across the Thu Bon River. Below in the rice paddies, at some 1,200 yards (1,000 meters), he spotted four enemy soldiers. There was only a light breeze, so he decided to take a shot. Resting his Remington on a sandbag, he turned the elevation on his scope to 1,000 yards (915 meters), then fired. His first shot missed, but the spotter saw where it fell. Mawhinney adjusted his shot. The Vietcong were lying down, but he could see them through the shoots of rice. His second shot hit one of them. Another two shots took out a second man. The other two jumped up and ran for the tree line, but a helicopter went after them.

On the way back, the helicopter stopped off to examine the two men Mawhinney had killed and collect their weapons. They reckoned the distance to be nearer to 1,500 yards (1,370 meters) than 1,200, making this Mawhinney's longest kill.

His shortest was about a foot (30 centimeters). He had been on a patrol when they ran into a squad of North Vietnamese regulars. The enemy scattered. Mawhinney chased after them through the village. In an alleyway, he ran straight into an enemy soldier. They both bounced back slightly stunned. The NVA soldier raised his AK-47 but hesitated. Mawhinney did not, and the man fell dead.

As it moved into an open area, another patrol Mawhinney was accompanying came under sniper fire. They were pinned down in the open, and no one could see where the shots were coming from. Mawhinney and his spotter moved around the flank to a rise in the ground. From there they noticed a patch of earth that began to move. It was the lid of a spider hole opening. The VC sniper popped up, took a shot, and disappeared again. When the next lid opened around 300 yards (275 meters) away, Mawhinney was ready, took aim, and hit the man in the head. Then another lid opened. Mawhinney shot again. Seconds later, another lid opened, and Mawhinney shot once more. The last sniper then opened his lid, looking around to see what had happened to the others. Mawhinney killed him as well.

But his greatest score in one day was on February 14, 1969. He was out on patrol with Delta Company of the 1st Battalion, 5th Marines. That evening, they dug in about 400 yards (365 meters) from the Thu Bon River. As night fell, a spotter plane flew overhead and saw a large formation of North Vietnamese soldiers on the other side of the river, heading their way.

Mawhinney and his spotter took a forward position, digging into the riverbank itself. He had brought with him an M14, as well as his bolt-action Remington, and kept watch through its Starlight scope. After a few hours' wait, he spotted movement in the brush about 100 yards (90 meters) away on the far bank. It was an NVA scout. He crawled down to the riverbank and slipped noiselessly into the water.

As the scout forded the river, the water came up to his chin. He reached the near bank around 25 yards (23 meters) from the sniper's position, so close Mawhinney claimed he could hear the water dripping from his uniform. In the field your senses are heightened.

"When you fire, your senses start going into overtime: eyes, ears, smell, everything," said Mawhinney. "Your vision widens out so you see everything, and you can smell things like you can't at other times."

Mawhinney kept the man in his sights. He did not want to risk him stumbling on Delta Company's position. But when he reached the edge of the elephant grass, he turned back. Then he crossed back over the river. Mawhinney told his spotter things were about to get interesting.

Around 30 minutes later, the North Vietnamese formation emerged from the undergrowth on the far bank. They were in full battle gear. One by one they began crossing the river with their rifles held above their heads. As the man on point reached the near bank, Mawhinney aimed at his head and squeezed the trigger. The rest of the column saw him go down, but they were unsure what to do. Should they go on and try and find cover on the bank? Or should they turn back? They were perfectly spaced with about 10 feet (3 meters) between then. While they tried to figure out what to do, Mawhinney picked them off one after another, all 15 of them, each one with a head shot. This would become known in marine circles as the Saint Valentine's Day Massacre.

These 16 kills were listed only as probables, as there was no officer on hand to see their lifeless bodies float away and no chance to search the corpses. More importantly, the NVA column did not cross the river that night, avoiding what would have been a large-scale engagement that would have been costly for both sides.

Mawhinney extended his tour twice, but his third request for an extension was rejected when a chaplain said he was suffering from "combat fatigue." He had been a sniper for 16 months. By then, while others would come back from a mission almost in tears, Mawhinney would be laughing when he described his kills.

"I used to worry about him cracking up," said Master Gunnery Sergeant Limpic.

Mawhinney admitted himself that he was near the edge. "You get to the point where you start living like an animal," he said. "You act like an animal, you work like an animal, you are an animal. All you think about is killing."

His days as a killer were over, and he was sent back to the States, where he became a shooting instructor at Camp Pendleton. By then American forces were withdrawing from Vietnam. In 1970, Mawhinney took an early discharge and returned to Oregon where, for the next 27 years, he worked for the Forest Service. He told no one about his exploits in Vietnam, not even his wife.

Then in 1991, Joseph T. Ward published his book *Dear Mom: A Sniper's Vietnam*, which mentioned Mawhinney and credited him with 101 confirmed kills. Peter Senich, author of *Long-Range War: Sniping in Vietnam*, looked into this claim with the intention of debunking it. It was easy to check out, as snipers have to provide a written record of their kills.

At the time, it was thought that Carlos Hathcock held the Marine Corps record with 93 confirmed kills. But Senich's study of the records showed that Hathcock came third after Eric R. England with 98 confirmed kills and Charles Benjamin Mawhinney with 103, though out of all the services, Adelbert Waldron held the record with 109 confirmed kills.

Of Mawhinney, Senich wrote, "Here was a seasoned combat veteran who had managed to do something no other marine had in over 200 years of Marine Corps history and he could not care less if anyone knew about it, or believed it, for that matter."

Mawhinney never liked the idea of league tables. In Vietnam, when an overeager platoon leader put up a "kill board" for the snipers, Mawhinney objected.

"It started making a competition out of it," he said. "Some of these young kids wanted to get kills so they were taking chances with their lives. We talked to the squad leader, the platoon sergeant, and the CO, and said 'This is BS. Take this board down.'"

After Ward's book was published, Mawhinney found himself in demand to speak at conventions and attend shooting competitions. Looking back at his time in Vietnam, he said, "It was the ultimate hunting trip: a man hunting another man who was hunting me. Don't talk to me about hunting lions or elephants; they don't fight back with rifles and scopes. I just loved it ... My rules of engagement were simple: If they had a weapon, they were going down. Except for an NVA paymaster I hit at 900 yards [820 meters], everyone I killed had a weapon."

He said he only gave the interview to the *Los Angeles Times* in 2000 and appeared at public events because he wanted to change the public perception of snipers as bloodthirsty assassins.

"A good sniper," he said, "saves more lives than he takes because he undercuts the enemy's will or ability to fight ... I was never ashamed of what I did. I was proud of it. I didn't go over there to kill people. I went to save lives—my guys' lives."

After his outing with Ward, Mawhinney was sent back to An Hoa to be central squad leader and handed his Remington to Ward with the words, "Take care of my baby."

Ward said that the rifle was in such good condition that he could have put it in a sports shop and sold it as new. He also took over Dan Collier as his spotter and was given an Australian bush pack, which he found better balanced than an American backpack and easier to open. This could be vital when they came under fire. However, he found that Collier's nerves were shot and soon replaced him.

Out in the field, Ward began to rack up the kills. But he was yet to be battle-hardened, and he began to smoke marijuana to distance himself from the death and destruction around him. When they gunnery sergeant found out, he took no action. After all, Ward was not getting drunk before going out on a mission. Ward was still alert enough to win a sniper duel. He and his spotter

Dave Sulley were going out on an early-morning hunter-kill mission when they saw a puff of smoke in the trees some 700 yards (640 meters) away. Less than a second later, a bullet landed barely a pace in front of them. Within seven seconds, Ward had raised his Remington, taken aim, and fired, hitting the enemy sniper in the face. When they found the body, the VC had been using an American M1 Carbine with a telescopic sight, and Ward wondered how his opponent could have missed him.

While the snipers could move about the country easily enough undetected, word spread that the Hanoi government had put a bounty on their heads. They offered $1,000 for a bolt-action rifle and $3,000 for the sniper, who would then be skinned alive. This was more than a little intimidating, and the NVA's intelligence was good. In a captured command bunker, US soldiers found a wall covered in photographs, drawings, and detailed descriptions of American snipers. Headquarters reacted by ordering that snipers take out firing teams with them. Then they were to take a squad or platoon. This only made them more vulnerable, as they could hardly employ their training in stealth and concealment in the middle of a noisy patrol. And they stood out. With their long bolt-action rifles, they were an easy target in an ambush.

These new regulations also brought snipers, who were usually lone wolves, into closer contact with the command structure. In a night ambush in August 1969, the patrol Ward and his new spotter, Dave Suttles, were with shot three North Vietnamese soldiers dead and captured two NVA regulars and a nurse. Agents from counterintelligence were along on the ambush and interrogated the prisoners there and then. When one of the NVA refused to answer, the agent rubbed his face in the brains of a dead comrade. Ward was sickened by this and volunteered to relieve the marine guarding the other two prisoners.

When he did, he found that the nurse was clearly in pain. He turned her over and found that the counterintelligence agent had tied her wrists together so tightly that her hands had swollen up and were turning black. So he went to the agent and insisted that the woman's bonds be loosened in a tone that was grossly insubordinate. He could have been arrested, even court-martialed. But the agent knew it was not wise to piss off snipers.

"To piss off one sniper is to piss off all the snipers," said Ward.

But the agent did not untie the woman's hands. So Ward pulled out his machete. He returned to the prisoners and, after finding a point where the swelling had not entirely covered the rope, cut it. He then went to find a corpsman, who said she would probably lose her right hand.

When two more prisoners were taken—one an NVA captain—Ward reminded the agent of the Geneva Conventions and took charge of the prisoners himself. But there was only so much he could do. After the prisoners were choppered out with counterintelligence, the agent radioed back the news that one of the prisoners had jumped out of helicopter. Ward drew a different conclusion.

The following afternoon, the patrol was caught in a hit-and-run ambush. Dave Suttles was injured by shrapnel from a mortar, and Ward had lost another spotter.

At An Hoa, grunts bribed snipers with marijuana and beer to man the most dangerous bunkers, as by then they could fire without asking permission. At midnight on August 29, 1969, Ward was scanning an area of no-man's land from an isolated foxhole with his Starlite scope when he saw movement around 450 yards (410 meters) away. He spotted two sappers coming in. These were essentially suicide bombers who were prepared to blow themselves up to make a break in the defenses where others could follow. They often wore nothing but loin cloths and had wire tied around their arms and legs so they could tourniquet a limb, if necessary, and continue with their mission.

Ward knew he could easily take one out. But the muzzle flash would blind the Starlite scope long enough to let the other one escape. However, he knew where the marines had strung their Claymore mines. He woke his partner and told him to call headquarters on the field telephone and stop anyone else firing on them. Through his Starlite, he could see the Vietcong sappers moving inexorably toward a line of Claymores about 50 yards (45 meters) away. Each Claymore would throw out 700 one-eighth-inch (0.3-centimeter) steel balls, which were deadly out to at least 100 meters (110 yards). When the sappers got to within 50 yards of them, Ward gave the order to fire. A marine pressed the detonator. They both ducked as the back-blast threw dirt and rocks over the bunker. Ward did not bother to go and examine the bodies, as sappers did not carry any documents. When the corpses were recovered, he heard that one had more than 100 holes in it.

The death and destruction were beginning to take their toll. Ward began having nightmares. But his new spotter, Ron Feekes, was a cheerful guy. This helped. On September 1, 1969, they were sent back out into Arizona. On their second night, they were bombarded by a barrage of mortars. In the dark, they fell into a deep bomb crater and only just managed to scramble out in time before two mortars crashed into it. Having cheated death, they lay out in the open until the bombardment was over.

The next day, one of the marines had his legs blown off by a booby trap. The lieutenant leading the patrol said the enemy had been spotted nearby and asked the sniper team to pin them down long enough for a helicopter to medevac the wounded man out.

Feekes scanned a distant tree line with his binoculars and spotted the enemy. He estimated that they were in platoon strength and at least 1,000 yards (915 meters) away. But Ward had a problem. There were no good firing positions in the vicinity. To make any effective shots, he would have to shoot standing up.

He rested his rifle on Feekes's shoulder to steady it and dialed the scope to 1,000 yards. He aimed above the first target, squeezed the trigger, and missed. So he aimed a little higher. This time the bullet hit. Now he had the range and took out a machine gunner. The enemy took cover. By then they had worked out where the shots were coming from and were keen to return fire. But as soon as they tried, Ward hit a man carrying a mortar tube.

As they tried to regroup, Ward managed to hit four more. They tried to return fire with their AK-47s, but Ward and Feekes were out of range and could see the tracer falling short.

The medevac helicopter was now on its way in. Ward could no longer see through his scope because so much heat was coming off the barrel. But he loosed off a few more harassing shots. Once the helicopter was clear, the enemy position was pounded by mortar and artillery fire.

Feekes was left stunned. His head had been right next to the muzzle, but the lieutenant reported that not one enemy bullet had hit the chopper. He was so pleased that he offered to sign the kill sheets before they had even gone out to inspect the bodies. At the tree line, they found 17 dead NVA soldiers. Six had been killed by sniper fire.

Later, a near miss by a mortar knocked Ward's scope out of true, and it would no longer hold a setting. He and Feekes used this as an excuse to take it to the armory at An Hoa in the hope of getting a better assignment. Instead he found himself in another confrontation with authority.

Ward and Feekes had been assigned to another company when it stopped at the edge of a plateau. Below, about 700 yards (640 meters) away, was a village. The snipers were called up. Ward and Feekes scanned the village and judged it to be friendly. The captain disagreed. He called in an air strike, and the village disappeared in a ball of flame. Then a figure came running out, straight toward their position, and the captain ordered Ward to shoot.

Through his rifle scope, Ward could see that the figure was a woman clutching a baby. He told the captain, who took no notice and again ordered Ward to shoot.

Ward balked. He offered the captain his rifle and said that, if he wanted them dead, he could shoot them. The captain said that he was giving Ward a direct order. Again Ward refused. The captain threatened him with a court-martial. It made no difference. A supply helicopter arrived. Ward and Feekes took it back to base. When he explained what had happened to his commander, the commander refused to allow the company to utilize any more sniper teams.

Intelligence came that an NVA officer made regular visits to his girlfriend in the village of Giang Hoa, some 13 kilometers north of An Hoa. Ward and Feekes were assigned to take him out. It was going to be a difficult task. They were going to have to travel eight miles across hostile territory and cross the Thu Bon River without being detected.

They set out at first light on September 22, wearing full camouflage and traveling light. They figured that carrying a radio would only slow them down. Along the way, they had to employ all their skills of stealth and concealment and frequently changed their route to avoid even the most innocent-looking peasant. If anyone saw them, they would have had to call off the mission.

The sun was almost setting when they reached the river. Their maps did not tell them how deep it was at that point. Ward waded into the water with his rifle held above his head, with Feekes going ahead to probe for any holes or obstacles that might be on the bottom. The Remington Model 700 is a precision instrument, and it was vital that he did not stumble and get the scope wet.

Dusk had fallen by the time they reached the far bank. Stripping off their clothes to dry them, they wrapped themselves in their ponchos, taking turns to sleep. It was still dark when they set off down the trail again, watching for booby traps every step of the way.

There was a certain trail the captain used to travel to and from the village. It was already light as they neared it, and they had to crawl the last 500 yards (450 meters) to avoid detection. Once they were in their firing position and well camouflaged, they set about observing the trail, which was soon full of people, carts, and bicycles—but no one who answered the NVA captain's description.

As the sun rose in the sky, they found themselves plagued by a swarm of tiny mosquitoes. More were attracted when they had to piss where they lay. Feekes scanned the trail that ran for about a mile down to the village. Ward watched the other end where it disappeared over a low hill. After a couple of hours, Ward noticed a man in civilian clothes come down the track. Feekes trained his binoculars on him and confirmed that he matched the description of the NVA captain. What's more, he could see a holster under his shirt. This made him a valid target.

Ward began to have doubts. The man looked nervous. Perhaps he was not the captain at all, but a common soldier being used as a lure to catch a bigger fish and flush out the snipers themselves. But at 900 yards (820 meters) he put these doubts away, and at 800 yards (730 meters) he fired. The match round hit the target in the chest and threw him backward. Those around him scattered. Then the snipers waited. They had revealed their position. Was gunfire about to rake their hide?

After 20 minutes, they moved warily down onto the trail. It could still be a trap. While Feekes stood watch, Ward searched the body. The bullet had gone through his heart, killing him instantly. Ward found no documents confirming his identity. But the man was well groomed and well fed, and he was carrying a pistol with a red star on the handle. Ward was satisfied. He put a match round on his chest, and they ran off. When they stopped for a rest, Ward filled out the kill sheet. Back at An Hoa, he handed it in for signing, then cleaned his rifle and went to bed.

After a shard of shrapnel hit him above the right eye during an action that saw three marines killed and seven wounded, Ward was awarded the Purple Heart. He went on to fight another sniper duel just two days later. On October 6, he was with Charlie Company of the 3rd Battalion, 5th Marines when India Company was pinned down for three hours by an enemy sniper. From a tree line 1,000 yards (915 meters) ahead, he had already killed two marines and injured three more.

Ward was called up. Charlie Company was 2,000 yards (1,830 meters) from the sniper's position, and Ward asked whether he would move in closer. Permission was denied as an air strike was due as soon as the cloud cover lifted. However, Ward eventually got permission to move 100 yards (91 meters) to the flank to get a better angle. Even though he was still 2,000 yards away, Ward decided to take a shot. After all, it was within the capabilities of his weapon.

Feekes and Ward scanned the tree line for a muzzle flash or a puff of smoke. But the enemy sniper was too clever for them. They decided that something drastic had to be done. Feekes loaded a magazine with tracer and emptied it at the trees. The sniper would now know exactly where they were. And when he popped up, Ward would be ready to take him down. But he did not show himself. Even waving a T-shirt around did not attract his fire. Instead he concentrated on India Company, killing another man.

The cloud cover lifted, revealing that the forest was hit with napalm and high explosives. But the sniper survived and wounded another marine. After that, he melted away. Another VC was not so lucky. Ward took him out at 1,800 yards (1,645 meters) through mist while resting his Remington on a gravestone.

Like other snipers, Ward was not a jealous man. He was happy for others to take a shot. When he and his new spotter,

Pat Zenishek, were dug in with Whiskey Company one night on a hilltop and came under fire, Zenishek grabbed his M14 with its Starlite scope and returned fire while Ward spotted for him. But when his magazine was empty, Ward pulled him back into the foxhole. He had been using tracer and the enemy would now know where they were.

Later Ward and Zenishek were hit by shrapnel. They were medevaced out direct to Da Nang. Ward arrived at the hospital still clutching his—Mawhinney's—rifle and only let go of it when the colonel arrived. Even then, he insisted that it was checked into the armory and the serial number recorded. As soon as he was up and about, he would limp to the armory and check on it.

By the end of November, Ward was back in An Hoa and out on sniper missions again. In January 1970, he and his new spotter, Terry Lightfoot, went out on a predawn mission. They were going into an area where Ward had taken down a large formation of North Vietnamese soldiers some months before. It seems that the NVA had also remembered the incident. When an enemy platoon came out of the trees, they headed straight for the sniper's position. It was plain that they stood no chance, so Ward called in an air strike. But it was going to take the planes 10 minutes to get there.

The NVA started across the paddy field toward them. They had already set up machine guns and mortars. There was no time to wait for the planes. The two of them would have to hold off the NVA until the air strike arrived.

They waited until the enemy was 700 yards (640 meters) away. Ward gave the signal. His first shot hit a machine gunner in the head, while Lightfoot took down the first three men before they could dive for cover. Bullet two took out another machine gunner. Bullet three downed a mortarman, and bullet four hit another mortarman just as he was dropping a round into the tube. The shot threw it off course, and it landed among his own men. Meanwhile, Lightfoot hit another four and pinned down the rest.

The NVA were firing back with AK-47s, but their fire came in random bursts. Plainly they had not located the snipers. But that would not matter if the machine guns got going and raked the whole area with fire.

Ward hit the man who had taken over the first machine gun. Then came his first miss. As the machine gun fire began to creep nearer their position, over the radio they heard that the bombing run was about to begin. Ward took out another machine-gunner. They only had to hold the enemy off for another few seconds, which Ward used to take out another mortarman.

Then they saw the enemy's position being strafed and rocketed. The tree line erupted in a ball of flame as the napalm hit. But farther back in the trees, heavy machine guns opened up. Ward could see the tracer arcing skyward. They radioed through, warning the second plane of the heavy ground fire, and it aborted its bombing run. He then called in the artillery to cover their escape.

As they made their way to safety, Ward found that the shrapnel wound he had suffered earlier was slowing him down. When he got back to base, he needed morphine to kill the pain. His days as a sniper were numbered, so he handed his Remington on to Lightfoot with the same words Mawhinney had used when he had given it to him: "Take care of my baby."

He spotted for Lightfoot. After Lightfoot had made 12 kills with the Remington, Ward got him a new spotter and took off for some R&R. Soon after that, he was rotated home and given an early discharge. During his time in Vietnam he had made 63 confirmed kills.

In 1996, the famed Remington Model 700 bolt-action sniper rifle, serial number 221552—designated an M40A1 by the army— that was used in Vietnam by Mawhinney, Ward, and Lightfoot was found at the Weapons Training Battalion at the Marine Corps base in Quantico, Virginia. It was retrofitted to the configuration that Mawhinney had used and is now on display in the National Museum of Marine Corps Iconic Artifacts exhibit.

Ed Kugler joined the marines at the age of 17 to get out of his hometown of Lock Seventeen, Ohio, a community of just 75 residents. During the US invasion of the Dominican Republic in 1965, Kugler was injured in the hand and eyes when his unit was pinned down in a field by a machine gun and an M79 round he was carrying was hit by a bullet. Fortunately, it did not go off. He recovered, only to be injured again in a car accident while drunk driving. He could have left the service then, but he had heard stories about Vietnam from the first marines to be rotated home and was determined to go—even though he did not know where Vietnam was.

Sent to California for jungle training at Camp Pendleton, he proved himself to be an expert rifleman, even though he had never fired anything but a BB gun before. Once in Vietnam, he volunteered to become a scout-sniper when a sniper team was being formed for the 4th Marines. To Kugler, taking on the enemy one-on-one with a high-powered rifle sounded a lot better than getting in a line and charging a machine gun.

He was sent to sniper school in Phu Bai, where he trained on a Winchester Model 70 .30-06. Then he and his partner, Zulu, were assigned to 3rd Force Recon. On his first outing, his patrol was attacked, and he found out how useless his bolt-action sniper rifle was in a firefight. He took a bullet in the backpack. Eventually, Zulu threw him an M14 taken from a wounded marine.

The following morning, the dead and wounded were choppered out. That left a patrol of just six. Kugler held on to the M14 but still had to carry his Winchester, which snagged on the undergrowth. He reflected on how useless it was to carry a rifle that could fire 1,000 yards in a jungle where you could barely see 20 feet.

They spent three days observing an enemy village, but when Kugler asked permission to take one of the villagers out, it was refused. When they moved out, an air strike took out the village completely.

On their next patrol, Kugler and Zulu carried .45-caliber Thompson submachine guns, but they found them too heavy to carry along with all their other gear. The next time, they traded them in for automatic M14s.

They were transferred up to an observation post on the top of a mountain peak known as the Rockpile near the demilitarized zone (DMZ). For two weeks they acted as spotters for the artillery and had still done no sniping. Then they spotted an opportunity. They saw enemy activity some 700 yards (640 meters) to the west and asked permission to take a shot. The lieutenant was amused by the suggestion, not thinking that they could shoot that far. But he gave his permission anyway.

It was 1000 hours, so heat would not be a factor, and they could judge the wind by watching the movement of the treetops between them and the target. Still it would be no easy shot. As he would be shooting down from a 700-foot (215-meter) peak, Kugler would not be able to lie down to take the shot. Sitting up, he rested his rifle on his backpack. He rehearsed his training in his mind and prepared to make his first real sniper shot. Then he squeezed the trigger. Zulu, spotting, gave his verdict. It was a kill. The lieutenant was impressed.

Then it was Zulu's turn. They kept their eyes on the corpse. Eventually, another enemy soldier came out to recover it, and Zulu scored his first kill. They continued watching the area for most of the day. By the end, Kugler had scored three kills, and Zulu two.

Kugler was accompanied by Pearl when a South Vietnamese unit requested sniper help at Con Thien, which was also in the

DMZ. They had no night sights, but their 7 x 50-mm binoculars worked well enough if there was moonlight. One night, Pearl saw lights that swayed to and fro like a group of people walking along together. Kugler called an ARVN lieutenant, who dismissed it as an optical illusion. After all, they had no night vision equipment. For the next two nights, they saw the same thing. It seemed as if the NVA was simply marching right by them. So on the fourth night, Kugler asked permission to call in artillery. Again the lieutenant said no. They began to wonder whose side he was on.

After two weeks of this, Kugler spotted movement during the day. It was some 1,420 yards (1,300 meters) away. He asked the lieutenant for permission to fire—after all, the ARVN had requested the help of snipers. The lieutenant laughed at the thought that they would make an effective shot over that distance, and he gave permission to try. Even Pearl thought it was impossible. But there was no wind. It was early afternoon and it was hot, so there would be less air resistance to slow the bullet. Indeed, hot air rising from the ground would help keep the round airborne. And 1,300 meters was within the range of the Winchester.

With Pearl spotting, Kugler got on the roof of the bunker and rested his rifle on his backpack. Through the scope he could see the target go in and out of a hootch as if he were building something. With the scope at maximum elevation, he squeezed off a shot. Pearl did not even see where it landed. He tried again with the crosshairs on the top of the man's head. Again he missed. The shooting was now drawing a crowd. Pearl though they should stop before they made fools of themselves in front of the ARVN. But Kugler was adamant.

This time he aimed over the top of the man's head. He missed again, but this time the man looked up. Plainly he had heard the shot, though he would not have imagined that it could be coming from so far away. The fourth round made the man duck. He fell to one knee and looked around for whoever was shooting at him. The ARVN were also wondering what Kugler was shooting at.

Kugler chambered the fifth and final round. He checked the treetops and the elephant grass. Still no sign of wind. With the vertical crosshair still on the man's body, Kugler aimed higher still. This time when Kugler fired, the man threw himself to the ground. Now Pearl spotted a puff of dust behind him. He was in the frame. Kugler needed one more shot. But there was no time to reload as the man ran inside the hootch.

The entire base had now turned out to watch Kugler, who worried that they could all be killed with a single grenade. He reloaded. Now he would have to play a waiting game. After two hours, he was rewarded. The man gingerly came out of the hootch. The air was still. Kugler raised his aim so that only the very top of the target's head was in the scope. Then he squeezed the trigger. Pearl could scarcely believe his eyes when the man fell dead. Strangely, the lieutenant was not happy. There would be no more work for the snipers to do, but every night the lights kept on going past the base.

Despite this, Kugler and Pearl were sent out on patrol with the ARVN to set up an ambush. But it seemed to the two Americans that the South Vietnamese soldiers lacked even the most basic of training. Nevertheless, they reached their dropping-off point without incident on the trail between a small village and a hill they knew to be booby-trapped.

After a night of heavy rain, they saw a Vietcong patrol making its way home. They could hardly see the ARVN at the far end of the village and tried to raise them on the radio. There was no answer. There were seven enemy soldiers walking in a line at about 300 yards (275 meters). Kugler took the tail-end Charlie, and Pearl the point. While they were reloading, the enemy quickly returned fire. Although the ARVN fired from the other side of the village, it was plain they were not going to ride to the rescue.

Soon rounds were landing perilously close to the two Americans. They dropped their Winchesters and grabbed their M14s. As Kugler turned to fire, his foot caught on something. He kicked it free. Then he saw a puff of smoke, and a Chincom grenade landed between his legs. He dived into the bushes and covered his head. The grenade did not go off. It was a dud. Only the detonator had exploded, not the main charge. Then they saw the Vietcong make a run for it and downed another one.

Pearl was killed soon after, and Kugler got a new partner, Greek. They went out on a patrol that split into two for a search-and-destroy mission. The snipers got permission to go out on their own and overlook the other two groups. As one of the groups approached a village, the snipers saw two Vietcong behind the houses. They got permission to fire and set up a camouflaged position about 200 yards (180 meters) from the targets. Their rifles were zeroed on 600 yards (550 meters), so they had to shoot low. Firing together, they took out the two VC.

The next day, the patrol was shot at by a sniper, wounding one man, as they were entering a village. Once the man was medevaced out, they went into the village and told the inhabitants that if they harbored snipers, the Americans would burn the village down. It did no good. That evening a sniper began taking potshots at them again. A corporal with the reputation of being a crazy man noticed a young boy and assumed he was spotting for the sniper. The lieutenant ordered Kugler to shoot the child.

Kugler protested that the boy was only about 11 and was not carrying a weapon. The corporal also insisted that he shoot the kid. Kugler refused. The corporal then took Kugler's gun and took out the boy at 150 yards (135 meters). The corporal was killed in a firefight the following day.

Another mission ended in disaster, partly due to the new M16s they had been issued. Thirty-five marines were dead. This convinced Kugler the snipers would be better off going out patrolling on their own, where they could use their skills to the fullest rather than act as inappropriately equipped grunts. Kugler requested that they be sent out in the free-fire zone of Co Bi Than Tan Valley and extended his tour for another six months to prove his point. When he returned from leave in the States, he found that sniper patrols were already out in Co Bi Than Tan valley, and he headed out to Hill 51, the center of their operations. The sniper patrols there had taken the call sign "Rogues."

They went on patrol in fives, carrying two Winchesters and three M14s. But Kugler's first kill on patrol was hardly a sniper shot. Through the jungle he saw a Vietcong in black pajamas holding a rifle just 15 feet (4.5 meters) away. He aimed at the man but hesitated, wanting him to turn and look down his gun sights before he killed him. But the man realized he had been spotted and raised his rifle. Kugler hit him with a burst of automatic fire from his M14. He felt no remorse when he saw that, with his antiquated M1, the VC also had Chincom grenades, the sort used in booby traps.

Figuring that the Vietcong would not expect them to return to the same spot, they went back there one night with charcoal made from burnt wood smeared across their faces. Nearby was a small mound covered in elephant grass. They took up position there, pulling up the grass they had flattened after them, a trick Kugler had learned in Force Recon.

The sun was already high in the sky when they saw a man coming down the track. They waited to make sure that he was not with a larger unit they could not handle on their own. When it turned out that he was alone, he got a third eye at 175 yards (160 meters). They waited through a long, hot afternoon. Finally another man turned up. He had a pack on his back, but did not appear to be carrying a gun. This was a free-fire zone though. Any male of military age was a legitimate target. They waited until he

was just 11 yards (10 meters) away before the shot rang out. Snipers are taught to shoot at great distances, not close up. The bullet
hit him in the leg and knocked him down. Despite the wound, he
got up again and ran. Two snipers ran after him, but then one of
them unslung his M14 and shot the fleeing man in the back. In his
backpack, they found more grenades and booby traps.

Although they were occasionally called in to scout for larger
units, they continued these five- or four-man patrols until they
felt they owned the valley. But there were failures. After going out
hours before dawn to set up an ambush, Kugler missed a shot from
440 yards (400 meters). The man ran for his life and had disappeared before Kugler could chamber another round.

There were still booby traps on the trails, but the Vietcong
made themselves scarce. This instilled a dangerous complacency.
After four days in the field, they were just 500 yards (450 meters)
from Hill 51, heading home, when a bullet whistled overhead.
Thirty yards (27 meters) down the trail, more bullets flew by. They
threw themselves to the ground again. It was hot, and at Hill 51
the inviting prospect of a cold beer beckoned. They decided to
head on. Another 50 yards (45 meters) down the trail, outside an
abandoned village, they were fired on again. This time they did not
even bother to get down. Instead they strolled into the village, looking for the sniper who dared fire on the snipers' team. More shots
flew overhead. It was clear that their adversary was not a very good
shot. Without a word between them, they charged the tree line,
shooting and hollering. When they got there, the man had fallen
from the tree. No one knew who had shot him. One of them cut
off his ear as a trophy. Back on Hill 51, the lieutenant had seen the
whole thing through the scope of a tank, and he was worried.

But there were some notable successes. Seven of them were
hiding in the grass on the top of a mound that overlooked the
valley floor. Thinking that no one was around, they were having

a lively debate about the merits of various race cars. Then one of them got up to relieve himself and quickly fell down again, telling the others to be quiet. Peering out through the grass, they saw 11 black-clad Vietcong walking down a trail directly across their field of fire. The seven snipers lined up in a row. The first aimed at the point man, the next at the man behind him, and so on. Kugler found himself aiming at a young woman wearing a uniform and carrying an AK-47. They fired simultaneously, taking down the first seven in the column. The remaining four ran for it. Only two reached cover. Nine had been killed in one go.

They waited for an hour to see if anyone else turned up. Then they sent two out to guard their rear. Two remained on the mound to give covering fire if necessary, while Kugler and two others went down to search the bodies.

But there were also moments of compassion. The snipers hit a group of men who had women and children with them when they saw the men pull a radio out of a basket, plainly to communicate with the enemy. A teenage girl was hit in the leg. Kugler called in a medevac chopper as if one of his marines had been hit. He found himself in hot water.

The Rogues had built themselves a fearsome reputation. But the NVA began coming in ever-bigger formations. Patrols of five snipers could not take on the enemy when it came in companies, so they found themselves depending on mortars and artillery. In response, the NVA brought up heavy artillery, something snipers have no defense against. Posted up to the DMZ, all they could do was dig deep and stay in their bunkers as 300 rounds of high explosives came in a day.

Kugler was back at the Rockpile when he heard that the NVA was infiltrating a whole regiment to take them on. Then A-6 Intruders appeared in the sky and doused the area with napalm. But as the battle continued to rage, Kugler and his partner Huffer were asked whether they would work their way around the back of the NVA to support Mike Company. Both of them set off with a Remington 700 and an M14. They headed out along one of the long fingers that extended down from the peak. Eventually they got within 1,650 yards (1,500 meters) of the battle and, through their binoculars, they picked out individual firefights. But Kugler insisted on getting closer, so they crawled forward another 750 yards (685 meters).

From there, they could see a squad of marines coming down Highway 9. On the other side, the NVA opened up with their AK-47s, taking down the marines' point man. Two more marines were hit. When another moved up to help them, he too was wasted. They searched in vain for the NVA's position. Then Huffer spotted a puff of smoke coming from under a bush at the side of the road.

They radioed through the enemy's position. Then, with Huffer spotting, Kugler prepared for the shot. The marines tried to move up under cover of fire from an M60, but another one was downed. This also served to confirm the enemy's position. Kugler squeezed the trigger. Huffer saw it fall. It was 100 yards (90 meters) short. One of the marines ran across the highway with a machine gun and shot up the bush. But when his machine gun was empty and he ran back, the NVA soldiers popped up out of his spider hole and threw a grenade at him. He threw one back. There followed an exchange of grenades.

Kugler was determined to take another shot. Though he lined it up carefully, the shot again fell short. It seemed his Remington would not fire that far. This was his last shot of the war.

A Huey came in. As it hovered about three feet (one meter) above the ground, the door gunner sprayed the area with rounds from his M60. Another squad of marines came up. Their machine gunner stood above the spider hole and emptied a whole belt of ammunition into it.

Kugler and Huffer climbed back up to the Rockpile. He was awarded the Vietnamese Cross of Gallantry and sent home.

On November 4, 1967, Sergeant Bobby Sherrill of the 26th Marines arrived at the Bon Son River junction south of Hill 65. At around 1100, the rain stopped and the sun broke through the cloud cover. It was then that Sherrill saw an old man propelling a long thin boat down the river with a pole. In the prow stood an officer in a Chinese army uniform. He was carrying a pistol in a shoulder holster and binoculars that glinted in the sunlight. Though China was not officially involved in the Vietnam War, it often sent military advisors to aid the Communists. This man was certainly not destined for the front line. He was wearing not camouflage fatigues but a new uniform straight from the parade ground.

Sherrill was carrying an M1D, a sniper's rifle first made in World War II, with an M84 scope. It had been made by "Wild Bill" Johnson of Barstow, California. The Chinese officer was well outside the M1D's normal range, and the boat was near cover, so he would have just one shot.

But there was no wind, and he had a bench rest with good sandbag support. Sherrill estimated the range to be 850 yards (780 meters), while the M84 scope only adjusted to 650 yards (595 meters). To compensate, he aimed 6 to 8 inches (15 to 20 centimeters) above the officer's left shoulder. Sherrill breathed in, then partially exhaled, held his breath, and squeezed the trigger. He got back to the M49 spotter scope in time to see the Chinese officer toppling over the side of the boat and the old man, panicked and poling desperately for cover.

When he reported the kill, it was relayed to Intelligence. They wanted to tell the Pentagon and perhaps even the president that Sherrill had killed a Chinese officer. But first they wanted to send a helicopter to recover the body. Sherrill knew that the enemy had two M2 Browning machine guns in the vicinity. He did not want them to risk any lives recovering the body, so he lied and said it was only a "probable."

Army Major General Julian Ewell of the 9th Infantry Division noticed his snipers were not making as many kills as the marines. This was because they were being sent out with regular infantry patrols, and although they had more accurate weapons, they were operating as ordinary infantrymen. Ewell was determined to do something about it. He told his officers to retrain and redeploy their snipers and set up a new snipers' school where all but two of instructors were in the "President's Hundred," the hundred highest-scoring marksmen in the US.

Army snipers trained on match-grade M14s. They were expected to make one-shot kills at 765 to 875 yards (700 to 800 meters). They were also trained on Starlight scopes, as the enemy usually moved at night, and were expected to make a hit at 600 to 650 yards (550 to 600 meters) at night. Soon the 9th Infantry Division had 72 snipers, six per battalion plus four per brigade. Newly trained snipers were deployed in pairs with a security element of five to eight men. They were allowed to engage up to five-man enemy groups while the rest of the group held their fire. The snipers also maintained surveillance on anyone they had shot in the hope of picking off other enemy soldiers who tried to recover their equipment or the body.

As the Starlight scope needed a little ambient light to work, a Xenon searchlight with a pink filter or flares was used to give some illumination to the scene. Snipers were sometimes set up behind a village that was going to be searched to pick off any fleeing Vietcong. Or they were used as stay-behind elements after a patrol had made a sweep through an area to take out any hostiles who came along afterward.

Sergeant Adelbert F. Waldron, who had 109 confirmed kills to his name, making him the highest-scoring US sniper ever, was out on a stay-behind mission on the night of February 4, 1969. That day, Company D of the 3rd Battalion, 60th Division had sent a medical assistance patrol into a hamlet some one-and-three-quarters miles (three kilometers) south of Ben Tre in the hope of gaining intelligence on Vietcong movements in the area. As they left, Waldron and his partner set up an ambush position at the end of a large rice paddy adjacent to a wooded area.

At around 2105, five Vietcong came out of the woods toward Sergeant Waldron's position. He shot the lead man. The other four men hit the ground. But Waldron had used a noise suppressor on his gun, so they were not sure what was happening. After a few minutes they got up and began to move off. Sergeant Waldron killed all four, one after the other.

At 2345 hours, four more Vietcong moved into the rice paddy from the left of Sergeant Waldron's position. Again using a Starlight scope and a noise suppressor, he picked off all four of them. The average range was 440 yards (400 meters)—not a long shot, but good shooting at night.

Unlike the marines, who used bolt-action rifles, Sergeant Waldron used a semi-automatic weapon—an accurized M14 rifle, known popularly as an M21. The gun Waldron used was a National Match–quality weapon with a Leatherwood 3x–9x Adjustable Ranging Telescope and standard leather M1907 sling. Rock Island Arsenal converted 1,435 of these firearms for use as sniper weapons, sending them to Vietnam in 1969. From then until 1988, it was the US Army's principal sniper rifle. The M21 was accurate out to 875 yards (800 meters) and fired the M118 standard NATO 7.62-mm round.

General Ewell said Waldron was the Army's best sniper and gave this example: "One afternoon he was riding along the Mekong River on a Tango boat when an enemy sniper on shore pecked away at the boat. While everyone else on board strained to find the antagonist, who was firing from the shoreline 985 yards (900 meters) away, Sergeant Waldron took up his sniper rifle and picked off the Vietcong out of the top of a coconut tree with one shot (this from a moving platform)."

Marine Lance Corporal Jim Miller was a man of simple rules. With the 3rd Battalion, 7th Marines in Vietnam in 1968, he believed that long distance was the next best thing to being there. He also said, "If I wanted to shoot a gook at a range of five hundred meters, I had to aim at his balls in order to get him in the chest. If I wanted to shoot one at twelve hundred meters, I aimed at his head to get his heart. Simple arithmetic. It was his balls below a thousand, head beyond a thousand, and heart at a thousand." And he never failed to take an opportunity for a kill. Out on a hunting party with another sniper, Corporal Jay Taylor, a radioman, and two grunts, they came across a dozen naked Vietcong. They had dumped their clothes and weapons on the bank and were having a swim in a jungle river. It was too good an opportunity to miss. The snipers opened fire, turning the water scarlet. Two or three VC made it to the bank—but no farther. The wounded were dispatched with a couple of extra shots. But they were not alone. As Miller's party retreated, enemy mortars came raining down. Miller and his men, who carried their rifles in cases, called themselves "Murder Incorporated."

Before Marine Captain Jim Land opened his snipers' school there, Hill 55 was harassed by a VC sniper. In just two weeks, three marines had been killed and another two injured on an outcrop known as Finger One. Land and his spotter, Master Sergeant Donald L. Reinke, were called in to solve the problem. The tree line was some 770 yards (700 meters) away. That was assumed to be where the shots were coming from, but there was a small pile of brush in the grass 165 yards (150 meters) in front of the trees. It was such an obvious place for a sniper to hide that Land almost dismissed it. There were any number of places for the VC sniper to use as a firing position.

While Reinke set up the spotting scope and rifle, Land visited the doctor to ask about the entry point of the wounds. Then he asked around about the circumstances of each of the casualties and drew a map to plot back to where the shots had come from. Meanwhile, Reinke had noticed that birds that fed in the grass between the marine fire-base and the jungle avoided one patch. This corresponded to the area Land had figured out the shots were coming from, near the brush pile. It was right out in the middle of the grass where no one would expect a sniper to be hiding.

The following morning, Land and Reinke went out on a reconnaissance patrol. They left Hill 55 on the north side, then worked around by way of the jungle and the river in the hope of intercepting the sniper's path. Approaching the grassy area from the tree line, they found a faint trail of bent grass that led from the river up to the brush pile. They followed cautiously in case the sniper was already in place. When they reached the brush pile, they noticed that several other faint trails converged there. The sniper used several different routes to get there.

One of the trails was like a tunnel through the grass. It let out into the middle of the meadow. Land and Reinke followed it. It ended 110 yards (100 meters) beyond the brush pile in a flattened area that the sniper had obviously used as his hide. It was the perfect sniping position. From there he got a good shot at anyone on Finger One. Even if the marines on the hill suspected that was the general area the shots were coming from, they would have concentrated their fire on the brush pile. Once they had finished firing, the sniper could safely withdraw and return again when he felt like it.

Land and Reinke carefully made their way back by the route they had come. On the hill, they got the platoon leader to aim a

106-mm recoilless antitank gun on the hide. The next time the sniper fired a shot, a 106 mm blew him to smithereens. As Land said, there is more than one way to get one shot, one kill.

Snipers did not always work on their own initiative. Sometimes they accompanied a patrol and were expected to kill on demand. Marine Corporal Gary Reiter was out with a platoon in Quang Tri Province early one morning in 1967 when they came across a man washing his clothes in a stream. The platoon leader, a second lieutenant, ordered him to take the man out. Reiter knelt to steady his Winchester, put the crosshairs on the man's chest, and squeezed the trigger. The round flew over the target's head. Reiter's rifle was zeroed for 600 yards (550 meters). The man was only 200 yards (180 meters) away. He ran for cover.

The lieutenant looked at Reiter but said nothing. Reiter then noticed that the man had not gone far. He was standing just behind a tree. The platoon commander again ordered Reiter to kill him. This was a more difficult shot. The target was half-obscured by branches. But Reiter made no mistake. He hit the man in the chest. He could see the shirt ruffle and the blood spray out. The lieutenant offered his congratulations.

Then five NVA wheeled into sight. Reiter needed no order to fire. He took out the second man. A firefight quickly developed. The enemy were in strength, so the marines withdrew.

After a month's leave in the States, Reiter found himself out on patrol again, this time in Thua Thien Province. The platoon was being led by a gunnery sergeant. As night was falling, they were just descending a valley when the gunny called the snipers to the head of the formation. He pointed out two silhouettes against the last glimmer of dusk. They were 600 yards (550 meters) away. The gunny said to take them out.

Reiter put the scope on the first of them. In the failing light, he could not make out any of the figure's features. The target was just a dark shape against the dim sky. As Reiter took up the slack on the trigger, the man bent down and disappeared from view. Reiter turned quickly to the second figure. He put the crosshairs on his head and squeezed the trigger. The man fell.

Suddenly the hillside was ablaze with muzzle flashes, and a ferocious firefight ensued. The gunnery sergeant was on the radio reporting the contact. The next minute he was giving frantic orders to cease fire. They had been firing on a platoon from the 4th Marines. The man Reiter had taken out was a sniper. He did not know him, but Reiter did know his partner—the man who had bent down at the crucial moment and saved his own life.

Reiter was arrested and kept under guard in a pit in Dong Ha combat base for five days before being exonerated. The gunnery sergeant admitted that he had given the order to fire. He was docked two months' pay and busted in rank. But a marine was dead. Years later, Reiter still found it hard to forgive himself.

Corporal Greg Kraljev was another marine sniper with good reason to have regrets. He arrived in Vietnam in April 1969 and was sent to An Hoa, where there had been heavy fighting. It was just four miles (six-and-a-half kilometers) from the border with Laos and the Ho Chin Minh Trail, which the Communists used to infiltrate men and materiel from North Vietnam into the south. Indeed, the base there was rocketed within minutes of his arrival.

Although Corporal Kraljev was a trained sniper, he had to serve as a regular infantryman—a grunt—for a week or two before he could join a sniper platoon. Eager to prove his worth, he nearly got himself killed on his first patrol.

When his moment came, he was assigned to Hotel Company of the 2nd Battalion, 5th Marines as spotter to Steve Suttles, one of the best snipers, who finished the war with 63 kills. Suttles took him in hand and taught him his trade. They operated as a separate unit, detaching themselves from a platoon and remaining hidden until an unsuspecting enemy walked by.

After a month or so, Kraljek was given a Winchester Model 70. His spotter was to be his best friend and fellow sniper, Jim Seely, who was happier in the role of observer. But Kraljek himself was not quite ready to drop the hammer. On his second mission, he was out with Seely and a radioman named Chambers. They were dropped off by a patrol and hid up near a large area of rice paddies. They were in Arizona Territory, a free-fire zone. That meant the civilians had been evacuated and they could fire at anyone whether armed or not, except other marines.

Kraljek had yet to make his first kill when a young Vietnamese male began crossing the paddy fields. He was about 700 yards (640 meters) away. It was an easy shot for a trained sniper. He studied the target. The boy was a young teenager, no more than 14 years old. Kraljek knew there was no such thing as a noncombatant in Vietnam. Kids as young as six had been trained to deliver grenades to GIs with smiles on their faces. Kraljek studied the kid for 20 minutes, then put down his rifle, deciding that the boy was too young to die. Seely was relieved, but it was a decision Kraljek would live to regret.

They returned to An Hoa. That night the marine base was hit. After the attack was driven back, Chambers radioed in that there were dead Vietnamese outside the wire. His platoon leader told him to go out and check on them. Even though it was the middle of the night, he did as he was told. But the enemy had not withdrawn completely, and Chambers was fatally wounded.

The party that did it got theirs, though. As they were pulling back, they ran into a marine observation post and were cut down. When Kreljek went out in the morning to check the body, he found that one of them was the teenager he had decided not to kill in the paddy field the day before. Had he dropped the hammer on him, Chambers might still be alive. It was a mistake he would not make again. He said the guilt and rage he felt turned him into "robo-sniper." At the end of the tour he had 15 kills to his name.

Marine Corporal Ron Szpond was just 19 in 1966, but he had already been wounded and seen several of his buddies die before he was "volunteered" to join Captain Bob Russell's 3rd Marine Sniper School at Hill 127 and join what was then called the "Dirty Dozen." Later, he learned, people like him who wanted to get even were rejected from the sniper school. But that early in the war, everyone was welcome.

After three days' training, he was returned to the 2nd Battalion, 4th Marines—aka the Magnificent Bastards—with a Winchester Model 70 and an x8 Unertl scope ready for his revenge. His instructions were simple.

"I don't want anyone shooting civilians," his captain said. "But if I see we have armed VC, I'll give you permission to take them out."

His first mission as a sniper was to set up at the rear of a Vietnamese village while the infantry went in the front way. Two men came running out into Szpond's sights. The first was in khaki, carrying a rifle and pack. At 800 yards (730 meters), Szpond took him down. He turned out to be a Chinese military adviser.

Then Szpond moved his crosshairs to the second man, who was wearing the traditional VC black pajamas. He was surprised. If the man had run to his left or his right, he might have escaped with his life. But he kept right on running straight ahead into the sniper's sights. Szpond squeezed the trigger again, but the man kept charging. A second shot brought him down. It went right through both legs, severing an artery. The man dragged himself into some bushes, where he bled to death.

A few days after he was told that the VC and NVA had put a bounty on snipers' heads, he walked with a patrol into an ambush.

The marine in front of him was cut down. Szpond immediately threw his Winchester—a bolt-action sniper's rifle is virtually useless in a firefight—and grabbed the fallen man's M14. Then, screaming like a banshee, he ran straight at the enemy. No matter how crazy that might seem, it was better than going the other way, where you were likely to run straight into a minefield or a blocking force. If you were dropped as you ran away, the ambushers would catch up with you and slaughter you like a pig. But if you ran straight at them you could, at the very least, expect a nice clean kill.

As it was, the ambushers melted away. Szpond returned the M14 to the wounded marine, who, as he was being medevaced out, gave Szpond his .38 revolver for his future protection. Soon he would have good reason to thank the man. From then on, Szpond wore the .38 and a .45 everywhere he went.

Szpond soon figured that the VC liked to pick up on a marine patrol then follow it until they found a good time and place to attack. So he would drop off into the bushes after the patrol had crossed a paddy field. When the VC tracker came out into the open, he presented an easy shot. But the VC got wise to this tactic. One squad simply outflanked him and attacked the patrol from the rear. Szpond found himself cut off. He was alone in a jungle crawling with enemy soldiers. When they captured prisoners, they tortured them to death, often castrating them and shoving their severed genitals into their mouths as a warning. What they would do to a sniper did not bear imagining, so Szpond quickly tried to rejoin the patrol.

He tried to outflank the enemy. As a result, he ran straight into the rear of a VC element of five or six men who were also trying an outflanking maneuver. They were taken completely by surprise—so much so that it took a second or two before they turned their guns on him. By that time he had thrown his Winchester aside and drawn his two handguns. Pistols blazing like a frontier gunslinger, he dropped two of them. The rest ran, which was just as well since both his pistols were empty by then.

Sometimes the hunter became the hunted. A farmer spotted Szpond in his hide and told the NVA, hoping to claim a reward. From his hide, Szpond could see the men coming to get him. He could have dropped one, two, or even three of them. But eventually, they would have gotten him. However, he had already scouted an escape route through the thickest part of the jungle. As he fled, he stopped frequently to listen for anyone following. Then he heard someone coming his way. It was a soldier holding an AK-47 with his finger on the trigger. Szpond had taken cover, but he was sure that the man had seen him. He seemed to be looking straight at him. Szpond made a plan. If the man turned his rifle in Szpond's direction, he would roll over and cut the man down with his pistols. He nearly did that anyway, knowing that it would give away his position and lead to his death. At least, he would get his revenge first. But then the soldier looked away. He called out something to a comrade and moved off. Once he was out of sight, Szpond crawled away and escaped. For Szpond, knowing that people were out to kill him made the war personal. He was determined to kill those who wanted to kill him and his fellow marines.

And he had plenty of opportunity. During a sweep across the A Shau Valley, Szpond followed a platoon into Bong Son village. VC in the schoolhouse took down two marines with automatic fire. The VC, in turn, were taken with a 3.5 rocket through the window. Then Szpond took up a position on the roof. A couple of marines pointed out an elderly Vietnamese man leading a water buffalo across a dike to the jungle beyond. Szpond looked through his scope and saw that the buffalo had too many legs. An officer gave him permission to fire.

Szpond shot the water buffalo. As it fell, he saw that the VC had strapped equipment to the blind side. Instead of running, they tried to recover it. In a couple of seconds, Szpond had killed both of them. Spzond ended the war with 12 confirmed kills and 12 more unconfirmed.

In January 1967, sniper Vaughn Nickell and his spotter, Ron Willoughby, were selected by Sergeant Tom Casey, platoon sergeant of the 5th Marine Regiment Sniper Platoon, to reinforce Hotel Company of the 2/5 Marines for the forthcoming Operation Tuscaloosa. Hotel Company was stationed at an outpost called Phu Loc 6, some six miles northeast of An Hoa. Nickell carried an M14, while Willoughby still had an old Garand M1D. At the time, rumor had it that the M1D was going to be replaced by a new Remington bolt-action rifle, but for Willoughby the M1D was good enough.

Phu Loc 6 was being harassed by a Vietcong sniper known as Six O'Clock Charlie. Every evening at 1800 hours, he would fire a few shots at the marine outpost. Usually the rounds did no more damage than make a couple of holes in the sandbags surrounding the bunker of Second Lieutenant Ed Smith, commander of 3rd platoon. He was such a poor shot that the marines would tease him by leaving their hootches and deliberately exposing themselves to his fire. But then a round hit a marine in the buttocks and he had to be medevaced out, so Captain Jerry Doherty ordered that the Vietcong sniper be eliminated.

Lieutenant Smith picked 3rd platoon's best marksman, Private First Class John Culbertson, for the job. He was told to position himself in a camouflaged spider hole next to Smith's hootch each evening and take on the Vietcong sniper the next time he fired at the command post. Culbertson was from Oklahoma. His father, a World War II veteran, had taught his son to shoot everything from rabbits to white-tailed deer. He was as keen as any marine to kill the Vietcong. But he complained that his M14 had no scope. Its stock had gotten wet and swollen, and it simply was not up to the job. But Lieutenant Smith was not interested in excuses. He told Culbertson to turn up at the command bunker the following evening at 1500 hours, dig in, return fire, and kill the Vietcong sniper.

Sergeant Casey and his sniper team, just arrived at Phu Loc 6, were walking by. Lieutenant Smith had not seen them before and asked who they were. Casey introduced the sniper team, and Lieutenant Smith asked them to join Culbertson the next day. Naturally, Casey and his men were delighted by the prospect.

Casey was from South Carolina, where he used to hunt rabbits and squirrels. He claimed to have been weaned on a Winchester. The next day he began work early, scanning the paddy fields beyond the wire with a battered pair of binoculars. He spotted a mound about 440 yards (400 meters) from the perimeter wire with a small pile of rocks on it. This, he decided, was the sniper's firing position. He then traced the sniper's pathway to his rocky hide, which took him across a furrowed field beyond the paddies' dikes. It lay to the west, so the sniper could crawl into position unobserved against the setting sun. That was why he always started shooting at the outpost at 1800 hours. Casey reckoned that he would be using an old Moisin-Nagant, a sniper rifle of World War II vintage. Its range was about 400 meters. Casey was confident that the marines were better equipped and trained and would prevail.

That evening, Willoughby and Nickell got in position by the command bunker. Around 1745, a bullet came whining over their heads and hit the sandbags of the bunker. It was clear that the Vietcong sniper was targeting them. Another shot range rang out. It missed them by inches. This time they saw the muzzle flash. It came not from the rocky sniper's hide but from the hillside over 3,200 feet (about 1,000 meters) away. They would have to wait until he got closer or showed himself before taking another shot.

Through his 7.5 x 50 binoculars, Willoughby spotted some movement. The Vietcong sniper was making his way along a ditch, coming closer to the marines' lines. Leaving aside his M14, Nickell picked up the Garand M1D and put it to his shoulder. It was loaded with a 173-grain match boat-tail bullet from Lake City Army Ammunition Plant. Through the 2.5x scope, he picked up the movement. The target was tiny. The VC sniper was straight on to him, but he could not even see the man's face. The wind was gusting, and Nickell did not hold out much hope of hitting the VC sniper at that distance, but a shot landing near him might make the man get up and run away, thereby presenting a bigger target. The M1D was zeroed on 330 yards (300 meters), so he aimed 6 feet (2 meters) over his head. Then he flipped the safety off and squeezed the trigger.

The rifle bucked, and the scope went out of focus, so Nickell did not see where the shot fell. But Willoughby did. It was slightly to the left and about three feet (one meter) short. It bounced off the hard ground and landed in a paddy field half a mile farther on. Nickell adjusted his aim. The second shot kicked up dust right next to Six O'Clock Charlie, who moved to get out of harm's way. A third shot hit him in his head, which exploded like a pumpkin struck with a hammer. The shot was over 1,200 yards (1,100 meters), the longest kill using an M1D.

Snipers Loren Kleppe and Ulysses Black, both 19 years old, were with Foxtrot Company during Operation Tuscaloosa. They were fording the Thu Bon River when they came under fire from Vietcong dug into the opposite bank. Soon they were pinned down. Then 81-mm mortars began falling on them. The company commander, Captain George Burgett, was wounded in the legs. His radio operator, who had taken a direct hit, was blown to pieces.

The marines returned fire, but the enemy was almost invisible, and targets were hard to find. Then Kleppe spotted the muzzle flash of an enemy machine gun. He took aim with his M1D and pulled the trigger. His 173-grain match bullet hit the gunner in the face, slicing his cheek off. Another VC gunner took his place. Kleppe kept his aim and fired again, killing him.

While Captain Doherty of Hotel Company called up artillery support, Kleppe and Black dug in at a sand dune at the side of the river. Shells from the 105-mm howitzers at An Hoa made the Vietcong keep their heads down. But between each volley, VC snipers would peer through the smoke and dust, looking for their next target. From his shallow hole, Kleppe saw one looking over the edge of a trench, taking aim with an ancient Moisin-Nagant sniper rifle. The sniper fired at a wounded marine, hitting his leg. The Vietcong's tactic was not to kill the enemy. Wounding a man would bring others to his rescue, who could also be shot at. They also knew that the cries of anguish of wounded men demoralized their comrades.

As the VC sniper hit another wounded marine, Kleppe raised his rifle. The shot was only 110 yards (100 meters). Through the smoke of the battlefield, he did not see the bullet hit, but there were no more shots fired from that trench. Kleppe and Black then swapped to their M14s to keep up harassing fire.

Willoughby and Vaughn were with Hotel Company as they forded the river farther downstream. They were halfway across with their rifles held high above their heads when the Vietcong opened up. They found cover on a sandbar and began digging in. Amid the screams of the marines who were being cut down by automatic fire from the far bank, Willoughby took aim with his M1D, picking off VC gunners in the enemy trench line, while Nickell peppered them with fire from his M14. But there was little they could do to stop the massacre, which only ended when the artillery zeroed in on the far bank.

When the artillery had done its worst, Willoughby and Nickell began picking off the wounded the VC had left behind in the trenches to cover their withdrawal. Slowly they advanced across the river and clambered up the far bank. After a short rest, the call came: "Snipers up!" The next objective was a Vietcong mortar position.

Captain James A. Graham, who had taken over from the injured Captain Burgett, decided not to attack the mortar position with his main force but rather to let the snipers pick apart its defenses first. Willoughby and Nickell were sent around the right flank, while Kleppe and Black, who had now been joined by Jim Flynn, were sent around the left. Their job would be to take out the machine-gunners who defended the mortars. They crept forward down the trail, looking out for booby traps, and headed for the sound of the mortars that had opened up again.

After 10 minutes, Kleppe and Black were overlooking the mortar position. Through his binoculars, Black saw a bush move. Under it, a VC sniper was crawling forward. Black indicated the enemy gunman to Kleppe, who took aim. The .30-06 bullet hit the man, flipping him over on his side. When another VC came up to see what had happened, Kleppe took his head off.

110 yards (100 meters) to Kleppe and Black's right, Willoughby and Nickell heard the shots. They were answered by a burst of fire from an enemy machine gun. Willoughby and Nickell crawled forward to within 44 yards (40 meters) of the machine gun position. Willoughby raised himself into a kneeling position and scanned the scene. It was then that he saw a VC rifleman moving toward him. The man was well camouflaged. Otherwise they would have seen him earlier. But the VC had seen Willoughby. His SKS rifle was already raised to fire. Willoughby raised his heavy M1D, already fearing that it was too late to defend himself. Then he heard a shot. The VC crumpled and collapsed. Nickell had had no time to aim. He simply raised his M14 and fired. From 33 yards (30 meters) he had shot the man through the chest, killing him instantly.

It was Nickell's first kill, and as he was a religious man, it troubled him deeply. Eventually he had to be taken for counseling. Meanwhile an air strike finished off the mortar position.

Two more 5th Marine Regiment snipers, Fred Sanders and Dennis Toncar, were sent with Golf Company to block the retreat of the Vietcong. They were choppered into the Que Son Valley by a CH-46 Sea Knight.

Almost as soon as Golf Company formed up, they came under fire. Toncar pulled out his binoculars, while Sanders shouldered his M1D, trying to spot muzzle flashes through its scope. Three marines in the point unit were hit—one killed, two injured. Then the enemy broke off.

After the casualties were medevaced, Golf Company headed out. Ten minutes later, they came under fire again. Another marine was killed, and two more were injured. The marines had not even seen the enemy yet. It was clear that specialized help was needed, so the gunnery sergeant told Sanders and Toncar to take point. Sanders explained that they would be no good on point, as the M1D Garand was useless in close-quarters combat. The gunny said that if snipers were no good on point, they were no good for anything. They would have to depend on artillery, so they radioed An Hoa and put the eight-inch howitzers on alert.

By the time they reached the next village, though, they were at the limit of the artillery's range, which was roughly 10.5 miles (17 kilometers), so Sanders and Toncar were called up to scope out the hamlet. They spotted a Vietnamese sentry holding an automatic weapon. The gunny radioed a situation report to battalion head-quarters in An Hoa. Sanders and Toncar were then told to take out the sentry.

Lying on the ground with his legs spread, Sanders tightened the sling to take the weight of the Garand. Then he put his eye to the side-mounted scope. He took his time. Settling the crosshairs on the sentry's chest, he breathed in, then exhaled slowly until the crosshairs fell back into place. He squeezed the trigger. The 173-grain match bullet went right through the sentry's heart and smashed him against the hut behind him. He was dead before he hit the ground. Then the rest of the marines opened up on the village with machine guns, grenades, antitank weapons, and small arms fire.

No sooner had the mayhem finished than the marines themselves came under fire. This time it was not the hit-and-run bursts of a small band of guerrillas but the all-out assault of a large and disciplined force. The two snipers and the rest of the marines quickly dug themselves in, and Toncar returned fire with his M14. An artillery barrage was called on the Vietcong's position. Sanders spotted a man in a dark green uniform—either a North Vietnamese soldier or a Chinese advisor. He was signaling the troops to bring them in closer. That way the American artillery could not reach them without the risk of killing their own men.

Plainly this man was the field commander. He was just 110 yards (100 meters) away. Sanders took aim and put a .308 bullet through the man's heart. The artillery did the rest. Fortunately, the ground was soft, absorbing the impact of the shells and limiting the spread of shrapnel. Nevertheless, in their hastily dug foxholes, the marines were terrified.

Meanwhile Casey and Willoughby, his acting spotter, were making a sweep to the north with Echo Company. Out on patrol, Casey kept an olive-drab towel draped over the scope of his M1D to protect it from moisture. On the first night, after digging in beside a paddy field, Casey and Willoughby took four-hour watches. After dark, two shots from a Moisin-Nagant sniper rifle came flying past Sergeant Casey's foxhole. He could tell from the noise they made that they came from a long rifle. It was too dark for Casey to fire back effectively, but a marine came up with an M79 grenade launcher. Casey pointed out roughly where the sniper was. He fired a number of 40-mm high-explosive grenades in that general direction, making a saw-tooth pattern out to 220 yards (200 meters). There was no more incoming fire that night, and in the morning a badly burned body was found in the paddy field.

Casey and Willoughby were sent to guard a sidewinder missile that had fallen off an F-4 Phantom until an EOD team could come to dispose of it. Scoping the surroundings with his binoculars, Willoughby spotted a crowd of Vietnamese running toward the marine patrol. Through his scope, Casey could see that some of them were armed. But they had women and children with them, so he dropped the rifle. Just then, another marine tripped a booby trap, and a fragment of shrapnel tore into Casey's leg. The two men were medevaced out, leaving Willoughby on his own.

Sergeant Casey was well enough to be back in action when Operation Newcastle kicked off in March 1967. He sent two sniper teams to support Bravo Company of the 1st Battalion, 5th Marines, going back into Que Son Valley. Vaughn Nickell was now teamed up with Tom Elbert. Loren Kleppe's new spotter was Fofo Tuitele, an American Samoan.

The snipers were accompanying a patrol that was fired on by heavy machine guns, badly wounding one man in the arm. The injured man was pinned down in a paddy field and would die if medical help did not reach him shortly. While the rest of the patrol went to clear the village that the sentries were guarding with their heavy machine guns, the snipers took on the machine gun crew with their M14s and their newly issued Remington 700 bolt-action sniper rifles. Under the weight of fire, the gunners fled.

When the village was searched, the two machine gunners were found in a spider hole. Meanwhile, a Navy corpsman attended the wounded man, but he died before a chopper arrived to take him to the hospital in Da Nang. One of the Vietcong machine gunners tried to escape. Having just seen his patient die, the corpsman put a gun to the prisoner's temple and shot him. Then the village was torched.

Later, Tom Elbert was teamed up with Ken Barden and sent back into Que Son Valley. Elbert carried a Remington Model 700, while Barden carried an M14 spotter rifle and 7 x 50-mm binoculars. They joined Lima Company of the 3rd Battalion, 5th Marines at Hill 10 north of Chu Lai. Then they set out on foot through the paddies, doing their best to keep their equipment clean and dry. Like Casey, Elbert had taken to covering his scope with a towel.

Ahead, the point man had just reached the crest of a low hill when the snipers were called up. In the valley below was a village thought to be under Communist control. Elbert and Barden were to cover the four point fire-team scouts as they went into the village ahead of the main column.

It was beginning to rain when they set up their hide. As the scouts went down into the village, Barden noticed three VC walking across the paddy fields directly toward them. He pointed them out to Elbert, who moved into a cross-legged position and aimed his Remington M-700 at the first VC. The range-finder said they were 440 yards (400 meters) away. The elevation knob on Elbert's Redfield scope was set at 330 yards (300 meters), and he intended to aim about 1 foot (30 centimeters) above the man's head. The wind was gusting up to 10 miles an hour, and he reckoned that it would carry the bullet about 6 inches (15 centimeters) to the left, so he would aim just to his right, over the man's right shoulder. That way if a gust of wind blew the bullet off-course by as much as 10 inches (25 centimeters), it would still hit his body. These details were passed back and forth between Elbert and Barden as they talked through the shot.

By the time he was ready to fire, the range was down to 385 yards (350 meters). Barden switched his M14 to semi-automatic and aimed for the second man's head. Elbert squeezed the trigger, and a 168-grain bullet hit the man in his chest, making an exit wound in his back the size of a baseball. Then Barden fired. As the shot flew across the paddy field, it dropped, hitting the second man in the stomach and breaking his spine. The two men flew backward across the field, Barden's target bent double. The third VC turned and ran toward the village.

The scouts were closing on the village. One of them knelt, raised his rifle, and took down the third VC. The scouts then turned their fire on the village. Barden joined in with a few bursts from his M14. Then he turned his attention back to the paddy field. Suddenly, two Vietcong gunmen emerged from some trees and, again, ran directly toward the snipers' hide. Elbert reloaded his Remington.

"You take the leader," said Barden. "I'll take the other guy."

Seconds after Elbert fired, Barden squeezed off his second shot. Both targets fell dead. Soon after, they watched as Lima Company entered the village, where they killed over a dozen VC and burned the place down.

Jim Flynn was teamed up with Tony Spanopoulos—inevitably known as Tony the Greek—who was from the Palisades, New Jersey. They were on patrol 7.5 miles (12 kilometers) south of Hill 51 when they were shot at across a paddy field by an enemy sniper. The bullet clipped Flynn's elbow, shattering the bone, and went on through the leg of another marine. Before Flynn was medevaced out, he told Spanopoulos to find the sniper and kill him. Spanopoulos had already worked out that the sniper was out of range of the M16 he was carrying, so he took Flynn's Remington.

As the helicopter carrying the two injured marines dusted off, the enemy sniper took another shot, hitting the platoon commander, Lieutenant Jewel, in the arm. Spanopoulos took a fireteam of four marines and went out after the sniper. He knew that their opponent was a seasoned sniper, so he moved position after every shot. As Spanopoulos surveyed the landscape looking for a place for a hide, another shot rang out, narrowly missing his head. About 660 yards (600 meters) to his right was a grassy mound. The sights were set to 330 yards (300 meters). He did not want to take the time to adjust it, so he aimed a meter high and scanned the crest and the sides of the mound, anticipating that the sniper would show up there.

Spanopoulos glimpsed a dark green shape on the left-hand side of the mound. He turned up the magnification on the scope to 9x. Just above the grass he could see a piece of canvas. This was the Vietcong sniper's hide. Plainly, the sniper had not moved on because he figured that no one in the patrol had a scoped rifle, and to the naked eye he was practically invisible at that range. It was a mistake.

With a knot in his throat, Spanopoulos aimed a few feet above the canvas, checked his breathing, and slowly took the slack on the trigger. As he fired the shot, the Remington bucked. When he got the sight back on the target, he could see the canvas had been blown away and bits of flesh and bone we strewn all over the hillside. The bullet had hit the sniper's rifle and exploded, blowing his head to pieces.

Sergeant Casey sent two sniper teams to support Charlie Company of the 1st Battalion, 5th Marines, South Vietnamese marines, and South Korean marines, known as the Blue Dragons, on Buddha Mountain on Highway 1 just outside Quang Ngai City. As Charlie Company moved off the mountain in two columns, the sniper teams were up front, just behind point in case they needed covering fire.

Ken Barden was teamed with Dave Kovolak. They were nearing a rice paddy when a couple of shots came whizzing by. They fell to one knee and tried to spot where they were coming from. Kovolak scanned the distant tree line with his binoculars when two more shots whizzed close by them. Plainly the enemy meant business. Then the call came: "Snipers up!" So they grabbed their gear and ran up to point.

The scouts were firing random shots at the jungle that lay on the other side of the paddy field. Barden was sweeping the undergrowth with his scope when another shot rang out. His scope was on 9x, and by sheer chance he spotted a muzzle flash. The sniper, too, was an expert. He stood well back from the tree line in the darkness of the forest where he would be more difficult to spot.

The range was 500 yards (540 meters). The elevation was set to 330 yards (300 meters), so he aimed around a foot high. He squeezed off one shot, then reloaded. Knowing that Vietnamese snipers often worked in pairs, he took aim at the same point again, hoping that there were two snipers in the hide. But he was beaten to it by the company's mortarmen. They walked mortar fire across the jungle until one landed exactly where Barden had seen the first muzzle flash. Barden did not claim even a probable, let alone a confirmed kill. He reckoned that the VC sniper was good enough to have slipped away after his last shot.

John Culbertson went on to become a marine sniper himself after a two-week course at Happy Valley—the 1st Marine Division Sniper School in Da Nang. After a brief R&R, he returned to An Hoa, then on to Phu Loc 6 with Hotel Company, relieving a platoon for Echo Company, who were manning the fire base there. After the relative comfort of Da Nang, Culbertson found himself back sleeping in a foxhole.

After a breakfast of hot coffee and C ration eggs the following morning, he stocked up with ammunition, loading three boxes of tracer into his pack. He kept two specially marked magazines loaded with tracer every other round so he could mark targets for machine guns or tanks. After lunch he went over to chat with the crew of an M48 tank that was dug into a revetment. While they were talking, the tank sergeant spotted three men walking passed a small coppice of trees about 550 yards (500 meters) away. They were in uniform but did not appear to be carrying any weapons. The tank commander came up. He focused his binoculars on them and ordered the tank's 90-mm cannon to be traversed. His sergeant informed him that Culbertson was a sniper, so he ordered Culbertson to take out the three men, insisting—as they were not American—that they were Vietcong.

Culbertson grabbed his gun and loaded a magazine carrying tracer. Concerned that the targets were unarmed, he asked the tank commander what he wanted him to do. The reply was, "Kill them." Culbertson climbed on top of the tank and sat cross-legged on its fender. Supporting the rifle with its sling, he took aim at the lead man. The men were now walking away from him diagonally, but through his scope it still appeared to Culbertson that they were unarmed. He informed the tank commander of this and asked once more what he should do. The tank commander, now growing angry, told him to take them out; otherwise he would fire a 90-mm shell at them.

The target was now 660 yards (600 meters) away. He reckoned that the bullet would drop a meter at that range, so he aimed a yard over the target's head and held off 1 foot (30 centimeters) in front of him so that the target would walk into the path of the bullet. The first round was tracer. It passed just under the man's chin and hit the ground 22 yards (20 meters) beyond. Aiming a little closer to the man's head, he loosed off a second shot, which hit the lead man in the forehead, killing him and spinning him around as he fell. Quickly, before the other two realized where the shots were coming from, Culbertson took a shot at the second man. The round dropped and hit him in the thigh. The third man flung himself to the ground.

Culbertson was taking careful aim on the wounded man when tracer came flying over their heads. Then more men came up to join the ones on the ground. Through his scope, Culbertson could see they were marines. An urgent message came through on the radio in the tank to cease fire. It was from a patrol from Golf Company. They had been bringing in three prisoners. Culbertson felt bad. He knew that he had shot unarmed men and could have faced a court-martial if he had not made sure that he had a direct order by an officer to fire. As it was, the tank commander congratulated him on his shooting. Even so, he thought it best to make himself scarce.

The following day, news came that a marine sniper team in the field had taken out a handful of VC. However, they were not guerrillas on their way home after a hard night's work but the lead element of unit of a least 100 men. Although the snipers had a fire team with them for protection, the Vietcong had surrounded them. Culbertson was to accompany a platoon to rescue them. Two Sikorsky H-34s dropped them at a landing zone nearby. From there, they would have to make their way by foot across the paddy fields. Culbertson would take point with his old buddy John Lafley. They headed off across the paddy fields, past villages that had been burned out on previous patrols to deny supplies of rice to the enemy.

As they neared the sniper's hide, where the last radio message from them had come, the platoon sergeant, Harold Wadley, a Bronze Star winner from the Korean War, told Culbertson and Lafley to make their way along the tree line and find the snipers' hide. They would be supported by Gary Woodruff and Gerald Burns while the rest of the platoon took up position to provide suppressing fire.

When everyone was in position, the area was raked with machine gun fire. Culbertson and Lafley moved forward. Then they began looking for the snipers' position. Burns found a radio riddled with bullet holes. When they found a bunker, it was dark inside. They found a dead body and lifted it out. It was a marine. There was a bullet hole in his temple.

Then a bullet flew over their heads. The Vietcong had left a sniper team behind. The platoon answered with machine gun fire, while Woodruff took careful aim with his M14 and loosed off three rounds. The Vietcong sniper put his head up again and sent two more shots over their heads. Woodruff flicked his M14 to automatic and marked the sniper's position with tracer. Then an M72 Light Antitank Weapon (LAW) fired an antitank rocket, which blew the sniper's position to smithereens. VC snipers often built a separate bunker behind their firing position where they could take shelter from artillery or air attack. But the response from the LAW was so quick, this sniper had no time to take cover.

They retrieved five bodies with multiple bullet wounds from the bunker. One of them was Culbertson's close friend Buddy Bolton, who had been at sniper school with him. The bottom of the bunker was full of cartridge casings. The sniper party had used up most of its ammunition before it was overwhelmed. Some of the marines were now out for revenge.

When they were next out on patrol, Culbertson spotted some Vietcong snipers behind a tree. He saw a spider hole open. As they flung themselves to the ground, bullets flew over their heads. They waited until the sniper came up for another shot. Culbertson and Lafley trained their rifles on the lid of the spider hole. When it opened and the barrel of a rifle emerged, they each put a couple of shots into it. Woodruff fired a burst from his M14, smashing the lid of the spider hole to pieces. Although the sniper was already dead, Burns walked over to the spider hole and emptied his magazine into the corpse. Disarmed, Burns was flown back to base.

In June 1967, Hathcock's former spotter, Corporal John Burke, was sent to the outpost on Hill 950 at Khe Sanh as the sniper team leader with the Headquarters and Services Company of the 1st Battalion, 26th Marines, 3rd Marine Division (Reinforced). The marine base at Khe Sanh was at the northwest corner of Quang

Tri province, on the border of Laos near the demilitarized zone that extended three miles (five kilometers) on each side of the border with North Vietnam on a major infiltration route. Early in the war it had been considered vital to defend this remote outpost to prevent the North Vietnamese Army from outflanking US forces; it was abandoned in 1968.

As the helicopter carrying Corporal Burke to his new posting approached Khe Sanh, holes began to appear in its thin skin as small-arms fire opened up from the jungle below. A door gunner used his .50-caliber machine gun to return fire.

Hill 950 overlooked the main infiltration route. From its slopes, marine snipers would take out Vietcong couriers carrying arms and ammunition to resupply their comrades fighting in the south. As this supply was vital to the VC, the base came under constant attack. Marines hung tin cans with pebbles in them on the wire to warn of anyone approaching.

Behind the coils of razor wire, conditions were primitive. The marines lived in a network of bunkers and trenches. Shielded by walls of sandbags, men slept under poncho liners on leaky rubber mattresses and subsisted on C rations. That summer, the temperature soared to 100°F, while regular showers kept the humidity over 90 percent.

On June 6, it was so hot that after the sun set around 2000 hours they brought their makeshift bedding outside to sleep in the open air in the hope of catching one of the light, cool breezes that occasionally played around the hilltops. The air was full of the sounds of exotic birds and forest animals. Some men even thought they heard a tiger roar. Seldom seen, the beasts were known to stalk the dark jungle below.

That night, the sentries heard the clanking of cans. Burke was alerted. In the darkness, the men on watch could see the enemy gathering. They carried AK-47s and RPGs, and it looked like sappers were preparing to blow a hole in the wire. An M60 machine gun on the listening post held them back temporarily. Then RPGs started coming in. One exploded in the middle of the camp, and Corporal Burke pulled the wounded men into the command bunker.

Sappers reached the wire with their satchel charges. The sky was lit up with flares. Corporal Burke began picking off the sappers. An incoming RPG injured one of Burke's snipers badly. Burke himself was hit in the hip by a large piece of shrapnel. Ignoring his own wounds, he rushed to tend the other man and carried him toward the bunker. They had barely reached the doorway when he heard the whistle of another RPG. He covered the wounded man with his own body. As the grenade exploded, he felt the sting of shrapnel on his back. Then he dragged his wounded comrade into the bunker.

The machine gun was still keeping the enemy at bay, but more RPGs came whistling in. Burke and another marine dragged several seriously wounded men into the bunker, but a grenade exploded nearby and sent them flying.

Then the machine gun fell silent. Corporal Burke knew that the outpost was about to be overrun. His wounded men were in position to defend themselves. Burke grabbed an M16 and loaded his belt with grenades. Offering a few words of encouragement, he left the bunker and charged directly at the enemy, hurling grenades at a dozen Vietcong who were coming through the wire and emptying the M16 into others. Such was the ferocity of Burke's attack that the enemy turned and fled. Burke had saved his wounded men—at the expense of his own life.

Corporal John Roland Burke was posthumously awarded the Navy Cross, the second-highest medal for valor in the United States. The citation read:

Mawhinney's Heirs

For extraordinary heroism while serving as a Sniper Team
Leader with Headquarters and Service Company, First
Battalion, 26th Marines, 3rd Marine Division (Reinforced),
in the Republic of Vietnam on 6 June 1967. Assigned
the mission of defending an outpost on Hill 950 at Khe
Sanh, Quang Tri Province, Corporal Burke's team was
taken under attack by a numerically superior enemy force.
During the initial assault, Corporal Burke was wounded by
an enemy grenade. Ignoring his wound, he administered
first aid to a severely wounded comrade and placed him in
a relatively safe position, covering the wounded man with
his own body to protect him from further injury. Heeding
a call for help from outside the bunker, he unhesitatingly
went to the aid of another Marine. While he and a
companion were moving the man to the security of the
bunker an enemy grenade exploded, knocking him and
his comrade into the bunker. Although seriously wounded,
he moved the wounded man to a tunnel to protect
him from the devastating enemy fire. With all his team
members' casualties, Corporal Burke unhesitatingly and
with complete disregard for his own safety armed himself
with grenades, and shouting words of encouragement to
his men, stormed from the bunker in a valiant one-man
assault against the enemy positions. While firing his weapon
and throwing grenades at the enemy positions, Corporal
Burke was mortally wounded. By his dauntless courage,
bold initiative and devotion to duty, he was instrumental in
stopping the enemy attack and saving his men from possible
further injury or death, thereby reflecting great credit upon
himself and the United States Marine Corps and upholding
the highest traditions of the United States Naval Service.
He gallantly gave his life for his country.

PART TWO
SMALL WARS

CHAPTER FIVE

Aden (1964)

The British had had a presence in the port of Aden, at the southernmost tip of the Arabian Peninsula, since 1800 as it was an important supply station on the way to India and the Far East. But in the 1960s, they decided it was time to pull out. This destabilized the region, and while rival factions fought for power among themselves, they also attacked the departing British. As always, the Special Air Services (SAS) were sent to hold the line, and their snipers were sent out into the rugged terrain inland to tie down the rebel tribesmen.

In April 1964, one SAS sniper—SAS men's names are never released to the public—was lying up in an observation post overlooking a wadi in the Radfan mountains near the border with Yemen. One evening, he was on his way down to the well when he spotted two guerrillas heading the same way. So he dropped down behind some rocks. The guerrillas were about 400 yards (365 meters) away when he got them in his sights. The first one got a bullet in the head. The second did not even have time to raise his weapon before he was downed, too.

By 1967, the fighting had moved into the city of Aden itself, and the British troops there were coming under sniper fire. This, they thought, came from Eastern European mercenaries. The sniper fire in the Al Mansoura district had become so intense that the only way in and out of the detention center was by armored car. Troops stationed at the detention center in Al Mansoura were warned to keep well clear when the main gates were opened because sniper fire came in from the surrounding houses. Guardsman Mike James, with the Household Division of the Irish Guard, was watching when the commander of an armored car was hit between the eyes as the vehicle was going out the gates. The sniper had put the round through the one-inch gap between the armored plates in front of his command position. The only respite the troops in Al Mansoura got was during the Six-Day War between Israel and the surrounding Arab states. The British even waved to the gunmen as they headed off to fight alongside the Egyptians. They waved back, but eight days later, when the war was over, they returned and resumed their sniping. James himself was almost a victim. Tired after a long night at a machine gun post, he was leaning on a sandbag talking to a fellow Irish Guardsman when he got the sensation that he was in a sniper's sights.

"I feel that someone has got a bead . . ." he said as he pulled himself upright.

He had not even gotten a complete sentence out when a bullet hit the sandbag he had been leaning on. From its trajectory, he worked out that it would have hit him in the temple if he had not moved.

Countering the threat of snipers, the Royal Marines sent their own marksmen to hold position to hold a ring of crags around the Crater District, the home of many of the rebels. In the dark around 0530 to 0600, Mick Harrison, a veteran of the war against the Greek National Organization of Cypriot Fighters (*Ethniki Organosis Kyprion Agoniston* or EOKA) guerrillas in Cyprus, hauled himself up on a rope to an old Turkish Fort, where he hid. When he saw a terrorist, he would get up and wave to draw the man out.

"They thought they were good," he said, "and I let them come to me."

He would shoot them at a range of 400 to 500 yards (365 to 460 meters), then move to another position.

"The first person I shot came out all dressed in black," he said. "I remember I shot him in the throat. They wanted to go to Allah's garden, and I just paved the way for them."

Although he made it sound easy, the citation for the gallantry weapon he was awarded says that he was under small-arms fire and was bombarded with explosives.

Over four days, for the expenditure of just 18 rounds, Harrison killed or wounded eight rebels and ended all terrorist activity in the area during daylight hours. He was also used in a counter-sniper role. When the armored car carrying a general in the Irish Guards was ambushed by rebels, Harrison was watching from a rooftop. But he had to ask permission to open fire. When he got his commanding officer on the radio, the CO said simply, "Get on with it."

Without waiting for backup, he shot three of the rebels.

"The sniper is the loneliest man in the world," he said, "and that's the way I like it."

When you returned home, he said, other people could smell it on you. They wanted to get away. You did not have any friends.

CHAPTER SIX

Northern Ireland (1972)

In Northern Ireland, the British Army was pitted again the Irish Republican Army (IRA) and loyalist terrorists, both of whom employed snipers. One of the IRA snipers was dubbed "One-Shot Willy" by the soldiers. On one occasion he put a round through the back window of a Saracen armored personnel carrier (APC). The bullet passed through the head of one man, killing him instantly. It took out the eye of a second man and damaged his nose before coming to rest in the rear end of a third man.

IRA gunmen would force their way into people's homes and use them as firing positions. On one occasion they took two elderly sisters hostage while they knocked a small three-by-six-inch hole near the floor of an upstairs bedroom. A high-velocity bullet fired from that position ricocheted off a wall and clipped the nose of a sentry.

On another occasion, a young soldier was sitting in an observation post when a bullet came through the narrow slit between the sandbags and hit him in the head. He was on the radio at the time. Although the wound was fatal, he managed to get out the words "I've been shot" before the radio went dead.

The soldiers had difficulty defending themselves again terrorist snipers. As Northern Ireland is part of the United Kingdom, they were constrained by British law, and shooting a suspected sniper could have invited a murder charge. So British snipers operated in three-man teams, equipped with scout regiment 20x telescopes. Under the rules of engagement, they had to agree that an armed target was a threat to them or the people it was their duty to protect. Even then, according to one sniper officer, when you squeezed the trigger, you had visions of courts-martial and boards of inquiry running through your head.

As IRA activity intensified in the 1970s, the British asked the best shots to volunteer for sniper training. At the time, the old Lee-Enfield .303 No. 4(T) sniper rifle was being replaced with the 7.62 mm L42. However, the new rifle had no brackets to fit a night sight, so snipers had to carry a self-loading rifle (SLR) with an individual weapon sight (IWS) Starlight scope for night work.

On January 29, 1972, a three-man sniper team was deployed to an observation post on top of a mill in Coalisland. There was a march that day from Coalisland to Dungannon, and their job was to prevent the IRA from firing on the security forces. The IRA used a tactic of parting a crowd, shooting, and then closing up the crowd again before fire could be returned. The British observation post was behind the march, cut off from friendly forces. They were to be in place by 0430 hours and remain hidden until 1300. To do that, they had to lie perfectly still in a narrow gutter in cold winter weather. At 1300, they were to become overt and move into sniper positions around the rooftop to discourage any IRA sniper from using the crowd to take a potshot.

Eventually, the crowd was broken up by a baton charge. The security forces retired while being covered by the snipers, who then had the problem of withdrawing themselves. The plan was for an APC to speed in, pick them up, and speed out again. On the first two attempts, the APC got lost. On a third attempt, it got as far as the mill's gates. But by the time the snipers had gotten down from the roof, the APC had been surrounded by an angry mob about 150 strong and was forced to withdraw. The snipers were stuck. They could not climb back onto the roof without making themselves vulnerable, so they had to hide in the mill yard. The crowd grew until there were two or three hundred people, whose mood was ugly. Taking advantage of the situation, they moved up to within 16 feet (5 meters) of the back of the crowd, where they could hear the speaker call for the destruction of the security forces. At one point, a car drew up and fired six shots up at the previous observation post, but the snipers could not get a clear shot to return fire. Eventually, around 2225, an APC careened down a side road beside the mill and managed to get the sniper team out.

Two Royal Marine snipers were stationed on an observation post on top of the police station in Brown Square. Just to get there they had to run the gauntlet of stone-throwing youth. The only protection they were afforded came from 50 sandbags. Otherwise, the position was overlooked by the surrounding flats. There was constant gunfire from Shankill Road below. At one stage, a group of women became hysterical when they were caught in the crossfire.

During the day, the snipers could use the scopes on their L42s for observation. After dark, they had to use their IWS night sights, but this caused a problem. Looking through it left the eye blind for a few seconds afterward. They were not supposed to look through it using their shooting eye, but the observation post (OP) was so cramped this was impossible.

Around 0100 hours, the gunfire had slackened. They heard the boom of an SLR, and around the corner a gunman ran with a pistol. He took cover behind a wall in full view of the OP. The lead sniper laid down his night sight and put his eye to the scope of his rifle, waiting for his vision to return. By the time it had, the gunman had changed positions and was hiding in a doorway. The sniper put the pointer of his sight on the man's chest and pulled the trigger. He quickly reloaded and aimed again, but the man was nowhere to be seen. Thinking he might have gone to ground, both marine snipers unloaded with magazines into the general vicinity where he had last been seen. But they saw nothing more of him and were convinced that they had missed.

However, at the end of his tour, the sniper was credited with the kill of a gunman who had been found shot through the chest. He was one of 56 kills the unit claimed. Later he was told by a soldier from another unit how they had been chasing a gunman that night who had been cut down by a barrage from Brown Square.

Soon afterward, marine snipers of 40 Commando came into their own in another incident. A Ferret armored car was disabled by a land mine, and the IRA moved in for the kill. A car drove up, and the terrorists began unloading rifles. More than a kilometer away, an OP overlooked the scene. As the IRA men were armed and about to join the attack on the armored car, it was decided that they were legitimate targets. The snipers had detailed maps of the area, so they could easily work out the range. The problem was, they were 1,200 yards (1,100 meters) away, and it was a windy day. But the sniper officer was a crack shot who had won competitions at the UK's National Rifle Association's range at Bisley, Surrey.

IRA hunger-striker Bobby Sands had died shortly before, so the whole area was festooned with black flags. This should have made it easier to correct for wind, though the distance was off the scale in the snipers' pocket calculator. When the sniper officer squeezed off his first shot, he slightly miscalculated the wind correction. But in the two to three seconds it took the bullet to fly that far, the target had moved, walking into the path of the bullet.

After that, the sniper officer and his sergeant continued picking off the gunmen. But they were at such a distance that the gunmen could not work out where the shots came from. Their shots were masked by fire from two platoons of B Company who had been sent in to rescue the crew of the armored car. Together they downed 10 gunmen—the officer taking seven with 43 rounds, the sergeant three with 40 rounds. The longest lethal shot was 1,470 yards (1,344 meters). They did not see most of the kills because of the dust kicked up from the sandbags, but spotters with binoculars and a 20x scout regiment telescope kept the tally. One man thought he had reached safety when he ran across the road into a house and slammed the door behind him. But as he leaned against the door in relief, a bullet hit the door and went right through it—and him, taking most of his chest away.

The IRA did eventually work out where the gunfire was coming from. They sprayed the OP with automatic fire, but the snipers ducked down behind sandbags. As this proved ineffective, they began to take more careful aim and homed in on the snipers.

Quickly the two snipers moved to another firing position, giving them an excellent field of fire but offering no protection at all, and a gunman began working around their flank. Fortunately, another OP in the area had not seen much action yet. The gunman was up on a balcony to the side when they loosed off the three shots. Other than slightly damaging the officer's hearing, they did little damage. Snipers in the second OP then opened up, and the man tumbled from the balcony, clearly dead. Other IRA men came to collect his body, which was wrapped in an old carpet and slung in the back of a van.

After that, IRA activity dropped. Around half the casualties wreaked on the IRA by 40 Commando were inflicted by the snipers. However, toward the end of their tour of duty, the sniper sergeant was wounded. Usually, whenever units were rotated, the IRA would make a big push at the incoming outfit. But when 40 Commando was replaced by the Scots Guards, they left their snipers in place. They paired up with their replacements so that the experienced snipers could show the new men the lay of the land. That meant the OPs were in full force, so the sniper sergeant was left outside on a wall doing surveillance when he was hit by a bullet that passed through his biceps. After a temporary dressing had been applied, the sergeant went back to base to have it attended to, leaving an 18-year-old sniper private in the OP. The private, too, was ordered back to base, but he figured that the gunman would try again, so he moved his position about 22 yards (20 meters) and waited. He was right. The gunman moved in, and the young private hit him in the chest at 220 yards (200 meters).

The British Parachute Regiment also used snipers. The 2nd Battalion—2 Para—would send out patrols to draw fire so that the snipers could pick off the gunmen. Even the presence of snipers instilled fear. While suspected terrorists took little notice of regular soldiers patrolling the streets, the sight of an L96 sniper rifle caused consternation. A local kid would be sent to talk to the man carrying it. He would either parry their questions or give loaded answers calculated to spread the fear. These tactics proved so successful in deterring IRA fire that, by the end of the 1970s, the IRA had largely abandoned the gun in favor of bombs.

But there was still work to do along the border with the Irish Republic. Again, snipers came into their own because the use of automatic or semi-automatic weapons often resulted in the injury of innocent bystanders—never a desirable outcome, particularly on home territory. In the 1990s, the IRA began a crossborder sniping campaign. At least one of their men was armed with a Barrett .50-caliber. A rumor spread that it was being wielded by a renegade from US Special Forces. This was discounted by professional snipers. While the Barrett had a range of over a mile, none of the shots made with it were over 440 yards (400 meters). It seemed that the weapon was not being used by a trained sniper but rather for its psychological and propaganda value.

When soldiers guarding the crossing points came under fire, British snipers were sent in to make a countersniper study. They visited the area during the day in civilian clothes and unmarked vehicles to take photographs. At night they went on patrol with regular army units, sometimes occupying IRA firing positions to check their fields of fire. Potential countersniper positions were also assessed. On occasions when sniping was expected, countersnipers were deployed. However, no one ever came to take a pot-shot at the security forces. By the end of the 1990s, the Belfast Agreement had been signed, and gradually the IRA began decommissioning their weapons.

CHAPTER SEVEN

The Falklands (1982)

When Argentina invaded the Falkland Islands in 1982, the British sent a task force to retake them. With the 2nd Battalion of the Parachute Regiment—2 Para—was the Army Chaplain David Cooper, a shooting enthusiast. Sailing across the Atlantic on the SS *Canberra*, which had been converted into a troops ship for the operation, he zeroed in some new night sights and ran shooting courses for battalion snipers. They practiced on moving targets: the garbage that was tipped overboard each day. The loss of the *Atlantic Conveyor*, which had been carrying transport helicopters, meant the troops would have to walk the 50 miles from the landing site in San Carlos Bay to the capital at Port Stanley. This presented the snipers with a particular problem. As resupply was going to be difficult, they would have to carry ample supplies of heavy sniper-quality ammunition, along with the laser range finders they borrowed from mortar crews.

However, 2 Para's newly acquired sniping skills were wasted during the battle for Goose Green, a settlement on the island of East Falkland. Their commanding officer, Lieutenant-Colonel Herbert "H" Jones, who died during the action, stationed the snipers alongside teams carrying Milan antitank weapons on a promontory over the water from the ruins of Boca House, a key position in the Argentine lines. The shot would be about 1,000 meters (1,100 yards) across the water. David Cooper pointed out the shot's difficulty: Over water, there was little indication of wind strength—and in the South Atlantic it was windy—and the attack was taking place at night. With night sights it was difficult to clearly make out the target at that distance. If you hit the target and the man falls over, that's okay. But if you miss, you cannot see where the bullet fell, so you could not make corrections.

When Major John Crossland and B Company got pinned down while trying to take Boca House, there was nothing that the snipers or the Milan teams could do about it. And by the time they had made their way around the water, Colonel Jones was dead and the situation had changed radically. When they reached the battle, they lent a hand to British units that had been held up. The Argentines were forced to surrender when snipers put rounds through the slots of their bunkers at 700 yards (640 meters).

When the Royal Marines reached Mount Harriet outside Port Stanley, they found themselves held up by Argentine snipers. Pinned down in the cold of the night, Corporal Steve Newland decided to do something about it. He stripped off the 66-mm antitank shells he was carrying and crawled around a large boulder to see if he could spot the sniper. What he found was around 10 of them lying on a small plateau overlooking the marines' positions, protected by a machine gun. Each time a marine moved, only one of the snipers would shoot, so it looked like there was only one of them who kept on the move. It was clear they hoped the marines would try to rush the position and be cut down by the machine gun.

Newland pulled back around the rock and put a new magazine in his SLR. Then he got out two grenades. Pulling the pin, he threw one grenade at the machine gun and lobbed the second at the snipers. As soon as they had gone off, he bounced back around the rock and gave three rounds to anyone who remained alive, emptying the whole magazine. He took cover again when 66-mm shells pummeled the position. Miraculously, one of the Argentines had survived. Newland had only hit him in the shoulder, and when the marine came around the rock again, the Argentine opened up with his automatic, hitting Newland in the legs. In response, Newland fired 15 rounds into the sniper's head.

According to David Cooper, the talents of the British snipers were wasted again during the next action on Wireless Ridge, where they were simply parceled out to any unit that was short of manpower. A man with a bolt-action rifle with a 10-round magazine was of little use to a unit equipped with automatic or semi-automatic weapons. Not only did the sniper lack the firepower for tactical combat, he was even less use when they closed on the enemy, as he did not have a bayonet.

CHAPTER EIGHT

Lebanon (1982)

American sharpshooter Chuck Kramer had been training Israeli snipers when the Israel Defense Force invaded southern Lebanon to oust the Palestine Liberation Organization (PLO) in 1982. He found himself in command of more than 20 snipers out of the 47 deployed with the Israeli invasion force that numbered more than 100,000 troops. The snipers were assigned an area south of the hippodrome near the French ambassador's house where there was a lot of PLO activity. Their job was to put the PLO west into Beirut, while Israeli artillery took down the buildings.

Kramer had confirmed kills at ranges of 656 to 875 yards (600 to 800 meters). The PLO were very bad snipers, he said, and they had old equipment, while the Syrians, who also entered into the fray, were well trained and well equipped. The PLO were terrified when they knew that a team of dedicated snipers was coming after them, but the Israeli troops were just as frightened when they found themselves under the sniper's scope. Advances would be held up for hours while they called in an air strike.

The action took place in the first three days. During that time, Kramer's team had 16 confirmed kills and 32 probables, most of them at long range. The closest shot was at 164 yards (150 meters). One of the snipers had lined up an enemy gunman only to find that he did not have a bullet in the chamber of his M14. So he pulled the bolt back, but when he eased it forward it did not lock, a common fault of that rifle. When he got the enemy in his sights, he squeezed the trigger. And there was a click. The gunman heard it and ducked inside a building. The Israeli sniper cursed, but put another round in the chamber and waited. A little later, an Israeli air strike came over. The PLO man came running out to watch it and the sniper cut him down.

A UN Multinational Force was sent in to support the Lebanese Army in an attempt to make peace. But on April 18, 1983, a suicide bomber blew up the US embassy, killing more than 60 people. In June, the US Marines were sent to join a Multinational Force in Beirut in an attempt to police a cease-fire between the warring factions there. Corporal Tom Rutter, a marine sniper, was with them. While the Battalion Landing Team (BLT) made their headquarters in a building in the airport, Rutter and Corporal Jon Crumley occupied an observation post on the roof of the four-story administration building at Lebanon University, which was across an open field from a warren of streets known as Hooterville, around 550 yards (500 meters) away. By then, years of civil war had turned what had once been the "jewel of the Mediterranean" into a city full of ruined buildings, burned-out cars, bomb craters, and hastily built defenses.

There was little to do. They had been told not to put a round in the chamber unless they got permission from headquarters. All they could do was watch as the Israelis and the local Amal militia, just one of the numerous Christian and Muslim factions, fought it out with rockets, small arms, and artillery fire. Rutter found this increasingly frustrating.

When the Israelis pulled out, the Lebanese Armed Forces (LAF) took over their positions. However, the militiamen were determined to drive the LAF out of Hooterville. One morning, Rutter and Crumley watched as two LAF armored personnel carriers drove along the street to the enemy-held quarters. What the occupants of the APCs could not see was that a mass of Amal guerrillas was hiding behind a building. But there was no way that the marines could warn them. Suddenly, the militiamen swarmed the APCs. Taken by surprise, the LAF surrendered. They came out with their hands up.

The guerrillas then took over the .50-caliber machine guns on the top of the APCs. Fearing that the Amal militia intended to kill their prisoners, the marines tried desperately to get permission to fire. But by the time they had radioed in a situation report, the militia had opened fire, cutting down the defenseless troops. The guerrillas then waved their guns and flags at the university building as if issuing a challenge to the marines.

Soon the Amal militia had driven the LAF out of Hooterville and surrounded the marine positions at the airport and the university. They set up bunkers and fortifications that gradually encroached on the marines' position. Every so often, the militiamen emerged from cover to squeeze off a burst of AK-47 fire, forcing the marine snipers to dive for cover.

It was all the more frustrating because, though the snipers were out of effective range of the AK-47s, the guerrillas were within easy range of the marines' M40A1. Rutter spent his time picking out targets through his scope and squeezing the trigger. But with an empty chamber, it was just a game. And because the marines returned no fire, the militiamen grew bolder and bolder.

Then one morning, Corporal David Baldree came bounding up the stairs. Finally, BLT headquarters had given them permission to return fire. They took up their firing positions, but the day was quiet. It was not until around 1730 hours that a heavy machine gun opened up. Rutter and Baldree dived back down behind their sandbags. Moving quickly from one firing point to another, they tried to locate the enemy gunman who was still loosing off shots at them.

Lebanon (1982)

"The rounds were hitting near the firing openings in the sandbags, but so far none of the bullets had come through," said Rutter. "I didn't want my head framed in the opening when the gunner finally hit it."

Baldree said he could not see the gunman, but then Rutter spotted something. He glimpsed a figure on the second floor of a tall building at two o'clock. The gunman knew what he was doing. He did not fire from the window, but stood well back in the shadows. However, through their scopes and binoculars, Rutter and Baldree could see the muzzle flashes of the machine gun light up the room. The problem was he was too far back for Rutter to take a shot at him. So he grabbed the field telephone and called Crumley, who was on guard on the ground floor of the administration building. Rutter said that he and Baldree would pick out the window where the gunman was with tracer, while the men below opened up with their M60s. According to Rutter's mil-dot scale, the range was 600 yards (550 meters). Two lines of trace streaked across the evening sky and into the window. Tracer from the M60s below followed. Soon the room was full of flying lead. After that, Rutter noted in his sniper log, the night was "all quiet."

But it did not stay quiet for long. Soon they had sporadic incoming from the bunkers and berms that surrounded them. They called in the other 10 snipers of the Surveillance and Target Acquisition (STA) platoon. They dashed to their firing points. Then Rutter saw a muzzle flash from the darkened firing port of a sandbag bunker at the corner of a street. The hole in the revetment was 6 inches high (15.2 centimeters) and a foot wide (30.4 centimeters). He waited for another muzzle flash, then put a single 173-grain bullet through the opening. Meanwhile, Crumley was pursuing an Amal gunman who changed position after each shot. But then the gunman made the mistake of falling into a predictable pattern. Hidden by a raised berm, he took one shot from one end, then the next from the other. Crumley zeroed in on the near end and waited. Eventually the gunman, who was wearing a patterned turban, stuck his head up once again. Crumley pulled the trigger.

"The high-powered bullet kicked up dirt in front of the man's face," said Rutter, who was watching through his scope. "At the same time, his face under the turban literally exploded."

A couple minutes later, an ambulance arrived, picked up the dead man, and sped off with barely a pause at the university building.

Other insurgents were taken by surprise by the change in the rules of engagement that allowed them to fire without asking permission.

Captain R. D. Bean, who served two tours in Lebanon, recalled that a sniper team had spotted a partly uniformed insurgent carrying an AK-47 on a concrete rooftop some 800 yards (730 meters) away. He loosed off a 30-round magazine ineffectually in the general direction of the marines' position. But he had misjudged the situation. Staying exposed just a little too long, he was taken down by a .308 match-grade round from an M40A1.

Soon after, a second insurgent came into view. He must have thought his partner had been struck down by a random bullet—they were way out of range. But as he approached his fallen comrade, he was downed by a second bullet.

It was not long before an observer saw a third man venture onto the roof, "apparently disbelieving what he saw, turning to look west toward the American positions," said Bean. "Crack! The 173-grain projectile took him squarely in the chest, buckling his knees, bending him into praying before he fell limply onto his side."

Then a fourth man approached to examine the bodies. He too was dispatched. But though the marine snipers waited until nightfall, no more insurgents showed their faces.

A few weeks later, Corporal Rutter's particular skills were called on again at Beirut International Airport, where the First

Platoon of Charlie Company had come under small-arms and RPG fire from the Shiite Amal militia. When Rutter and his partner, Corporal James "Rock" McGlynn, turned up, they were briefed by Charlie Company. Immediately across the field there was a place called Danielle Café where there seemed to be a lot of activity. Next to it was a huge poster of the Ayatollah Khomeini.

As they watched, the Amal militiamen collected their weapons from the café and took up their positions. They loosed off a few rounds over the marines' heads, but kept under cover. At dusk, they withdrew and all was quiet. The following day, the pattern was repeated, but this time the marines opened fire.

"I'll take the first one," said McGlynn. The man was wearing a uniform and a green helmet liner and must have been a deserter from the Lebanese Army. He was carrying an AK-47.

McGlynn picked him out with his M40A1. Rutter said he saw the helmet liner fly in the air and brain matter erupt from his skull like a "pink puff." The two other militiamen ran for cover.

Then a small red car arrived. Two men jumped out of the back, raced for their fallen comrade, and dragged him toward the car. One sprayed bullets toward the marine line. It was 520 yards (475 meters) away—long range for an AK-47, but not for an M40A1. Rutter put a single shot in the center of the shooter's chest. The other dropped the man he was dragging and jumped back into the car.

Corporal Frank Roberts, another Marine Corps sniper who was on the scene, put a bullet through the windshield. The driver threw the car into reverse and sped off. The street began to fill with people running around in a state of confusion. An old woman screamed and waved her hands, pointing at the poster of Khomeini. Rutter and McGlynn took the hint and put two bullets into the radical cleric's face.

Eventually the Marine Corps became a target, and on October 23, the headquarters of the Battalion Landing Team at Beirut

International Airport was blown up by a suicide truck bomber, killing 299 American and French servicemen. Corporal Rutter was about half a mile away when the bomb exploded and spent half a day recovering bodies and identifying the dead. While marines tried to rescue the wounded, they were fired on by enemy snipers. One marine was killed, another wounded. The marines returned fire and claimed to have killed five snipers who were shooting at them. After that, marine snipers were issued night-vision goggles and .50-caliber sniper rifles.

Corporal Roberts was at the airport with another sniper named Forbush. They had reached it on foot as their driver had refused to take them within a mile of it. Their infiltration route had taken them through Hooterville, and their final dash was across a wide boulevard strewn with the wreckage of burned-out vehicles. Forbush covered Roberts as he made the dash, and he was halfway across when a gunman opened up on him. Roberts did a combat roll into a shallow ditch. For a moment, he thought he was safe. Then, out of nowhere, a puppy came running up. It licked his face and scampered about with joy. Nice though this display of affection was in war-torn Beirut, the dog was drawing attention to his position. A second gunman opened fire. Bullets pinged off the concrete near Roberts's head. It was only a matter of time until one hit him.

Roberts had no choice. He jumped to his feet and ran toward the airport. Forbush and the puppy came racing after him. Together they flung themselves under the concertina wire then found safety inside the bunker there with Rutter and the other snipers.

Roberts teamed up with Rick David. Forbush and his partner, Moore, were on their left; Rutter and McGlynn on their right. They spent the night taking out targets in the ruined buildings beyond, but no one went out to check whether they were confirmed kills.

Soon after dawn, five men walked into the open some 400 yards (365 meters) away. They seemed to imagine they were safe at that distance. They should have known better. These were not the usual lowly militiamen the marines had seen in the streets of Beirut dressed in T-shirts and jeans. They were wearing brand-new Soviet camouflage. One of them, plainly the leader, had an AK-47 slung over his shoulder and a German shepherd dog on a leash.

Roberts watched them through his scope. They appeared to be measuring the depths of the craters made in the walls by M203 grenade launchers. This could be viewed as merely a defensive matter, but Roberts soon determined that they were, in fact, reconnoitering lines of approach and fields of fire, ready to make an all-out assault on the snipers' position. He adjusted his scope, put the crosshairs on the commander, and squeezed the trigger. As the man fell, the dog leash slipped from his hand. The dog ran for cover, followed by the dead man's comrades.

Within 20 minutes, the militia retaliated. The snipers returned a few shots, but the militia soon changed their tactics and resorted to guile, moving to the left. Rutter took out one or two of them. Others tried to sneak down an alley to the left. Forbush and Moore took out another two. After that, the militia thought better of their plan.

Soon a jeep with a white flag on it arrived and the leader of the Amal militia got out. He remonstrated with the marine commander, insisting that the snipers be called off. The Americans were there in a peacekeeping role, after all. While the marine commander explained that he would be happy to keep the peace provided the Amal militia did, Roberts emerged from his bunker and stood there cradling his Remington M40A1. Without a word, he went back inside.

Marine Corporal Carey Fabian did two tours in Beirut, one before Grenada and one after. In 1981, the marines went into Beirut where Yasser Arafat and the PLO were surrounded by Israelis. The US Marines and the French Foreign Legion secured a corridor from the Palestinian enclave to the docks so that the PLO could board a ship and leave the city. They would walk down the corridor or ride in trucks, firing their guns in the air as if they were celebrating a great victory.

Fabian and Lance Corporal Jeff Graham took up position on a grain elevator at the docks where they could oversee the evacuation route. They saw one PLO fighter jump off a truck with his finger still on the trigger of his AK-47. As he landed, his finger jolted, putting a bullet through the head of the man on the truck behind him. The marines were left to bag up the body and dispose of the corpse.

Later, a black limousine pulled up. The snipers had it in their crosshairs. A short man wearing a khaki tunic and a kaffiyeh headdress got out. Plainly he was a dignitary. Fabian did not recognize him, but Graham did. It was Yasser Arafat, leader of the PLO.

Graham asked Fabian, who was on the spotting scope, to determine the wind for him. He had already set up a range card. Fabian stared at him in disbelief. Nevertheless, he called the wind speed and the range. For a moment, Fabian thought Graham was going to pull the trigger, but then he relaxed and dropped the gun. Arafat went on to win the Nobel Peace Prize and become the first president of the Palestinian National Authority.

Returning in 1983, after the BLT command center had been blown up, Fabian found the marines under siege. He and Graham were at the airport, where there was another marine artillery battery, which was shot at each night. As one of the senior snipers of the STA platoon that assigned sniper teams, Fabian was determined to put a stop to this.

The battery had set up opposite the abandoned PLO field hospital. Beyond that was a 30-foot (10-meter) cliff and a factory. Roberts set up an observation post on top of the cliff and noticed that not all the men who arrived at the factory in the morning left in the evening. He then led a patrol that found a well-worn path leading up onto the cliff and around the abandoned hospital to the outer wire of the airport. The militiamen had even left cardboard there to lie on while they were taking a shot.

The STA platoon had seismic sensors that could detect vibrations in the ground within a defined radius. The sensors were sent up in the bushes. The artillery zeroed in on them, and next time the militia's gunmen headed to the airport they were met with a couple of high-explosive artillery rounds.

A different faction then set up an 82-mm mortar on a nearby roof and began mortaring Echo Company's position, badly wounding one marine. The mortar was hidden behind the low wall around the flat roof, and it took the snipers a few days to locate it. When they did, one of the snipers targeted it with an Iver Johnson .50-caliber rifle. This smashed the wall and destroyed the 82-mm tube behind it—and probably some of the mortar crew as well. But the fighting was anything but one-sided. Later a mortar hit the observation post, killing two of Fabian's snipers.

In the latter half of 1983, the militiamen adopted a new tactic. Their snipers would move up toward the airport behind a crowd of kids. Marine countersnipers could have taken them out, but their 173-grain ammunition was made for accuracy and penetration. If it hit one of the militia's snipers, the round would pass right through him and possibly hit a child.

Delta Force was brought in. They had lightweight bullets, high-velocity rounds that were just as accurate and deadly as the snipers', but they remained lodged inside the body. The problem was that a lightweight round is far more susceptible to the wind, so they were accurate only to 440 yards (400 meters). The militia snipers were usually 1,100 yards (1,000 meters). That meant the Delta Force men would have to go out and get them.

The two men assigned the task—Sergeant Andres Benevides and Sergeant Eric L. Haney—spent a day with their binoculars examining the area that the militia snipers frequented. They drew up detailed range cards and identified possible hides. That night, they headed out with their rifles and ammunition, enough food and water for four days, and plastic bottles and plastic wrap to dispose of their waste.

The set up in a pile of garbage and rubble that had once been a house. From there, as the sun rose, they identified and designated possible enemy positions. Then they waited. They had been told that the gunmen usually came out in the late afternoon, but they took turns at looking out through the spotter scope—half an hour on, half an hour off—to prevent eyestrain.

The first two days passed uneventfully. Nothing happened on the third day either until about 0735. Then a crowd of boys began to form up. There were about 20 of them, and they pointed toward the marines' positions. Then they were joined by two militiamen with AK-47s, whom they treated as heroes.

The two militia snipers raised their guns, confident that the marines would not shoot into a crowd. But this time they were being observed from just 350 yards (320 meters) through the scopes mounted on M24 rifles; Benevides and Hanley were close enough to count on a head shot. When they both had a clear shot, they squeezed the triggers. The two militiamen fell. The boys scattered. The braver ones tried to drag their heroes' bodies away. Benevides and Hanley sat out the rest of the day in silence. They had completed their mission, but did not necessarily feel good about it.

CHAPTER NINE

Grenada (1983)

In 1983, there was a military coup on the Caribbean island of Grenada by hard-line Marxists. There was already a large number of Cuban construction workers and military on the island. They were building a 10,000-foot (3,000-meter) runway that President Ronald Reagan feared might be used for military purposes. He decided to invade, ostensibly to protect the Americans on the island, which included 1,000 US medical students attending school in St. George's, the island's capital.

Five troop ships carrying the Amphibious Ready Group on their way to relieve the marines in Lebanon were diverted. With them was USMC sniper Corporal Carey Fabian. He and three other marine snipers were assigned to Echo Company, who were to make an airborne assault on Pearls Airfield at the north end of the island, while the 82nd Airborne took the south. The snipers' job was to stay 1,100 yards (1,000 meters) ahead of the invasion force, take the flank of the airfield, and stop any counterattack coming through the jungle undergrowth there.

On the morning of October 25, 1983, they clambered aboard CH-46 Sea Knight helicopters in full gear. Cobra attack helicopters went in first, and the marines could hear the sound of warfare as they approached the coast. Then the order came to lock and load.

When they landed, Fabian raced for the tree line carrying his M40A1. With his partner, Lance Corporal Jeff Graham, Fabian took one flank while the other two snipers took the other as Echo Company advanced down the airstrip. An enemy soldier appeared but then fled for the jungle, stripping off his uniform as he went. Corporal Fabian knelt down and got him in his crosshairs, but the man had disappeared into the undergrowth before he could fire.

The airfield had been abandoned. The defenders had even left their weapons behind when they fled. Fabian and Graham were sent with a platoon to take a nearby hill that had already been raked with fire by a Cobra. Again there was no resistance. They then dug in for the night. Their job was to watch for anyone infiltrating through the jungle.

No counterattack materialized, but they heard a couple of shots after it got dark. Fabian borrowed Graham's M16 and used its AN/PVS-2 Starlight scope to scan the jungle. In the trees directly in front of them, he saw the man's silhouette. Fabian locked him in his crosshairs, but waited until the man emerged from the trees. As the man crept forward, Fabian controlled his breathing and prepared to fire. But some other marine must have spotted the man and lobbed a grenade. The flash from the grenade viewed through the night sight temporarily blinded Fabian in one eye. In the morning, they found no body and no blood. It seemed the man had escaped.

A sniper team with SEAL Team Six saw more action. They were sent in to rescue the British governor-general, Sir Paul Scoon, and 14 hostages being held in the Government House. One of the helicopters flying them in was hit by ground fire and had to return to the USS *Guam*, where it crash-landed. Thirteen SEALs from the second helicopter fast-roped it to the ground, but their radio was hit by a bullet, robbing them of communications, but they reached Government House without serious injury. The Grenadian policemen holding the hostages threw down their guns.

The SEALs found the governor, his wife, and his staff in the cellar and announced that they had come to rescue them. But here were 13 American Navy SEALs surrounded by a large force of Grenadian and Cuban soldiers. The governor-general wondered who was going to rescue them.

The Grenadians had three Soviet BTR-60 APCs armed with 12.7 machine guns that took up positions around Government House. Two infantry units also moved in. A SEAL sniper and a spotter on the second floor ensured that they kept their heads down. They had no answer to the BTR-60s, but the sniper's well-placed shots held them at bay.

Although they had no radio, Lieutenant Bill Davis discovered that the telephone was still working. He got through to the airfield at Port Salines at the south of the island, which the Airborne had already taken. Two Sea Cobras were sent in, but they were shot down by the antiaircraft emplacements at nearby Fort Frederick. So an AC-130H Spectre gunship was sent in. At 10,000 feet (3,000 meters) it was safe from antiaircraft fire. When one of the BTR-60s approached Government House, the Spectre took it out within 20 feet of the door. The other two BTR-60s quickly withdrew.

For the rest of the day, the sniper was left to hold off the infantry. That night, the BTR-60s tried again to reach Government House. The Spectre gunship returned. The BTR-60s made a futile attempt to shoot at it, and in reply, the AC-130H peppered it with 20-mm rounds. Again, the SEAL sniper was left to hold the infantry at a respectful distance until, at 0712, a column led by five Abrams tanks arrived to relieve them.

CHAPTER TEN

Panama (1989)

In 1988, Manuel Noriega, the military ruler of Panama, was indicted by a US Federal court on drug charges. He responded by deposing the elected president of Panama, canceling forthcoming elections, and making himself dictator. In the National Assembly, stuffed with his hand-picked appointees, he declared that a state of war existed between Panama and the United States. The US took him seriously and invaded on December 20, 1989.

The invasion of Panama lasted a little over three weeks, so it did not present much scope for snipers. However, with the 82nd Airborne was Sergeant First Class William Lucas. As a marine sniper in Vietnam, he had logged 38 kills. In Panama, he was employed as a countersniper. The Panama Defense Force (PDF) had been supplied with a number of American-made M24s, but when the PDF's armory was taken, some of the weapons were missing. Then came reports that enemy snipers were harassing US troops in Panama City and the suburbs. One of them was in a hide in the downtown area of the capital. He had already wounded an American soldier and would have hit others if his shooting had not been so poor. Sergeant Lucas's job was to stop him before he killed someone.

Lucas and his spotter set up shop on the 15th floor of the Marriott Hotel, which gave them an unimpeded view over the area where the sniper had been working. By then, the invasion was over and the streets were filling up with civilians going about their everyday business. There was now the danger of innocents getting in the line of fire.

From the reports of the enemy sniper's activity, Lucas put the sniper in a high-rise block some 820 yards (750 meters) away. Sitting at the back of the darkened room, Lucas kept his M21— essentially an upgrade of the M14 he had used in Vietnam with a telescopic sight—resting in his lap, until he spotted something of interest in a window, when he raised the scope to his eye. Sniper versus sniper, he knew, was the deadliest game of all. One slip and you are dead.

But the PDF sniper did not have the years of experience that 43-year-old Lucas had behind him. He showed himself in fleeting silhouette against an open window. It was enough to catch the eye of Lucas's spotter. Now both men concentrated on that window. The mosquito screen had been removed and the drapes flapped in the breeze. Then the sniper appeared again. He was looking down at the boulevard below, trying to acquire a fresh target. He would not have long to wait. US troops were patrolling the streets of the capital.

Through his scope, Lucas could see the features of his thin face. He was out of uniform and wearing a black sweater. Then he lifted a scope rifle to his shoulder. He was clearly a threat. Lucas aimed directly at his heart. His M21 was zeroed on 100 yards (90 meters). However, as he was shooting downward, the bullet should not drop too much.

Lucas began applying pressure to the trigger. As he took up slack, he slowed his breathing, then held his breath. At that moment, the target disappeared inside the apartment again. But

Lucas did not move. He knew once the sniper had acquired a target below, the temptation would be too much for him.

Then Lucas saw a shadow on the window. Through binoculars, his spotter saw a glint from the sniper's barrel.

Lucas closed down his breathing again, then squeezed. The report echoed around the room. The spotter saw the sniper fall. They kept their eyes on the window. There was no further movement in the room.

Marine Sergeant Earl Schooley was also deployed as a sniper in Panama, but he was not with the invasion force. He was with the Surveillance and Target Acquisition (SAT) platoon of the 3rd Battalion, 6th marines who were sent to the Canal Zone in October 1989. They were stationed at the Rodman Naval Air Station at the west end of the Panama Canal.

It was clear that trouble was brewing. US personnel guarding the Canal Zone were harassed. On December 16, Marine Second Lieutenant Robert Paz was shot and killed by the PDF when returning unarmed from a restaurant in Panama City. At 1810, the STA platoon were put on standby.

Soon antiaircraft fire filled the skies and mortars began to rain down on the US bases in the Canal Zone. With guns blazing, US Marine Light Armored Infantry (LAI) took over a PDF military outpost, losing one man. One Panamanian was also killed, and three were taken prisoner. The LAI were about to move on when Sergeant Schooley and his spotter, Sergeant Gama, joined them on December 20 when the invasion started. They clambered about the marines' light armored vehicles (LAV), each equipped with an M60 machine gun and a 25-mm cannon. They headed into Panama City with helicopter gunships giving cover overhead. Their aim was to take the PDF base at La Chorrera.

Drawing to a halt outside the main gate, a marine demanded the PDF's surrender—three times. Then one of the LAVs smashed through the steel gate. Others followed, the 25-mm cannons pummeling the buildings. Through the smoke, a few muzzle flashes showed that the PDF intended to put up some resistance. The marines dismounted to engage them.

Schooley and Gama remained outside with the commander's vehicle. They leapt out and took cover behind it. They took aim at the largest building, expecting the stiffest resistance to come from there. Through holes blown in the walls by the 25-mm shells, they could see a man peering out. He was no more than 50 yards (45 meters) away. Schooley's weapon was zeroed on 100 yards (90 meters). That was the minimum range he had been taught to fire at. Marine snipers were not trained in close-quarters fighting. But, Schooley reckoned, there should not be too much difference between a shot at 50 yards and one at 100.

Only the top half of the man's head could be seen over what remained of the wall. Schooley could see the man's eyes looking directly at him. He put the crosshairs on the center of his forehead and squeezed the trigger. The skin sheared away from his skull and the man went down. It was Schooley's first kill. Gama later confirmed it with Fox Company, who had been inside the building. They said they found a man with the top of his head blown off.

CHAPTER ELEVEN

The First Gulf War (1990)

Saddam Hussein invaded Kuwait in August 1990 and, under the auspices of the United Nations, the United States led an alliance to eject the Iraqi invaders. Before the land campaign went ahead, coalition air forces attacked Iraqi airfields, communications centers, and strategic industries. Meanwhile, allied patrols probed the Iraqi defenses, with snipers taking the lead. As well as the standard M40A1 Marine Corps sniper rifles, the marines had just received .50-caliber Barretts. These could knock out LAVs even at a range of over 2,200 yards (2,000 meters).

At night, snipers and scouts, with painted faces and camel-colored camouflage smocks, would move across the Kuwaiti border toward enemy lines. Most were hunters, who were used to stalking their prey, and dedicated skeet-shooters, who had trained in the sniper craft for years. Some boasted that they could put a bullet in a man's head from 800 yards (730 meters). They made no bones about "the art of killing," saying that when they pulled the trigger, they could see the expression on a man's face when the bullet hit. However, they would avoid thinking about their quarry as a man with a wife and children. They were simply the enemy.

If a sniper betrayed any sympathy, he would be ineffective, and marine snipers were all too aware of the Iraqis' reputation for maltreating American prisoners.

And they had little time for other marines, who were irritated by their arrogance.

"We are as cocky as hell," Staff Sergeant Douglas A. Luebke told the *New York Times* in February 1991. "It is the image we portray, because we are the best in the battalion."

The men from his platoon would crawl unseen within yards of enemy lines and fire three shots from an exposed position, taking out Iraqi soldiers one at a time. They would concentrate on men who operated antiaircraft guns, machine guns, and other heavy weapons, usually hitting them at dawn or dusk. Then they would call in air strikes and artillery fire. However, the snipers of the 1st Marine Division made 39 kills—11 at ranges of over 800 yards (730 meters)—for no losses.

CHAPTER TWELVE

Yugoslavia (1991)

With the collapse of Yugoslavia, Croatia sought its independence by waging war with Serbia. Although there was a tradition of hunting in the Balkans, the locals knew little about military sniping, so John L. Hogan, a veteran American sniper from Vietnam, began training Croat marksmen. He recruited 30 men and divided them into 15 teams of two. They all thought they were crack shots, a notion of which Hogan quickly disabused them. On a breezy afternoon, he set up a 2 x 4-foot (60 x 120-centimeter) target at a distance of 710 yards (650 meters). Not one of them managed to hit it.

Using the US Marine Corps Scout-Sniper Manual, he set about training them fieldcraft, camouflage, concealment, undetected movement, and how to be a dead shot from anywhere from 330 to 990 yards (300 to 900 meters). Then came the baptism of fire. Hogan learned that ex-Yugoslav Special Forces men had taken over a nearby village and were snipping at Croat troops in the area. This would put his men's countersniper training to the test.

The village had been fought over, so there was plenty of rubble to give them cover. During the night, they built five hides in the debris. Hogan stationed a team each in two of them. They were to fire no more than two shots before moving to another hide. Hogan then led a third team forward 220 yards (200 meters) to a house where they set up on the second floor. This had a good view out of the back, overlooking the hides, so that they could cover them if they were attacked.

At 0700 the next morning, one of Hogan's team heard noises outside. They went on the alert. While one man stayed on the second floor to provide security, Hogan and the other man readied themselves on the ground floor. They heard movement, but no voices. Then there was the grunt of a pig—a hungry, carnivorous pig tearing into a dead cow. Hogan's companion wanted to kill it, figuring that a hungry pig could attack humans, but Hogan was afraid of giving away their position. His main worry was that the pig would sniff out the other snipers and draw attention to their hides. That afternoon, the pig stuck its head through a hole in the wall and one of the Croats slit its throat.

As the evening drew on, they awaited a Croatian patrol to escort them out of the village. But then two shots rang out, one from each hide. Then the team in one of the hides fired again. This was answered by a shot from another position. Hogan and his team went to the other side to see whether they could identify where it had come from. Then there was another muzzle flash from a group of houses about 220 yards (200 meters) away. One of Hogan's men homed in on him. When there was a third muzzle flash, the man squeezed the trigger of his .300 Winchester Magnum. No more muzzle flashes came from that direction.

When the Croatian patrol turned up and searched the houses, they found a man in Yugoslav Army camouflage with an entry wound just about his collarbone, where he had been hit by an 180-grain Barnes X bullet. The exit wound had practically severed his spine between his back and neck. The man was not carrying a gun. This had plainly been taken by a companion, but 7.92 x

57-mm rounds with Cyrillic markings were found. The dead man was a sniper who had not learned to move after his second shot.

As they left the village, the other two teams explained their three shots. A Serbian patrol had come out of the fields. The teams had taken out a man each at (330 yards) 300 meters. Then a third man had left cover to check on his buddies. The third shot had taken him down too. The Croatian snipers had fired four shots and scored four hits, one of which was a confirmed killed in action (KIA). They were coming along.

Also in Croatia was an ex-British Army sniper code-named Rose. With him as a heavy-weapons backup was a veteran of the Australian Army named "Skippy" Hampstead. When there was no major offensive going on, they would go out at night had find a position overlooking the enemy lines across the valley. Rose carried a Yugoslavian M76—a copy of the Soviet SVD Dragunov sniper rifle—with a night sight zeroed to 440 to 550 yards (400 to 500 meters). Hampstead had an MG42 machine gun with a tracer every third round. Rose would pick his target and fire. Hampstead would follow with a short burst that would zero in on the target, killing anyone who had come to help the fallen man. On one occasion they used a 66-mm antitank rocket launcher in a similar role to great effect.

The pair moved on to Bosnia to fight the Serbs there. In Mostar, they came upon a Serb sniper who had a reputation for killing women and children. He had also killed one of Hampstead's friends, and Hampstead and Rose were determined to kill him. Others had gone after him before and had either gotten nowhere or ended up casualties.

The Serb usually worked along a section of road where there was heavy civilian traffic. From that information and a few missed shots they had witnessed, they worked out his angle and distance. Scanning his likely position, they saw him among the rafters of a house. Although he stood back in the shadows—plainly he was a trained sniper—he was clean-shaven, and they glimpsed his white face ducking in and out of the shadows. It was a small target at a distance of 380 to 440 yards (350 to 400 meters), but they could not afford to miss. One fluffed shot and he would disappear. They waited for about 10 minutes. Then he showed himself, raising his rifle, about to take a shot. Rose downed him with one bullet.

Having killed from a distance himself, Hampstead felt the moral dilemmas of a sniper. He said that you felt like the hand of God, deciding whether someone lived or died. The people you killed had parents, siblings, wives, and children, and usually they were no direct threat to you. In the moments you watched them, you felt an affinity for them. Although they were soldiers in uniform, aggressors, they were still human. On one occasion Hampstead saw two Serbian soldiers trying to light their cigarettes, and he had to decide which one to kill. He decided to take out the one who lit his cigarette first. It was that arbitrary. One man lived; the other had his head blown to pieces.

Former British paratrooper Lee Marvin led a small unit of Croats against a Serb machine gun platoon in a trench. He put his own machine gunners on the flanks, then crept forward with his M76 over his shoulder and an AK-47 in his hand. It was quiet, and the unsuspecting Serbs were laughing and joking. There did not seem to be many of them, but there could have been any number inside the main position.

Marvin had told his men to wait until they had heard him fire three shots, while he moved up to the end of the trees he was using for cover. Now he was as close as he could get to the enemy, and his life depended entirely on his camouflage. Then he put down his AK-47 and took up his M76. He lodged the butt against his shoulder and twisted the sling around his right arm to steady the weapon. The first sentry was now in his sights. Then he moved on to the second, then the third. He returned to the first and repeated the process several times, so he knew instinctively where each one was. The first was just 75 feet (23 meters) away. The second was around 110 feet (34 meters), the third 200 feet (60 meters). He had to take out all three before they could fire back at his position. The problem was that, after the first shot, the other two would move, grab their guns, and return fire.

Gently Marvin flicked off the safety catch, then returned his hand to the grip, taking care not to disturb his aim. As he breathed in, the sights moved down the target; as he breathed out, they moved back up again. In an attempt to control his breathing, he inhaled and exhaled several times. Then, exhaling slowly, he squeezed the trigger. The first sentry fell. The second was hit before he could move. The third had time to move, but the bullet hit him in the shoulder blade and took him down. He grabbed his weapon, but to no avail. Marvin pulled the trigger again, hitting the man in the side of the neck. By then the machine guns had opened up. The Serbs were quickly overwhelmed, but the Croats lost several men to enemy mines.

As the war in Bosnia dragged on, Sarajevo became a sniper's paradise, for the Serbs at least. They occupied the high ground around the city and spent their time targeting Bosnian civilians in the streets below. The only answer was for the Bosnians to form teams of countersnipers. These consisted of two or three marksmen and an observer equipped with a 40 x 42 spotting scope or binoculars. Once they had identified a target, they would take a potshot from a window or shell hole, then move quickly to another hide. It was a game of shoot and scoot, as one sniper round was often answered by an artillery shell from a tank.

Although they had maps and sketches of the enemy's positions, the countersniper's task was not an easy one. The hillside occupied by the Serbs was built up. There were thousands of empty windows, and just 330 yards (300 meters) from the Bosnians' positions was a cemetery with hundreds of tombs and gravestones where snipers could hide.

The Bosnian and Serb snipers knew each other by name. They had worked together in the same police counterterrorism unit before the war. The most feared of the Serb snipers was a former shooting instructor who had an Olympic medal for marksmanship. One week he would pick out firemen, the next journalists, the next women—and he never missed. Once he had you in his sights, you were a dead man.

In Sarajevo, the UN peacekeepers came under fire from all three warring sides—the Serbs, Croats, and Bosnian Muslims. Sometimes the factions were just 20 or 30 yards (18 or 27 meters) apart. They were using the same weapons, which made them hard to identify. The French paratroopers who were holding the line in Sarajevo had teams trained for search-and-destroy missions, but the snipers occupied territory that was out of their jurisdiction. Consequently, they had to take the snipers out one at a time, using five-man countersniping teams that moved around the city in APCs. The marksmen were equipped with 7.62-mm bolt-action FR F2s—the standard sniper rifle of the French army—and McMillan Tac-50s, .50-caliber long-range sniper rifles made in Phoenix, Arizona. The APCs also carried a 7.62-mm coaxial machine gun and a 20-mm cannon.

Five of these APCs would drive down the sniper alley about 165 yards (150 meters) apart with their guns turned toward the Serb-held territory on the other side of the river. A sketch of the view showing the coordinates was taped to the APC's bulkhead. Each building had a code name, and each window or other sniper position had a letter. They would run through the coordinates several times every day to make sure everyone was up to speed. Reports on sniper activity on the other side of the river was radioed in. As they went into action, a spotter scanning the area with binoculars would call out coordinates. The target would then be verified by a trooper looking through the scope of an FR F2.

One of the UN countersnipers was Corporal Chevardez, a veteran of Chad and the Congo. He carried a .50 McMillan. His spotter picked up an enemy sniper setting up in a white apartment block about 380 yards (350 meters). He already had the target in his sights when he heard shots. Puffs of gun smoke gave him visual confirmation, and he loosed off two explosive rounds. These were followed by rounds from the 20-mm cannon, which took out part of the wall. There were no more shots from that position.

CHAPTER THIRTEEN

Somalia (1992)

In December 1992, the US led a United Nations force into Somali in Operation Restore Hope, an effort to still the fighting there enough to get humanitarian aid into the war-torn country. On January 6, 1993, after they had entered the capital, Mogadishu, they insisted that the Somalis surrender their heavy weapons the following day. It seems that warlord General Mohamed Ali Farrah Aidid had no intention of doing so. At 2130 hours, the marines who were billeted in the national stadium got a call from the headquarters of the US Army's 10th Mountain Division saying that they were being threatened by tanks and heavy antiaircraft machine guns some 600 yards (550 meters) away. They were also being harassed by small arms, but they did not return fire as they were only armed with M16s and machine guns.

More than 300 marines were sent to surround the area. Then five marine scout-snipers took up position on the roof of the 10th Mountain Division's headquarters at around 1930. That night a storm swept in from the Indian Ocean, instantly turning the African heat into an icy chill. One of the snipers ripped the canvas top from a Humvee to make a makeshift shelter, but it offered no real protection against the driving rain. The rain destroyed the effectiveness of the scout-snipers night-vision goggles, leaving them blind to what was going on around them. As dawn broke, they could clearly see that two 220-mm howitzers, two APCs, and two M48 tanks had their main armaments trained on the 10th's headquarters building.

Cobra gunships were on their way carrying missiles to take the insurgents out, but seeing that the enemy had a Soviet ZSU-23-4 four-barreled 23-mm radar-guided antiaircraft gun known as a Zeus, the forward air controller called off the Cobras. Marine Sergeant Jack Coughlin was asked to take out the Zeus. He trained his .50-caliber Barrett M82A1A Special Applications Scoped Rifle (SASR) on the ammunition feed tray of the Zeus 600 yards (550 meters) away. One shot and the weapon would be disabled.

By then the Cobras were hovering behind the 10th Mountain Division's headquarters. The Zeus gunner began to elevate the cannon so that he could take out the gunships when they came into sight. Coughlin could see him beyond the feed tray between two of the Zeus's gun barrels. On receiving the orders of General Jack W. Klimp through his headset, Sergeant Coughlin pulled the trigger. The heavy round punched through the feed tray and knocked the gunner over the back of his seat. There was little doubt he was dead.

Another Zeus opened up, raking the building in response. As the snipers hid behind the parapet, the cannon blasted lumps of concrete off the building. Marine Sergeant C. Johnson took out the gunner with one shot from his M40A1. Johnson also knocked out a rifleman who was aiming at the headquarters building, while Coughlin disabled the Zeus with armor-piercing rounds from his M82A1A.

Other insurgents ran for the tanks. None of them made it. Lance Corporal Andrew Lopez also took three of them out. Sergeant Johnson dropped another at 600 yards (550 meters) with a single round. Though wounded in the hip, one guerrilla escaped from the battlefield. Meanwhile, Sergeant Coughlin put armor-piercing bullets into the tanks at around the position the driver would be and began searching for other targets of opportunity, while machine guns poured down rounds on other militiamen. TOW missiles from the Cobra gunship then took out the insurgents' buildings. The cease-fire was called four minutes after Sergeant Coughlin fired the first shot.

Then another Somali appeared at a window with an RPD light machine gun. He was spotted by three marine snipers simultaneously. Coughlin's spotter worked out from the range card he had sketched earlier that the Somali was 623 yards (570 meters) away. When he was found, there were two bullets in his body. A second cease-fire was called.

But still the snipers were vigilant. With a fresh clip in his M82A1A, Coughlin spotted a man on a balcony, waving to the insurgents in the compound below. He locked onto him, but did not fire. Under the rules of engagement, he presented no immediate threat. But when a truck with a machine gun pulled up, it seemed the man was organizing a counterattack. Coughlin reported the situation and was told that if the gate to the compound opened he was to take him out.

But before that happened, Coughlin was spotted. The militiamen began pointing at him, and the man on the balcony turned. He was staring directly into the huge fish-eye of the scope on Coughlin's SASR. The man went inside, leaving the mob below without a leader.

Later it was discovered that the field pieces, the APCs, and the tanks' main armaments all had shells in the barrels. If it had not been for the quick and accurate work of the marine snipers, the 10th Mountain Division headquarters would have been no more.

In 1993, US Marine sniper Travis Mitchell found himself in Mogadishu, Somalia, seven days after the Black Hawk Down incident in which two Special Forces helicopters were downed by rocket-propelled grenades fired by Somali insurgents. In the ensuing fire-fight, 18 US service personnel were killed, 73 wounded, and one captured, along with another four United Nations personnel killed and 45 wounded. Estimates of Somali casualties vary wildly.

Mitchell and his eight-man team set up two observation posts. One was on top of the US Embassy. The other was outside the compound with the secure perimeter established by the Pakistani contingent of the UN forces. It was seven stories up and was code-named K7.

They quickly abandoned the use of binoculars for observa-tion. The insurgents moving around the streets below were only out in the open for two or three seconds. In that time, it was impos-sible to drop the binoculars, raise an M40A1 rifle, take aim, and fire. Besides, the 8x magnification of the binoculars did not match the 10x magnification of the Unertl scopes the marines were using.

Mitchell was on the top of the Embassy with his partner, Cor-poral Schmitt, who was cleaning his Barrett .50-caliber. The heat and humidity in Mogadishu meant a weapon had to be cleaned every day to prevent it from rusting. Mitchell was observing when Schmitt, who had just finished polishing the optics, said he was going to look through the scope. Then—*bang!* He fired with-out warning. An insurgent had been brandishing an RPG, he explained, and he had to pull the trigger suddenly. The Somali now lay dead with the RPG beside him.

A crowd gathered, and another Somali grabbed the RPG and ran off with it. He was too fast for either Schmitt or Mitchell to engage him, though Schmitt loosed off a shot from his Barrett anyway.

Soon after, word came from the 5th Special Forces that insurgents had been seen wearing black body armor taken from the men from Delta Force who were killed during the Black Hawk

Down incident. These men were a "target of opportunity"—they could be taken out without permission. They had also taken a sniper rifle, two M60 machine guns, and other equipment from the downed helicopters. The snipers were to watch out for them.

Mogadishu was awash with guns at the time. When the 5th Marines had first entered the city, they had confiscated all the guns they could find. But when the locals complained that they could not defend themselves against the warlord General Aidid—the target of the Black Hawk raid—the UN put tags on the guns and gave them back. It soon became clear to the Somali insurgents that they could put a tag on any gun they liked and it could be handled freely. Observers could see fresh guns coming into the city hidden in grain shipments. Intelligence said that 70 percent of the information they dealt with came directly from sniper teams.

One day Mitchell watched as a white Toyota Corolla drove up. When the driver got out, he had an M60 with him. They were under orders to shoot anyone with an M60. He passed it to someone behind a wall that was about 350 yards (320 meters) away. But the weapon was handed back to the driver, who took off before Mitchell or Schmitt could do anything about it. The incident was duly recorded in their log and reported up the chain of command.

Then the Toyota came back. The driver still had the M60 with him, but Mitchell could not get a clean shot. The car drove off again, and returned a third time. This time the driver got out of the car and walked around it in clear sight. Another man with an AK-47, possibly his bodyguard, was nearby. Schmitt said he would take him out, while Mitchell dealt with the driver.

Mitchell lined up the crosshairs on the man with the M60. He squeezed the trigger. The M40A1 bucked in his hands and the driver fell. The man with the AK-47 pointed up toward the observation point, but a few seconds later, Schmitt's Barrett roared and the man was felled. By that time, Mitchell had another bullet in the chamber and he scanned the area. Then he saw another man in the back of the Toyota who began to raise a weapon. Mitchell fired again and hit him through the back of the window. Mitchell could see he was dead when another Somali dragged him from the car and his bright red blood splashed on the dust in the street.

For Mitchell, these were his first and second kills in rapid succession. He told Schmitt he could not fire anymore. He was so pumped up on adrenaline he could not focus. Schmitt found he could not shoot either. The incident brought protestors out into the street. Mitchell and Schmitt realized they were now an easy target for the insurgents, and they had to be rescued by a rapid reaction force.

Though Mitchell was from Montana and a huntsman from the age of eight, shooting a man, he said, was very different from shooting an animal.

"You hear all of these guys talk about how they can shoot people and get right back on the gun," he said. "Well, I probably could have shot if I'd had to, but it would have been difficult."

The incident stayed with him. Mitchell returned to the States and went on to become head urban sniper instructor of the Special Operations training group.

US intervention in Somalia was not popular, and the press picked up stories fabricated by the Somali insurgents. According to one tale, a US marine sniper had killed 12 people with one bullet. In another, when marine snipers had taken out an insurgent armed with an RPG on top of a truck, the guerrillas said they had killed a pregnant woman with a .50-caliber slug. A team from the Army Criminal Investigation Department was flown in. They discovered the dead woman had actually been killed by the truck, but still the story of marine snipers taking out innocent women and children circulated.

Even so, Lance Corporal Andrew Lopez managed to put into action some of the more unconventional techniques he had learned at the 1st Marine Division Scout Sniper School. His target was hiding, but Lopez managed to ricochet a bullet off a wall alongside him. It was not a clean kill. Later a patrol picked up the man and found that the bullet had passed right through his nose. Lopez visited the man in the hospital, explaining that this time he had been merciful. The next time the injured insurgent may not be so lucky.

In September 1993, Sergeant Howard E. Wasdin was one of four snipers from SEAL Team Six in Somalia. He and his partner, nicknamed Casanova for his legendary womanizing, set up an observation post on top of the safe house they occupied in downtown Mogadishu. From there they spotted an old man with donkey pulling a cartload of bricks. When he came back again, they noticed that he was carrying the same bricks. They learned from an intelligence source that under the bricks he was transporting mortar rounds, and they got permission to kill him.

The next time he came by, Casanova acted as spotter. The old man was 500 yards (460 meters) away when Wasdin took aim. When Casanova gave the command "execute," Wasdin squeezed the trigger. The old man remained on his feet, but the donkey fell dead. Wasdin figured that there were a lot of old men in Mogadishu. A donkey would be harder to replace.

Along with the US and others, Pakistan had sent a peacekeeping force to Somalia in 1992. Wasdin and Casanova moved into the Pakistani compound and set up at a firing position on the top of a six-story tower there. Around dawn each day, they climbed the tower, lay there, and watched the comings and goings below from the home of Osman Ali Atto, one of Aidid's major backers, and the garage that Aidid's militia used as a base.

Wasdin kept his scope dialed to 500 yards (450 meters) so he could take anything between about 200 yards (180 meters), the garage below, and 650 yards (600 meters), a distant intersection, by aiming a little high or low.

From 0600 in the morning, Wasdin would go through the routine of dry firing. He would acquire a target through his Leupold 10x scope, check his breath, simulate pulling the trigger, then go to find another target. Their job was to cover a team from Delta Force who were going into the garage below with the aim of capturing Atto, whom intelligence reported was holding a meeting there. The idea was that if they could cut off his money supply, Aidid would be a spent force.

Again they were hampered by the rules of engagement. Even if a man appeared carrying a gun, he was not necessarily hostile. He could be with a clan that was on the government's side. They had to wait until he actually pointed the weapon at US or UN forces before he became a legitimate target. In the cluttered urban landscape of war-torn Mogadishu, an enemy could take one potshot at American troops, jump back into a building, then emerge again without a weapon. Under those circumstances, disposing of a target with one clean shot was vital. There was no time for the usual spotter-sniper relationship in which the spotter identifies and ranges a target, conveying the information to the sniper to take the shot. So both Wasdin and Casanova were equipped with .300 Winchester Magnum sniper rifles.

As the choppers carrying the Delta Force came in, Wasdin could see a militiaman firing at them through a window. He fixed his crosshairs on the target, took a moment to lower his heart rate, then squeezed the trigger. The bullet passed through the man's chest from left to right. He would be no further trouble.

Having fast-roped to the ground, the Delta Force men surrounded the garage. Another militiaman pointed his AK-47 at the

Delta Force from the fire escape of a building some 300 yards (275 meters) away. Wasdin put a bullet through his chest. When he fell, Wasdin could see hands trying to grab the AK-47. A third round discouraged this.

Then Wasdin spotted a more challenging—and more vital— target. At over 800 yards (730 meters), a militiaman was aiming an RPG at one of the helicopters. He had to make this shot count—and fast. The range on his scope was set at 1,000 yards (915 meters). Making a quick calculation in his head, he aimed for the man's chest and hit him in the face. But instead of flying backward, the man toppled forward from the weight of the RPG. As he did, he pulled the trigger, firing it straight down into the street, where it exploded.

Delta Force took 15 prisoners without casualties. But the Rangers, who were supposed to have formed a cordon, did not arrive in time, and Atto slipped away. A check with the laser range finder measured the distance from the tower to the militiaman with the RPG to be 846 yards (774 meters)—the farthest in Coughlin's career. Atto was later captured when the CIA had managed to give him an ivory-handled cane with a radio beacon in it.

Wasdin and his fellow SEAL snipers were then involved in the Battle of Mogadishu—the Black Hawk Down incident—where he was hit in the back of the knee and the ankle. But armed with a CAR-15 carbine, his role was more that of an assault troop than a sniper. Eventually, their Cutvee ran over a land mine and was disabled. The militia closed in on them, but they were rescued by a quick reaction force and taken to Germany, where Wasdin was patched up. He was awarded the Purple Heart and the Silver Star.

On October 3, 1993, members of Delta Force, the US Rangers, SEAL Team Six, and the 160th Special Operations Aviation Regiment tried to capture the warlord General Mohamed Ali Farrah Aidid when he was having a meeting in the Olympic Hotel in downtown Mogadishu. Two of their Black Hawk helicopters were hit. One of them, *Super 61*, flown by Chief Warrant Officers Cliff "Elvis" Wolcott and Donovan "Bull" Briley, was hit by an RPG and crashed near the hotel. The second, Super 64, flown by CWOs Mike Durant and Ray Frank, were circling over scrubland to the north when they heard *Super 61* had gone down. They were on their way to take over *Super 61*'s position when *Super 64* was hit by another RPG. The grenade hit the helicopter's gearbox. Oil sprayed out, but she still seemed to be airworthy.

Super 64 turned home toward the Ranger's base three miles away, near the beach. In *Super 62*, CWO Mike Goffena and his copilot, Jim Yacone, decided to follow. As *Super 62* turned, Goffena saw *Super 61*'s gearbox tear itself to pieces. The nose dipped and the helicopter went into an uncontrollable spin. It made a hard landing on a shanty town, where the flimsy huts cushioned its fall. The search-and-rescue team was already on the way to the crash site of *Super 61*. There would be no one coming to rescue the crew of *Super 64*.

Already, crowds of Somali militiamen, high on *khat*, an amphetaminelike plant, were racing toward the crash site. On board *Super 62* along with the pilots and two crew chiefs were three snipers from Delta Force—Team Sergeant Gary Gordon, Weapons Sergeant Randy Shughart, and Sergeant First Class Brad Hallings. *Super 62* was already coming under fire. The crew chief manning one of the Black Hawk's two door-mounted miniguns was hit. Hallings took over from him. As Goffena took *Super 62* low over the crash site, their job was to take out anyone who appeared to be aiming an RPG. Shughart was carrying an M24 Sniper Weapon System; Gordon a short-barreled CAR-15, more suited to close-quarters combat. They lay on the Black Hawk's steel floor to steady their aim as they took their pick of the militiamen below.

Goffena flew so low that the rotor wash forced the Somalis back. He made a low pass over *Super 64* to check for survivors. He could see Mike Durant, who had been knocked unconscious by the crash, coming to. He had a broken thigh. Ray Frank had a broken leg. He was also dazed, but Goffena could see him move his head. Out of sight in the back of the downed helicopter, Staff Sergeant Bill Cleveland was bleeding and delirious, while Sergeant Tommy Field was also a stretcher case.

The intense ground fire made it impossible to rescue them from the air, and there was no ground force on the way to rescue them. The search-and-rescue team sent to the crash site of *Super 61* had been ambushed repeatedly, and there was a danger that it might not make its way back to base without being massacred. Meanwhile, a new rescue convoy heading for *Super 64*'s crash site was taking heavy fire and was unlikely to make it in time.

The crowd was now closing in on *Super 62* and, although Mike Durant had opened up through the broken windscreen with a Heckler & Koch MP-5K, the survivors were in no fit state to defend themselves. They were as good as dead unless help arrived right away.

Immediately, Shughart and Gordon, both veterans in their mid-thirties, volunteered to go in and hold off the crowd until help arrived. They reckoned that with accurate and concerted fire, they could hold off a disorganized rabble of militiamen. This was conveyed to the mission commander, Lieutenant Colonel Tom Matthews, and Delta Force's Lieutenant Colonel Gary L. "Shooter" Harrell, who were in the command-and-control helicopter circling above. Matthews asked Harrell whether he should put his men in. There seemed no other choice.

Shughart and Gordon had already made up their minds to go in, despite the appalling odds. Hallings would stay behind to man the mini-gun. The crew chief popped a smoke marker on the downed Black Hawk. *Super 62* then headed for a small clearing between the shacks about 50 yards (45 meters) from the crash site. It hovered about five feet from the ground above a hut and a fence, while the two Delta Force men jumped out and then streaked skyward again as Hallings fired on the crowd. *Super 62* then resumed its position, giving cover to the crash site while Shughart and Gordon clambered over the shanty toward the smoke.

By the time they arrived at *Super 64*, Ray Frank had clambered out of the stricken helicopter and disappeared. Shughart and Gordon pulled Durant from the wreckage and propped him up against a tree. They checked around for an empty space big enough to set a helicopter down in. By the time they got back to help the others, the militiamen had arrived, occupying all the pathways back to the main road. CWO Keith Jones and copilot Karl Maier had put their Little Bird, *Star 41*, nearby, but there was no way the two Delta Force snipers could get the wounded men to them. There was no way out.

Shughart and Gordon set up a perimeter as best they could. Shughart picked off targets with his bolt-action M24 while Gordon fired short bursts from his CAR-15. Then Gordon was hit. Above, an RPG hit *Super 62*, tearing off Hallings's leg and knocking Yacone unconscious. Somehow Goffena nursed the crippled helicopter back to base.

Durant realized that the end was near when Shughart came around the helicopter to hand him Gordon's CAR-15. He wished him good luck, then walked away. Durant heard bursts of AK-47 fire. With a bolt-action sniper's rifle, Shughart stood no chance against automatic weapons at close range.

Over the Black Hawk's radio, Durant heard observers overhead saying that indigenous people were closing in. He kept firing until he ran out of ammunition. He still had a pistol strapped to his thigh but did not even reach for it.

All the other Americans were now dead. Durant was an unwilling onlooker as the Somali militiamen tore their bodies to pieces. When they found Durant was still alive, they stripped him and beat him with sticks. He was surprised to find that they spared his life. He was shoved in a car and taken to Aidid's headquarters. After 11 days, he was returned to US forces, along with the mutilated bodies of the others.

Sergeant First Class Randy Shughart and Master Sergeant Gary Gordon were both awarded the Medal of Honor and the Purple Heart posthumously.

Marine snipers oversaw the pull-out from Somalia in 1994. Five months after the Black Hawk Down incident and the deaths of Sergeants Shughart and Gordon, the last US combat units had pulled out of Mogadishu. Sergeant Michael Carr and his partner, Sergeant McFarland, both with the 1st Platoon, Fleet Antiterrorism Security Team (FAST) Company, and 50 other marines had stayed behind to guard the American embassy compound until the last of the diplomats were withdrawn. While Aidid's gunmen were now involved in internecine war in the city, they expected him to get around to attacking the embassy sooner or later. Indeed, they even saw clansmen practicing their assault in the streets below. When they did, the snipers were supposed to hold them back.

Carr and McFarland were on the roof of the White House— the main building at the embassy compound—when they came under fire. Their commanding officer was convinced that this was merely "spillover fire" from the gun battles in the surrounding streets. Under the rules of engagement, they were only allowed to fire if they actually saw someone firing at them. In this case, they thought it safer to keep their heads down.

When the Somalis brought up a truck with a 106-mm recoilless rifle on the back, Sergeant Carr was designated to keep an eye on it. He was ordered to fire if the clansmen so much as pointed it at the embassy compound. Carr got out his M40A1 and his spotter, Corporal Middleton, took up position with an M49 spotter scope and an M16 with a 6x Leupold scope. A convoy left for the airport, evacuating more men and equipment to Kenya. By then there were just eight marines left guarding the compound.

Once the convoy had gone, the 106-mm recoilless rifle left as well. But after two hours, it was back. Carr and Middleton rushed back onto the roof. This time it was pointing at the compound. Carr got out his sniper rifle, loaded a round in the chamber, and put the crosshairs on the man with the gun. But at that moment, the man turned the recoilless rifle away from the compound—saving his life. Car and Middleton kept an eye on the gun, but it was not brought back to bear on the compound. For Aidid, it was enough of a victory to push the US out of Somalia and force them to close their embassy. On September 15, 1994, the flag was hauled down. The last of the embassy left for Nairobi, while the marines went to Mombasa.

CHAPTER FOURTEEN

Chechnya (1999)

After the collapse of the Soviet Union, 18-year-old Nicolai Lilin from the breakaway region of Transnistria was conscripted into the army of the Russian Federation. He had already been in juvenile prison twice, once for attempted murder. Unwilling to serve in the army, he found himself beaten up, flung in a cell, then taken by train to a military base. He was to be trained as a saboteur and put in the charge of the *Spetsnaz*—Russia's Special Forces.

The training was grueling. Several of his fellow trainees were injured during exercises, but Lilin showed a natural aptitude for marksmanship and earned himself a place on the sniper course. He had been taught to hunt in the Siberian forests by his grandfather, a veteran of the Great Patriotic War, as the Russians call the war on the East Front during World War II.

Lilin was trained on a Dragunov and a VSS—that is, a "Special Sniper Rifle" with a folding stock and a built-in silencer. It had an effective range of just 440 yards (400 meters) and was used in urban conflicts. After three months, again against his will, he was sent to Chechnya. The enemy were Chechen nationalists, Muslims said to be backed by the Taliban. The Russians dismissed them as "Arabs."

Deployed to a mobile saboteur unit, his first job was clearing up the corpses after a battle. Then he went to work as a sniper. After his first kill, he took a Canadian-made bayonet from the body as a memento. Later he used it to kill a man.

The saboteurs did not wear uniforms like other soldiers. Not even helmets and boots. They wore sneakers, jumpsuits, light jackets, and informal headgear. They also wore their hair long and grew beards in case they had to go behind enemy lines.

After 60 Russian paratroopers were surrounded and butchered by the Chechens, the saboteurs were sent in to exact the Russians' retaliation. They were carrying AK-47s, but they sawed off the metal hooks that held the guns' slings as they clanked and made too much noise. Instead, each sling, or some rope, was held in place with electrical tape. In urban battles, they would tape their rifles to their jackets so their hands would be free but the rifle would be handy. And rather than carry revolvers in holsters on their belts where they might impede movement, the saboteurs held them in chest pockets they had sewn inside their jackets. Before they went out on an operation, they jumped up and down to make sure that nothing on them was loose or would make a noise.

After booby-trapping the far side of the trail a Chechen column was expected to come down, Lilin took up position to fire on the front of the column, while an infantry sniper was in position to prevent anyone escaping from the rear. The enemy often made things easy for the snipers. Commanders picked themselves out by carrying the 7.62 x 39-caliber AKS rifles with a folding stock and an American-made scope. These were the men the Russian snipers would pick off first.

There were 25 men in the Russian ambush. They were to take on a column estimated at 60. Five scouts appeared first, but the snipers held their fire. The rest of the column followed 330 yards (300 meters) behind. Machine guns opened up on the rear of the column while Lilin picked off the men at the front.

As men fell, others took cover behind their bodies and returned fire. The Chechens concentrated on those providing precision fire, but they focused on the infantry sniper who had no silencer. No one could hear Lilin's deadly shots. Some of the enemy soldiers tried to find cover on the other side of the trail and were blown up. Others simply stood there not knowing what to do. The machine guns stopped, allowing the Russians with ordinary rifles to pick them off.

One ran, dodging bullets. The Russian captain, a veteran of Afghanistan, ordered Lilin to bring the man down but not to kill him. He aimed in front of the runner. When the front of a limb brushed the crosshairs, he pulled the trigger. The round hit him in the leg, crippling his knee. By then, the rest of the column were dead, except for one man who seemed totally disorientated by what had happened. When he was beaten to the ground, a video camera fell out of his clothing. It showed Russian prisoners being beheaded. He was tied up to be delivered to counterintelligence.

The captain then carved the shape of a bat—the symbol of the mobile saboteur unit, as they often infiltrated at night using black parachutes—in the crippled man's belly. But he refused to allow another officer to shoot him, preferring to leave him to the tender mercies of his own side. The men were then allowed to strip the bodies of their valuables.

The mobile sabotage unit was employed in general skirmishing when they were called up for a counterstrike. Their job would be to take out the enemy snipers. They would be supported by a special paratroop assault team. Much of the fighting was over and the streets were full of the dead and dying. Lilin's job would be to stalk through the rubble and find and kill the enemy snipers who remained behind to harass Russian troops.

They reached a five-story building that had been half burned out. A young infantryman had been shot through the head. This, the captain decided, was a deliberate tactic to get them to attack the building, and he imagined that there was a machine gun inside. The infantry were to keep up their fire on the front of the building while Lilin and the rest of the saboteurs outflanked it and infiltrated from behind. He was carrying an AKMS—the latest AK-47 with a folding stock designed for paratroopers—with a dioptric scope that produced a red spot they called "Lenin's lamp," and he had five 10-round clips.

Lilin covered the rest of the men as they crossed the road outside without firing a shot. Then they took up position in an old bar where they could observe the back of the house. Two Africans appeared and were hit by a grenade launcher. The Chechens' grenade launcher was also taken out, and this provoked them to attack, only to be cut down by machine gun fire. Lilin spotted three enemy snipers trying to climb up on the roof and took them down, but only after one of them had fatally wounded an infantry sergeant.

When Lilin was next assigned a task, he feared he was going to face the type of sniper duel last experienced at Stalingrad when Russian infantrymen had been caught behind the Chechen lines and had been surrounded. Again a group of Russian infantrymen had been beleaguered behind Chechen lines, and Lilin and his team went in to rescue them. A Russian sniper had managed to hide in the sewers with details of the Chechen position, which Lilin was told to memorize. He feared that he was going to be sent back into the sewers—which were often mined—alone. But when his captain discovered that the senior officer, a major, had planned an air strike that would kill not just the Chechens but the besieged Russians, too, he insisted that there was time before the first air strike to take the saboteurs through the sewers and get the remaining infantrymen. Reluctantly, the major gave his permission. The saboteurs also voted unanimously to take along a Cossack officer, Vasily Ustinov, whose son was with the beleaguered Russians.

The captain led the way but stayed in the sewer when they reached the exit. Lilin was to go first. There were just 16 infantrymen left alive. One of them was the Cossack's son, Yury. Hurriedly, they descended the sewers once more, constructing a makeshift booby trap behind them. Lilin and his partner, Moscow, brought up the rear, hearing the booby trap detonate when they were 330 yards (300 meters) before the exit on the Russian side of the lines.

The captain was sure that the explosion of the booby trap would have alerted the Chechens, who would now be dropping explosives down the sewers. The Russians scrambled out of the nearest manhole right in the middle of the Chechen's second line of defense. Lilin and Moscow were sent to scout the area. Fortunately, there were no enemy snipers about. They found a captured armored car. The captain killed the guard who was sleeping in the back with a stab to the heart.

The Chechens liked to display the corpses of the Russians they had killed, so the dead guard was dressed in a Russian uniform and tied under the gun turret. The infantrymen got in the back, while the saboteurs, whose unshaven faces and scruffy clothes meant they could pass as Chechens, rode on top. They even found a Chechen flag to wave and shouted, *"Allah Akbar."*

Lilin and his partner disguised themselves as Chechens as best they could and clambered on, while an infantryman drove the armored car toward the Russian lines. When they reached an enemy checkpoint, the captain threw a hand grenade at a cannon. Lilin and Moscow opened up on the Chechens.

They were within sight of Russian lines when enemy machine guns began firing from upstairs windows. The armored car swerved and crashed into a building. The Russians quickly dismounted and ran for cover as the machine gun fire came after them. Through the din, Lilin would hear the sound of a Dragunov as a shot hit a Russian soldier. It went right through his bulletproof vest, his chest, and out the other side. Lilin yelled out a warning that there was sniper in the area. When a bullet grazed another man, the captain ordered Lilin to deal with the enemy sniper.

The sniper had been firing down into a courtyard where the armored car had crashed. Lilin ran into a basement and found a room with small windows that let in light from the courtyard. He chose one that was in shadows. It was high up, so he grabbed a table and knelt on it, then unfolded the stock of his VSS. Recalling the shot that had passed through the soldier's bulletproof vest, he worked out the angle that bullet had come from. In that direction were two five-story buildings, and behind was a taller one that was nine or ten stories, only the top two of which were visible.

It was also possible to tell by the extent of a wound how fast the projectile was flying, and hence how far away it had been fired. Professional snipers sometimes reduce the powder charge in the cartridge or use a misshapen bullet to fool an observer, but Lilin did not think that the enemy sniper was that much of an expert. The shot had been traveling fast enough to go through two layers of bulletproof vest, as well as a man's body, so he must be close. Lilin scanned the roof of the five-story buildings. On the top of the stairway in between them there was a small service shack. Through the window, Lilin could see a young blond-haired man smoking a cigarette as if he did not have a care in the world.

Sports marksmen from the old Soviet Union—often Estonians, Lithuanians, and Ukrainians—came to Chechnya as mercenaries. But just because they were good shots did not make them good snipers. The enemy sniper had left himself completely exposed on the rooftop, and he had not left mirrors or rods that looked like the barrel of a gun sticking out elsewhere that might fool anyone looking for him.

Lilin pulled out a small piece of cardboard that he kept in his hat and put it over his left eye. His grandfather had taught him this trick. It was difficult to keep one eye closed and the other open for any length of time, and it also distorted your vision when you opened it again. Then he took careful aim.

He was just about to fire when he realized that the enemy sniper had someone with him. A blonde woman appeared with her hair tucked into a military cap. It was plain that she was a tourist from the Baltic come to watch Russians die. When the sniper got up to kiss her, Lilin took aim at his chin. The bullet hit his temple and he disappeared, leaving only a red stain on the wall. A second shot killed his girlfriend, too. Then quickly, Lilin moved position in case there was another sniper out there.

The party was now ready to pull out. Several more Russians were dead, so they disabled their guns. The captain lodged a grenade behind the door of the armored car so it would blow up if anyone opened it. The infantrymen headed off carrying their dead and wounded. The saboteurs followed, pursued by about twenty Chechens with AK-47s. At one point the Chechens ducked into a building for cover, and the saboteurs responded with their grenade launcher. As the Chechens fled, Lilin hit one of them in the back.

The retreating Russians were then raked by machine gun fire. They dived into the buildings on either side of the street, but Yury Ustinov and been hit in the legs. He could not move and took what cover he could behind a cement pole. One of the saboteurs stripped off his bulletproof vest and ran out to his rescue. The captain hit the machine gunner with a grenade, and Lilin pulled out his VSS had shot another Chechen gunman who was firing at them. The saboteur then ran back into the building unscathed with Ustinov over his shoulder.

They crossed the street under fire. Then the captain and Moscow dumped most of their ammunition and ran for the Russian lines to get help. The Chechens had stopped firing, giving those who had remained behind time to reflect. Lilin recalled feeling an impact and found a bullet lodged in one of the clips in his pocket.

Half an hour later, paratroopers arrived, followed by an armored car. They jumped on and were whisked back to Russian lines.

The saboteurs were also sent out into the mountains to fight the Chechens. They were dropped in the rain at night near a small bridge. From there on, they would have to travel by foot. The captain told Lilin not to carry too much, as he did not want his sniper to get tired. They walked for almost two hours before they took a rest. The rain eased up and the sky cleared, and after another hour they reached a valley. But they would still have to stick to the higher ground. If they took an easier route lower down, they risked running into the enemy. But it was hard to clamber over the rocks and dead leaves without making a noise or slipping.

News came from the two-man reconnaissance team sent ahead that they were nearly there, and Lilin reached for his VSS, which he kept wrapped in a cloth for safekeeping. The reconnaissance team returned to say that they had found the enemy position. The Chechens had planted four mines on the trail, but they had defused two and removed the others. The enemy were by a stream 220 yards (200 meters) farther on. There were about 40 men well armed with grenade launchers, at least one RPG, and four heavy machine guns, two of which had night scopes. They had also spotted one man with a high-tech sniper's rifle. And there were just two guards who, judging by the smell wafting up the hillside, were smoking hashish.

The saboteurs took up position in the rocks above the Chechens' camp. The captain and Moscow crept up on the guards and killed them silently with their knives. After that, they surrounded the camp with mines and set up their machine guns and grenade launchers.

Lilin quietly open the stock of his VSS rifle and loaded it. He was to lead the attack. There was a fire lit behind a tent so it could not be seen from below, but Lilin could see it well enough. Dawn was approaching, and five men were sitting on a log warming themselves by the fire. As they were already awake and the most likely to respond, Lilin decided to hit them first.

The man on the left had an AKS. Lilin put the cardboard in his eye and aimed for the back of the man's neck. Without taking his eye from the telescope sight, he told the captain he was ready. The captain gave the order to fire. Holding his breath, he squeezed the trigger. Then he moved along the line firing four more shots. The rounds passed easily through each man's neck without alerting the man next to him. Four slid to the ground. The fifth fell to his knees, clutching his throat. Another shot to the head extinguished his life.

A yell went up. But before the Chechens could respond, they were being hit by grenades and machine gun fire. One returned fire from a bush. Lilin took aim, but the man stood on a mine before he could shoot him. Others tried to run the Russian lines. They, too, blew themselves up on mines. Lilin hit another man in the chest. He went down, but tried to get up again. Another shot took away half his face. But that still did not kill him. So Lilin finished him off with a shot to the back of the neck.

The captain was trying to give Lilin an order, but he could not hear over the sound of the machine guns, so he crawled forward with his AK-47. The captain drew his attention to an RPG that was peeping out from behind a tree. Lilin aimed at it, and his second shot detonated the grenade. A man then stumbled out, clutching his belly. Lilin hit him in the head.

It took some time for the Russians to realize that no one was returning fire. Everyone in the Chechen camp was dead. But the place was ablaze, and rounds were cooking off in the flames. Then they saw a green flare lower down the valley. There was another enemy camp down there.

While the others went down to the camp, killed the wounded, searched the dead for documents, and destroyed their weapons, Lilin pulled a young infantry sniper aside, showed him his cardboard eyepiece and briefed him on how, as a sniper, to avoid getting shot—a topic he often found that had been omitted from their sniper training. Against orders, one of the saboteurs, named Zenith, had taken an enemy machine gun with a night sight. The captain ordered to check that the scope had been calibrated correctly. If so, the man could keep it. It passed muster, and Lilin found that the rounds that came with it could cut through Kevlar. They were made in Texas and cost five dollars each.

Lilin, Moscow, and Zenith, with his new machine gun, were sent ahead as a reconnaissance party. Lilin was to take the lead so he could scope the path ahead. A little way down the path, through his night scope, he saw a man walking up the hill carrying a lot of ammunition. Behind him was a party of 34. More chillingly, they had with them two mules, which meant that they were bringing up .85-caliber mortars.

These were particularly lethal weapons in the mountains, as they turn rock into shrapnel. If the Russian patrol was caught out in the open, they stood no chance. And there was no time to turn back and report to the captain. By then, the caravan would have disappeared into the forest. They only option was to take out the mules.

Lilin figured that Arabs usually tied the mules together, meaning if one stopped, the other would pull it along. So if he hit one, the other would tumble with it down to the bottom of the valley. But it was a long shot, not one that could be trusted to the VSS.

So he swapped his sniper rifle for Zenith's new machine gun. It had a night sight, and its special rounds were not only tipped to cut through Kevlar, they had extra powder in the cartridges.

The bullets were polished and lacquered, and filled with mercury, which helped keep the trajectory true.

There was no time to waste. He moved the selector to single-shot, looked through the scope, aimed at the first mule, and fired. The first round fell short. He adjusted his aim and fired again, and again, and again. The two mules were down, followed by a number of men. Moscow and Zenith also opened up. The caravan scattered. They soon began returning fire. But as far as Lilin could see, they did not have a sniper with them.

He put in another clip. But this time, he had taken out about 10 of them and their ammunition was exploding when hit by the machine guns rounds. They were on a slope with nowhere flat to set up a mortar or a machine gun, but they did have an RPG. Lilin was temporarily blinded by the flash in the night scope. The RPG hit the rock wall behind, pummeling them with sharp pebbles, but Lilin kept on firing. There were explosions below where he hit RPGs or mortar rounds, and the place was strewn with bodies. Then they returned to the captain to report that all 34 of the enemy and the two mules were dead.

But when the Russian patrol moved back up the trail to the firing point, they found themselves coming under fire again. They dived for cover. The incoming was so heavy they could not raise their heads. Only one infantryman returned fire, but Lilin persuaded him not to, as the enemy could see his muzzle flash. When he stopped, the incoming tailed off. But still they could hear the sounds of a pitched battle nearby.

When Lilin finally raised his head, he saw three Chechens moving down into the valley some 220 yards (200 meters) away. The captain told him to kill them. Four rounds took down the first two. The third man returned fire, inaccurately, then made a run for it. Lilin followed him with his scope. The man climbed back up the mountain, but when he stopped to rest, Lilin shot him in the leg.

Another man appeared from the trees. Lilin hit him in the chest. But more Chechens were coming. Plainly they had lost the battle against the Russians on the valley floor and were now making their escape. That meant that Russian soldiers were following them. The saboteurs traveled light and did not carry a radio when out on a mission. They had no means of communicating with the comrades and were in danger of coming under friendly fire.

The patrol began firing mortars at the enemy fleeing toward them. When they turned to run, Lilan took down one and wounded another, who was finished off with a grenade.

They were about to take a break when bullets began to rain down on them from the top of the mountain. The infantrymen hid behind some boulders and began to return fire, drawing the fire away from the saboteurs, who had taken cover under the rock face and then tried to move position. An enemy soldier fell from above followed by a grenade that left Lilin stunned.

The captain launched an RPG, and the saboteurs put up a wall of fire so the infantrymen could join them. Bombs dropped and the Russian patrol began to withdraw, but Lilin stayed behind with his VSS. As the enemy did not seem to have any snipers, he felt he had a good chance of holding them off. It was only when he heard the sound of AGSs—Russian automatic grenade launchers—that he followed.

As they withdrew, the captain was hit. Though a round had cracked his breast plate and knocked him out, he did not seem badly injured. Lilin himself collapsed from exhaustion, but eventually they made it into the safety of the forest. When they reached a road, they saw an armored car that fired on them until it realized they were friends. Then they hitched a lift back to base.

The next time Lilin went into action, much of his role had been taken over by the Speynaz attached to the FSB—the Federal Security Service—he had their own countersniper teams. To add insult to injury, a new guy turned up in the unit with a Dragunov, though he had only fired a few practice rounds on the range. Lilin taught him how to use it in combat.

But while he continued killing, Lilin grew careless. When he was finally discharged, he was a wreck. He found it hard to adjust to civilian life and eventually headed back to Siberia where his grandfather had first taught him to shoot. In 2003, he moved to Italy.

PART 3
IRAQ & AFGHANISTAN

CHAPTER FIFTEEN

Iraq

Born and raised in Waltham, Massachusetts, Jack Coughlin enlisted in the US Marines in 1985 at age 21. He had no experience handling guns, but when he hit the rifle range he discovered shooting was easy and soon found himself in the Marine Corps Scout-Sniper School. After a tour of the world's trouble spots, including his time in Somalia, he was sent to Kuwait on Operation Iraqi Freedom.

As his column rolled into Iraq, most Iraqi resistance was dealt with by the armor or the infantrymen who went ahead. But then the headquarters and communications units came under fire from enemy stationed in an oil refinery. The use of artillery would risk blowing the whole thing up, while spraying the place with machine gun fire risked unacceptable casualties among civilians. Clearly this was a job for the snipers.

Gunnery Sergeant Coughlin was called up. He saw that he could easily reverse the situation if he took out whoever was behind the enemy machine gun. It would only take one shot, but first he had to find the man, and he swept the area with his scope. Coughlin's driver, Corporal Orlando Fuentes—aka Panda Bear— checked the distance to the refinery with a laser range finder. It was

911 yards (833 meters). Coughlin's M40A1 was zeroed in at 1,000 yards (915 meters)—the length of 10 football fields. He adjusted the elevation fine-tuning ring of his scope to nine plus one, zeroing it at 915 yards (836 meters). Smoke drifting by showed Coughlin that the wind speed was no more than three miles an hour (five kilometers an hour), so it could safely be ignored.

Random fire was still coming from the direction of the refinery, but it could not be ignored. Sooner or later, the enemy would get lucky. He scanned the front of the building. Then, to his surprise, he found a man there firing an RPK light machine gun from behind a bush. Although at that distance the man and the muzzle flash were obscured by the foliage, through Coughlin's scope he was clearly visible. Coughlin could even see that he had a thick black mustache. No amount of leaves and twigs could protect him from a 173-grain round of Lake City Match ammunition. Coughlin locked his crosshairs on him. Two seconds later, the machine gunner was dead.

Corporal Fuentes spotted movement three stories above. Someone had taken cover behind a wall. But Coughlin was sure that his curiosity would get the better of him. He would want to know whether his buddy behind the machine gun was dead. So Coughlin took aim at the edge of the wall and reloaded. He was not distracted by the sounds of battle in the background—or by the Iraqi prisoners who were watching him, unguarded.

Fuentes grew impatient. He was convinced that the second man had escaped. But Coughlin held his aim on the edge of the wall. Then a head was tentatively poked around the wall. Coughlin squeezed the trigger. The head snapped back and the man tumbled off the building. The ambush was over and the advance could recommence.

By the time they reached the town of Afak, nearly 200 miles (320 kilometers) from the Kuwaiti border, Coughlin had abandoned a sniper's usual first priority of blending into the background. He lay in a shooting position on top of his Humvee, sweeping the doorways, windows, and rooftops with his scope. Almost immediately, he spotted two men setting up an RPK light machine gun in a window. He could see the machine gun barrel pointing at the tactical headquarters's Amtrac and the marines below. He knew the marine who was in the turret of the Amtrac, but yelling to him might alert the machine gunners. Plainly, the two men had to die. Coughlin fired at the one on the left first. The bullet hit him two inches below the head and he fell dead. It was then that Coughlin realized that the other man was the gunner. But instead of opening up or taking cover, he simply stood there in shock, looking down at his dead comrade. Then he looked for the guy who had shot him.

This gave Coughlin the time to reload. He knew the range and windage were accurate. The crosshairs were on his neck. Coughlin squeezed the trigger. The round knocked the man back into the room, taking the machine gun with him.

A few minutes later, Coughlin's attention was drawn to two more armed men on a rooftop. He hit the first guy in the middle of the chest, but the second took cover before Coughlin could reload.

He moved up to a rooftop. Through his scope he saw an Iraqi man who seemed to be in authority 127 yards (116 meters) away. Coughlin could hear machine guns firing elsewhere in the city, but that did not mean he could simply take this man out. He kept him in the crosshairs, with his finger resting lightly on the trigger.

He thought he saw a pistol in the man's pocket, but he could not be sure. Several times, he put two pounds of pressure on the trigger—it took three pounds to fire—then slackened off again. Eventually the man went for his pocket. Coughlin tensed his trigger finger again, but the man produced a cell phone. The company executive officer, Lieutenant Casey Kuhlman, was also keeping his binoculars trained on the man. After 15 minutes, he told Coughlin to put his gun down. Without any positive reason to think the man was hostile, they could not simply waste him.

Back on top of his Humvee, Coughlin and his team moved on to the village of Al Budayr behind a heavily armored column flanked by Cobra gunships. They arrived to find that their commanding officer, Lieutenant Colonel Brian McCoy, had dropped an Iraqi soldier at 200 yards (180 meters), but others had gotten away. Coughlin now stood on the hood of his Humvee and braced himself against the windshield. He could not have been more obvious.

He scanned the scene in front of him through his scope. Then, in a second-story window, he saw an Iraqi solider with an AK-47. He guessed the range and dialed 430 yards (393 meters) into his scope. Then he took aim and checked his breathing. As the Iraqi moved forward to point his rifle out the window at the marines below, Coughlin squeezed the trigger. The round knocked the Iraqi back into the room. The threat neutralized, Coughlin pulled out his laser range finder. The window was exactly 441 yards (402 meters) away. McCoy was less than pleased at this one-upmanship.

His cover now completely blown, Coughlin walked around openly with his M40A1, even stopping to talk and trade cigarettes with the locals. As they left down Route 17 for Al Diwaniyah, Coughlin saw the man he had had in his sights for 15 minutes who had then been spared, thanks to Lieutenant Kuhlman.

On April 1, they launched their attack on Al Diwaniyah. Again, they took the enemy completely by surprise, and those who could ran away rather than put up a fight. Coughlin had resumed his position on top of his Humvee. Scanning the outskirts, he saw a gunman in a foxhole. He took him out at 286 meters (313 yards) and watched the body twitch as the man died.

However, in the center of town there was a blistering battle, with tanks and RPGs exchanging fire. The Humvee stopped near a bunch of marines. As he got out, Coughlin saw an Iraqi emerge from around a corner about 75 yards (70 meters) and point his rifle. This was practically point-blank range for a sniper. Coughlin leveled his gun, but hesitated, as the other marines might get in the way. The Iraqi then turned his eyes on Coughlin. This sealed his fate. The Iraqi was dead before he could get off a shot.

As they moved into the town, they saw three men in green uniforms carrying AK-47s running across their path. The laser range finder said they were 470 yards (430 meters) away. Although it was not yet 10 in the morning, the sun had been up long enough to create a slight mirage. Its shimmer moved from right to left, indicating that there was a slight wind. Coughlin adjusted his scope and aimed at the first man's torso. He was a moving target. The bullet hit him in the throat.

The second man turned and ran away. But he was still carrying his rifle, so Coughlin shot him in the back. Although the bullet hit him, he kept on running. A second bullet brought him down and he disappeared from view. By then, the third soldier had also vanished.

As they moved off, the rest of the team began ribbing Coughlin, saying that he had missed. Coughlin soon stilled the criticism with an 817-yard (747-meter) shot, with a crosswind, that took out an armed soldier who had taken up position in a burned-out bus.

While he was washing the dust off at lunchtime, Coughlin was told that the security patrol had taken prisoner an Iraqi who appeared to have been hit by sniper rounds. He went to the prisoner pen and found a 20-year-old with one bullet in his left arm and a second that had hit him in the back and come out through his chest without, miraculously, hitting any vital organs.

Coughlin called over an interpreter, but the wounded man refused to talk. Coughlin looked him in the eye, then began swearing at him. Under further interrogation, he described the place where he had been hit. It tallied with the area Coughlin had shot the second soldier. The wounded man said that the first round had hit him in the arm, sending him stumbling forward, while the second brought him down.

He said that he had been trying to surrender. So why had he not dumped his rifle and taken off his boots? He said that his own side would kill him if he had done that. Coughlin then told him that he was the one who had shot. The Iraqi looked at Coughlin's sniper rifle and nodded.

Coughlin was relieved that he had not missed his target. He was also relieved that the Iraqi had survived. He had him moved to the front of the line at the first-aid station and told the doctor, whom he knew, to patch him up.

"He is the only man I've ever shot who lived through the experience," said Coughlin.

The doctor then took fright, assuming that he wanted the Iraqi to die to keep up his record. But Coughlin explained that he wanted just the opposite. The interpreter explained to the wounded Iraqi that he was getting priority treatment.

Suddenly came the warning of a gas attack. All the marines dropped what they were doing and rushed to put on their gas masks. The Iraqi prisoners had none, so Coughlin called his driver to bring a gas mask for the wounded man.

The alert passed. The doctor finished patching up the Iraqi. The interpreter explained to him that he was going to be okay and that Coughlin would come back later with some food. But when Coughlin returned, the Iraqi had been moved to another prisoner pen.

Coughlin moved to the outskirts of Baghdad where the advance was again held up. Tanks were attacking a bunker complex. A marine had already taken out three Iraqis with his M16A4, a newer version of the standard assault rifle with a better scope. But still, it was not terribly accurate over 800 yards (730 meters). Even Coughlin only scored four hits from seven shots, which he admitted was a "terrible ratio for a sniper." But the visibility was poor and the battlefield was cluttered. The targets were moving and he had no spotter. Even so, with his contribution, the bunker complex was quickly cleared.

Poor visibility did not hamper Coughlin's last kill in Baghdad. He had climbed on top of his Humvee to cover India Company, who were clearing a building, when he saw a man with an AK-47 creeping up on them. He was shrouded in smoke. But at 168 yards (154 meters), he dropped the man with two shots. It was cold blooded, but as Coughlin's commanding officer Lieutenant Colonel Brian P. McCoy used to say, "My idea of a fair fight is clubbing baby seals."

On September 11, 2001, ex-US Ranger John LeBleu was due to meet friends for lunch at Windows on the World, the bar and restaurant on the top of the north tower of the World Trade Center in New York. He was just five blocks away when the first plane hit. Soon after, he heard that three of the members of his Rangers platoon had been killed in Operation Anaconda in Afghanistan. He knew what he had to do. He re-enlisted as a Ranger. In July 2003, he was at the US Army Sniper School in Fort Benning, Georgia, where he qualified on the M24 US Army sniper rifle, a military version of the Remington 700 with a Leupold 10x scope, and the XM 107 Long Range Sniper Rifle, a semi-automatic .50-caliber Barrett with a Leupold 4.5x14 variable scope. He was also trained in reconnaissance, surveillance, covert movement, tracking, and countersniping. The following month he was sent to Iraq.

His first mission that September was to take a sniper team into Fallujah. Although the city had fallen to the 82nd Airborne in April 2003, US forces were still meeting stiff resistance five months later. On their way into the city, their convoy was hit by an Improvised Explosive Device (IED). They were assigned to go out on night patrols, jumping the wall from Camp Volturno on the outskirts.

LeBleu carried his M24, now in desert camouflage, with PVS-10 day/night vision scope. There was one round in the chamber, five in the magazine, 10 more on a sleeve on the buttstock, and another 30 in his rucksack. He carried a Beretta 9mm semi-automatic on his upper right thigh and five knives, including two scaled-down versions of the World War II Fairbairn-Sykes British Commando knife looped into his belt on his lower back. There was a small knife on his left shoulder for close-quarters fighting, a four-inch, double-edged, fixed-blade knife in the top of his left boot, and a Smith & Wesson Bullseye Extreme Ops knife on the inside of his right boot. The reasoning was that a knife never jams or runs out of ammunition. They were all taped into place with military-issue 100-mile-an-hour tape, so the sheaths would not shift when he ran.

By October, Volturno was being hit with mortar fire and rockets every night. Then a US Army Special Forces major turned up with a present for LeBleu. It was an SR-25 7.62-caliber sniper rifle stamped "US Navy." The SR-25 was the preferred sniper rifle of the US Navy SEALs and other US Special Forces. He was going out on a "leaders' recon" with the 10th Mountain Division the next day.

After assembling the SR-25, he checked the round of 118LR, special long-range 7.62-caliber ammunition that had come with rifle, for any burrs or other defects. They were going out to check an unused factory complex on the southern edge of the city, an area known as the Boneyard. He jumped in the Humvee carrying his SR-25 with one 20-round magazine in place and two spare magazines. He also carried three 15-round magazines for his Beretta.

Out in the streets, LeBleu scanned the locals and got the feeling they were in for trouble. He was right. Their Humvee ran over an IED. But somehow, he knelt over his scope to protect it. When he came to his senses, he quickly scanned for the triggerman, whom intelligence said would be at least 330 yards (300 meters) away.

The convoy quickly drew up in a herring-bone formation. Some three meters to their rear was a village where there were people on the rooftops. Crowds began filling the streets. LeBleu set up his SR-25 on the roof of the Humvee. Beyond the crowd he could see a white pickup with men carrying AK-47s on it. These were the insurgents who had set off the bomb.

LeBleu shouted to the MK19 gunner on the lead vehicle to take out the white truck. Until May 1, 2003, the rules of engagement had been that they could only fire if they were fired on first. Now they could use deadly force on anyone carrying an AK-47 or any other weapon, but their mind set had not changed and they let the truck get away.

The crowd was fast approaching, and they feared another situation like Black Hawk Down in Mogadishu. But LeBleu took action. He aimed at a crack in the wall of a building just in front of the crowd 330 yards (300 meters) down the street. When the round hit, it sprayed fragments of concrete and dust over the crowd, sending them fleeing.

It was then that they saw movement on top of buildings to the northwest. Then AK-47s opened up from the rooftops, as well as from alleys and street corners all around them. About 110 yards (100 meters) to the northwest was a crane. LeBleu figured if he could make it there, he could set up and provide covering fire, while the 10th Mountain moved up behind a dirt berm to take on the enemy at close range.

With his rifle in his hand and a small field radio tucked in his vest, he jumped over the side of the Humvee and made a dash for it with bullets kicking up dust all around him. Once he reached the crane, he crawled underneath it to take cover. He flicked the SR-25 to semi-automatic and fired three shots at a man on the rooftop with an AK-47. The man disappeared.

LeBleu got on the radio, informed the 10th Mountain of his position, and told them to move up behind the dirt berm 55 yards

(50 meters) to the west. Bullets were now raining down on his position. Once the 10th Mountain moved into position, he picked up his three spent cartridges and moved out behind the crane. A sniper should never fire more than three rounds from the same position, nor should he leave spent cartridges behind so the enemy can track him.

Switching to the scout frequency, he called Staff Sergeant Jason Martin, a fellow graduate of sniper school whom LeBleu had brought along as a spotter. LeBleu told Martin to meet him behind the dirt berm.

With the 10th Mountain now in position to take well-aimed shots at selected targets, the insurgents' fire slowed. LeBleu took up position next to a rifleman taking single shots with the M4. As a sniper, his training was to blend in with the rest of the unit. When Martin arrived, he and LeBleu concentrated on the road while the 10th Mountain dealt with the insurgents on the rooftops. In Iraq, as in Mogadishu, the insurgents mounted heavy machine guns on pick-up trucks. So if enemy reinforcements were on their way, they would have to come down the road.

Soon they saw a man on a red motorbike coming up the road. LeBleu suspected that he was the triggerman for the IED. He studied him closely but he could not see an AK-47 or any other weapon. Then Martin spotted the white truck they had seen earlier. It was about 880 yards (800 meters) away and LeBleu elevated the scope accordingly. There was no wind, but the truck was traveling at between 20 and 25 miles per hour. It was headed toward the Boneyard, where LeBleu feared that they might pick up more insurgents and weapons.

Looking through his scope, he could see four insurgents on the back. He could not get a clean shot on the driver, but there was a broad-shouldered man holding an AK-47 standing up at the back of the truck.

Martin looked through the ACOG 4x32 scope on his M4.

"Eight hundred, no wind," he said, confirming LeBleu's estimate.

The 10th Mountain platoon leader asked if anyone had got the truck in their sights. Only LeBleu had. It was out of range of the other weapons they were carrying.

"I've got it," said LeBleu.

"Take the shot," said the platoon leader.

With the truck moving at between 20 and 25 miles per hour, LeBleu aimed ahead one mil-dot. He relaxed his breathing and squeezed the trigger. The bullet kicked up a puff dust some 220 yards (200 meters) behind the truck. By then the truck must have been 1,100 yards (1,000 meters) away.

Without taking his eyes off his target, who was still shouldering his AK-47, LeBleu reached up to the elevation knob on his scope and gave it a quarter turn.

Martin said, "One thousand meters."

LeBleu relaxed his breathing again and squeezed the trigger. The bullet hit the target on the right side of his midriff. He fell flat on the bed of the truck as his AK-47 tumbled over the side. The other three insurgents were in consternation. They dropped their guns and took cover. The pickup screeched to a halt in a cloud of dust. They threw the dead man over the side. Meanwhile, two more armed men jumped on the back, and the truck sped off before LeBleu could get in another shot.

LeBleu could see no movement from the man on the ground. There was no rise and fall of the chest, and a pool of blood was forming on the ground. When the blood is light pink, it came from the chest area. If it is dark crimson or even purple, it means you have hit a main artery.

Two women appeared and dragged the dead man away. LeBleu looked up at the elevation on his scope. It read 1,100 yards (1,000 meters).

On June 16, 2006, a US marine convoy of amphibious assault vehicles was making its way along a dusty street in Habbaniyah, some 50 miles (80 kilometers) west of Baghdad. The drivers took little notice of a silver automobile parked at the roadside. Fortunately, they were being overlooked by Sniper Section Four. With them was Sergeant Kevin Homestead, an infantry man from K Company of the 3rd Battalion, 5th Marine Regiment, who was serving as their spotter that day. From their hide he noticed a military-aged man in the rear of the car videoing the vehicles. As al Qaeda paid up to $5,000 per kill, it was important for gunmen to document their actives.

Through his 10x optic, Sergeant Homestead saw a rifle stock by the man's side. The sniper team radioed the passing marines and warned them they were being watched by an enemy sniper and should stay low. Then they saw the insurgent raise the weapon and prepare to fire. A 21-year-old marine sniper aimed in at the gunman's head. Controlling his breathing, he squeezed the trigger and shot the man through the rear quarterlight. The window smashed. The gunman fell dead, his rifle in his lap.

Then Sergeant Homestead saw another man of military age get into the passenger side door. He was plainly surprised to see the other insurgent was dead. He leapt out of the van and ran around to the driver's seat. With the marine sniper acting as spotter this time, Homestead took aim with his M4 Carbine and put three bullets in the man before he could drive off. It was not the clean "one shot, one kill" that the sniper had delivered. Indeed, the second insurgent was still alive when a squad of marines from K Company arrived at the van. He died shortly after. The first insurgent had been carrying a sniper rifle. It was an M40A1 that had belonged to a team of snipers from the 2nd Battalion, 4th Marine Regiment, who were overrun in Ramadi two years earlier. They also recovered dozens of 7.62-mm rounds, a hand grenade, a pistol, several license plates, and a number of camcorder tapes from the trunk. But it was the sniper rifle that was of interest.

It had originally belonged to the 3/5 Marines—aka the "Dark Horse" battalion—during Operation Iraqi Freedom I, but it had been turned over to the "Magnificent Bastards" of 2/4 Marines. Then on June 21, 2004, four marines from 2/4 were on a rooftop outpost in Ramadi, 17 miles (27 kilometers) from Habbaniyah. They were Lance Corporal Deshon Otey, the sole survivor of an ambush that killed his entire squad two months earlier; Lance Corporal Juan Lopez, a combat replacement pulled in to beef up the ranks; Lance Corporal Pedro Contreras, a veteran of firefight alongside Sergeant Major James E. Booker, who had been a sniper for 20 years; and Corporal Tommy Parker, Jr., the team's only trained sniper.

Booker believed that the four were killed at about 1040. After failing to make regular check-ins by radio, a quick reaction force was dispatched. By the time they arrived, video footage of the dead marines was already being aired on Arabic-language news channels. The four men lay dead in a pool of blood on the rooftop. The last entry in the logbook was at 0730. The marines had been shot repeatedly in the head and stripped of their weapons and equipment: two sniper rifles, four M16A4s, and a thermal sight.

The Homestead rifle recovered in Habbaniyah had belonged to Corporal Parker. He had shot thousands of rounds—in practice and in combat—with the rifle. Booker, who became a sniper in 1986 and later lead the 1st Marine Division Scout-Sniper School, explained how a sniper felt about his weapon.

"That's sacred, the relationship you have with that thing," he said.

Although the rifle had been in enemy hands for nearly two years, it was thought that the insurgent they killed had been one of the men who had killed the four marines, or was closely associated with them.

"I don't believe that weapon passed hands," said Lieutenant Colonel Paul J. Kennedy, 2/4's commander in Ramadi. "I think it was at least probably part of that cell. The very fact it was one of our snipers that killed theirs trying to use our rifle is poetic justice."

The weapon was probably used against US and Iraqi forces numerous times in the sniping war that was going on.

"He was a very good sniper," said Homestead of the insurgent. "But he got cocky and slipped up and it was our time to catch that… We were in the right place at the right time."

"It was more than being in the right place at the right time," said the Sniper Platoon's commander 1st Lieutenant J. H. Cusack. "It was the culmination of all of the training and planning the section leader had done up until that moment, being absolutely alert and focused to detect a small clue during a period of apparent inactivity, and a perfectly executed shot… The credit has to go to Sergeant Homestead and the sniper section leader who made the kill."

Corporal Angel S. Villalobos, who was with the Magnificent Bastards in Ramadi in 2004, was wounded the day after the four marines were killed and wondered if Parker's rifle was responsible.

"We were going through Ramadi, knocking down every door trying to find it," he said.

After they recovered the rifle, the snipers of 3/5 removed the powder and primer from the 7.62-mm round found in the chamber when the rifle was recaptured. They mounted it on a plaque and presented it to the Magnificent Bastards' snipers as a memorial to their lost marines.

Although the paint was chipped, the rifle itself was in good working order. However, its Unertl scope had been replaced by a Tasco. Booker did not want to see the weapon be used again knowing that insurgents had used it to kill marines.

"There are evil spirits on it," he said. "I would like to see it sit in a place of honor."

Besides, the marines were phasing out the M40A1 in favor of the newer M40A3.

The Dark Horse battalion had been dealing with sporadic sniper attacks since they arrived in Iraq in January 2006. Now, the marines had one less sniper to worry about.

"It's very rewarding to take them out the way we did," said Lieutenant Colonel Patrick G. Looney, the battalion commander. "Doubly rewarding that it's a 2/4 sniper rifle, even though it won't bring back the four marines who were killed that day."

Even more rewarding was that it would not be used on another marine or soldier.

Iraqi military snipers put in an appearance during the invasion of Iraq in late spring 2003. Then, like the rest of Saddam's army, they took off their uniforms and faded into the general population. Insurgents occasionally took potshots, but after US forces crushed resistance in Fallujah, showing that opposition was futile, the insurgents changed tactics. They would not depend on asymmetrical war, using car bombs, IEDs, and snipers.

Unlike US forces, enemy snipers were unencumbered by international law. Dressed in civilian clothes, they could open fire from behind human shields or mosques and make their getaway in an ambulance. While American quick-reaction forces could rush to the scene, they would find the hit-and-run sniper long gone. With his rifle safely stashed, he was indistinguishable from the rest of the population. The answer was for the US to deploy more snipers.

US Army Sergeants Daniel Osborne and Cyrus Field had already proved the sniper's worth in the increasingly hostile streets of Baghdad. They were part of a team of a dozen snipers with standing orders to shoot to kill anyone who fired on US troops or equipment. In their first two weeks, this team alone recorded more than 20 enemy kills.

Osborne, 27, and Field, 23, had been called in by Lieutenant Colonel Jeff Ingram of the 2-70th Armored Battalion to deal with insurgents who had repeatedly attacked his base with a .50-caliber machine gun. Most of the rounds had either hit a brick wall surrounding the compound or gone over the heads of soldiers. Nevertheless, the danger remained. A single round from a gun of that caliber can cut a man in two.

One night, Osborne and Field climbed a 125-foot (40-meter) radio-transmission tower near the base, each carrying 50 pounds (23 kilograms) of body armor and a rifle, looking for the Iraqi insurgents. They spotted them, but could not get a clear shot, and under the rules of engagement, no shot could be fired without first clearing it with a superior.

Two nights later, at around 2300, with loaded weapons strapped to their backs the two men sidestepped piles of garbage to climb a dark and musty stairwell before finding a good firing position on top of a four-story building. They were carrying high-powered M24s, which are sold to civilians as Remington 700 deer-hunting rifles, and M4s, more compact versions of M16s. They also had long-range night-vision equipment that enabled them to see up to 1,500 yards (1,370 meters).

That night they had another problem. The electricity had just been restored to some parts of Baghdad, and thousands of people had taken to the streets to fire guns in the air in celebration. Some were firing pistols while others had fully automatic machine guns that had been dropped by retreating Iraqi soldiers.

Osborne and Field decided that they would have to wait until they could tell who was deliberately firing at them. They took the opportunity to clean their guns. Shortly after midnight, they heard the sound of a .50-caliber machine gun firing short bursts from a clump of trees 800 yards (730 meters) away.

They radioed the base to confirm that it was coming under fire. The call was patched through to Lieutenant Colonel Ingram, who was preparing for bed.

"We've spotted these guys," said Field who already had them in his night-vision scope. "They're back in action off to the west. Four of them."

"There's no change in my previous order," said Ingram. "Take care of it."

This was good enough. Within 30 seconds, they were in position, one with his rifle on a bipod, the other resting his on the parapet. Muzzle flashes could be seen from the machine gun as the insurgents fired on the base before scurrying back to hide in some bushes. They men were in civilian clothes, but, no matter—they were firing on a US base.

Osborne and Field fired simultaneously. Two of the Iraqis fell. An empty shell casing was ejected from the M24. The snipers fired again, this time felling the other two Iraqis as they ran away. All four lay face down within 15 feet (4.5 meters) of each other. These were not yet confirmed kills. A soldier from the nearby Bradley Fighting Vehicle needed to inspect the bodies. Meanwhile, the two snipers smoked a cigarette. They had no doubt that they had done the job. Within 20 minutes, they got the news: All four kills were confirmed. Now they must move on.

In Samarra, Army sniper Sergeant Randall Davis twice defeated enemy snipers, engaging them from a rooftop. Firing an accurized M14 rifle, the 25-year-old from Nashville, Tennessee, patiently waited out an Iraqi sniper who had fired on Americans three days earlier. Then as the sun was setting at the desert's edge on December 18, 2003, when he was just finishing his countersniping duty for the day, he spotted his target about 300 yards (274 meters) away.

"It was just getting dark. I saw a guy step in front of the light," said Davis.

He knew the man was another sniper by the way he stepped back into the shadows and crept along the roofline to track a squad from Davis's unit, B Company of the 5th Battalion, 20th Infantry Regiment.

"Most people, when they get on a roof, will just move around and do what they've got to do," said Davis. "This guy was moving slowly, trying to have smooth motions, trying to stay in the shadows."

From his own rooftop position, Davis followed the target through the sight of his M14. He did not have to wait long before he got his opportunity.

"The guy made a mistake when he silhouetted himself against the rooftop," said Sergeant Davis, who has 20/10 vision. "He was trying to look over to see where the guys were in the courtyard."

As the gunman rose from the shadows to fire, Sergeant Davis saw his head and the distinctive shape of a Dragunov SVD Russian-made sniper rifle. Sergeant Davis carried a standard M24 sniper rifle with an adjustable Kevlar stock, a thick stainless steel barrel, and a mounted telescopic day/night scope. Like other sniper rifles, it was bolt-action rather than semi-automatic. It set up on a bipod and fired 7.62-mm ammunition, hitting targets up to 1,000 yards (915 meters) away. In the desert, he kept a plastic bag or condom over the muzzle to keep the sand out. Snipers also carried their weapons in padded green canvas bags.

"We baby the hell out of them," Davis said.

He drew a bead on the shooter with his special optic sight that had crosshairs and a red aiming dot.

"I went ahead and engaged him."

Davis fired one shot.

"I hit him in the chest," he said. "I watched him kick back, his rifle flew back, and I saw a little blood come out of his chest. It was a good hit."

It was Davis's eighth confirmed kill. Earlier, he had killed seven of the enemy on a single day.

"We had been engaged by snipers in here before, so I was hoping it was the same guy," he said. "It's kind of a professional insult to get shot at by another sniper."

Three days earlier, Company B had walked into an ambush in downtown Samarra. Gunmen on motorcycles used children leaving school as cover to attack the patrol. Sergeant Davis, then armed with an M4 rifle, shot 7 of the 11 attackers in a 45-minute skirmish. Normally, snipers do not get involved in sustained firefights. But fortunately, they were on hand to avoid casualties among the schoolchildren.

"We don't have civilian casualties," said Davis. "Everything you hit, you know exactly what it is. You know where every round is going."

Two days after taking out the rooftop sniper, Davis killed another Iraqi sniper with a 750-yard (685-meter) shot with a Barrett .50-caliber XM-107. The action took place during Operation Ivy Blizzard, which aimed to clear insurgents from the city of 250,000, where support for former leader Saddam Hussein remained strong among fellow Sunni Muslims. Samarra was a nest of guerilla activity in the "Sunni Triangle," 70 miles (112 kilometers) north of Baghdad.

"I shot one guy in the head, and his head exploded," said Davis, who was one of about 40 snipers in the Army's new 3,600-soldier Stryker Brigade, based at Fort Lewis, Washington. "Usually, though, you just see a dust cloud pop up off their clothes, and see a little blood splatter come out the front."

It was the first time he had been in conflict.

"Really, it was just like targets downrange," he said. "You just hit your target and acquire your next target. I thought I'd have a harder time shooting. Shooting someone is pretty unnatural."

But serving in a war zone was an opportunity to make a dream come true.

"It's one of those things I wanted to do since I was 12," he said.

Sergeant Davis worked in a two-man team alongside Specialist Chris Wilson. But Davis had done most of the shooting since Operation Ivy Blizzard began, though he acted as spotter and mentor to his less-experienced teammate.

"Properly employed, we can break the enemy's back," said Davis. "Our main targets are their main command and control elements and other high-value targets."

He had few moral qualms.

"As soon as they picked up a weapon and tried to engage US soldiers, they forfeited all their rights to life, is how I look at it," he said.

US snipers had been particularly effective against insurgents planting IEDs. Three US Army snipers from the 3rd Infantry Division's "Shadow Team" sniper detachment, under Staff Sergeant Jim Gilliland, lay motionless for 18 hours near Ramadi. Then in the darkness of the early morning, they were rewarded. They saw an Opel sedan stop on a major road and cut its lights. While the driver stayed at the wheel, two men got out and took two heavy objects out of the trunk. They unrolled wires and proceeded to dig a hole into a pile of garbage at the roadside to hide their heavy load. As soon as these were identified as 130-mm artillery shells, Sergeant Gilliland and his men opened fire, killing the three terrorists.

Army and marine snipers quickly proved their worth in Iraq when, like Gilliland's Shadow Team, they went after terrorists planting roadside bombs. Most such teams inserted in darkness or as stay-behinds when a larger patrol passed through, and they hid away for days. Because of their stalking, concealment, and observation skills, these sniper teams made bomb planting extremely hazardous for the Iraqis.

In August 2004, Marine Sergeant Joshua Clark and Navy Petty Officer 3rd Class Jeff Pursley saw two vehicles halt at night to plant a bomb inside the remains of a junked car. While the insurgents were unrolling the wires to the detonator, the American snipers crept forward and fired. They captured one insurgent. The others fled.

Illinois Army National Guard sniper Sergeant Bruce Hartman used precision fire to defeat a car bomb. Hartman's unit saw a vehicle parked on a busy road, and squad leader Staff Sergeant David Jensen examined it with his binoculars. He spotted a suspicious-looking package. Wired to it was a cell phone—the insurgents' favored means of remote detonation. Hartman fired just two shots. The first blew out the car's window, the second destroyed the cell phone, disarming the bomb.

Staff Sergeant Steve Reichert and his spotter were in a dangerously exposed position on top of an abandoned oil storage tank in Lutifiyah, 15 miles south of Baghdad, when Reichert saw a dead animal in the road just ahead of the marine patrol he was covering. Ever alert for IEDs, Reichert turned his spotting scope on the carcass.

"I could see the slight reflection of wires coming out of the animal," he said.

As he radioed a warning, an enemy ambush fired an RPG at the patrol. Then they were pinned down by enemy fire, the deadliest of which was coming from a 12.7-mm machine gun on the top of a nearby building. Reichert aimed his .50-caliber Barrett rifle at the insurgent and fired. His first shot missed, but his spotter saw where it fell. Reichert adjusted his sights and his second shot hit the machine gunner. The distance was 1,765 yards (1,614 meters)—

over a mile. The 31-pound, 10-shot semi-automatic Barrett was by then in use by all US services. It was considered accurate—and lethal—at 1,650 yards (1,500 meters). It also allowed snipers to punch through walls, take out gunmen behind barricades, halt vehicles, boats, or aircraft, and disable mines by sheer impact energy. On one occasion, a marine sniper used a .50-caliber Barrett to take out a gunman hiding behind an automobile by shooting right through the car.

Soon after, a few insurgents began to climb a set of stairs on the backside of the building where the firefight was taking place. Reichert aimed at the brick wall where he thought the men were taking cover, and he fired. The armor-piercing round penetrated the way, killing one insurgent. The other two also fell, possibly wounded by flying fragments of bullet and brick.

"I was concerned about my marines making it out of there in one piece," said Reichert. Besides, he and his spotter were out of the gunmen's range, so he was essentially shooting fish in a barrel.

Reichert then saw two marines get separated from the rest of the platoon. A small group of insurgents maneuvered into position to ambush them. Once they stopped moving, Reichert shot one. The other two fled. Twenty-five-year-old Reichert was awarded the Bronze Star with a combat "V" for valor.

Many snipers pride themselves on their ability to engage multiple targets. Twenty-six-year-old Marine Sergeant Memo M. Sandoval from El Paso, Texas, was with the Scout-Sniper Platoon, Headquarters and Service Company of the 3rd Battalion, 5th Marine Regiment in Fallujah in November 2004 when his battalion executive officer ordered him to "make the mortars stop."

"I took it personally and went out specifically to stop the insurgents," said Sergeant Sandoval. He went out deep into the city and lay hidden in a one-story house, scanning the area through his scope before he finally spotted the three insurgents responsible for two earlier mortar attacks.

"When I finally spotted them along a tree line, I realized how far they were," said Sergeant Sandoval.

Then he saw that one of the insurgents was about to drop a mortar round in the tube, and he knew he had to make a 950-yard (870-meter) shot—that's more than nine football fields. He cleared his mind, slowed his breathing, and gently squeezed the trigger of his M40A3. The 7.62-mm round slammed into the chest of the first insurgent.

But there were two more insurgents ready to continue the attack. With his next shot, Sandoval took down the mortarman's assistant. It took two more shots to take out the driver of the vehicle that carried the weapon.

"It was surprising how easy it was," said Sandoval.

Sergeant John Ethan Place was awarded the Silver Star for his sniping during the battle of Fallujah in April 2004. In just 13 days, the 22-year-old marine clocked up 32 confirmed kills. Many of the kills came after he maneuvered amid the rubble of the city and then waited for hours in a concealed position for insurgents who were trying to sneak into position to attack marines from Echo Company of the 2nd Battalion, 1st Regiment. It is likely none of the 32 insurgents knew Place had them in his rifle sights before they died.

"He didn't kill 30 people. He saved numerous lives by protecting our perimeter," said Sergeant Major William Skiles. "That's how the marines look at it."

The commander of the 1st Marine Division, Major General Richard F. Natonski, said the insurgents were so afraid of Place and other snipers that they pleaded with the US to withdraw them while negotiations were under way.

"It's hard to believe that one individual could have had such an impact on our combat operations," Natonski said.

The citation accompanying the Silver Star said, "Place's keen observation skills ensured his supported rifle company maintained a lethal, long-range response to enemy attacks."

As a youth back home in Lake St. Louis, Missouri, Place hunted quail and deer with this father, a retired school administrator. But when he went on to marine sniper school he took to heart their motto—"Kill one man, terrorize a thousand."

At the award ceremony, Place said he would never forget the faces of the enemy he killed to protect his fellow marines.

"You can make your peace with it," Place said. "But you think about it every day."

There were snipers on both sides in Fallujah. Thirty-year-old Marine Sergeant Sean Crane from Fort Lauderdale, Florida, saw an Iraqi creeping along a rooftop. Then the man slid down a palm tree and paused for his rifle to be handed down to him. From more than two blocks away, Crane shot him in the leg. A second shot to his chest killed him, throwing his body out of the tree. The man became Sergeant Crane's eleventh kill in Fallujah.

"For the first few days, we were hitting five a day," Crane said. "The word is out. It's tapered off to ones and twos." The insurgents had learned which streets to avoid.

Sergeant Crane lead a squad of marine snipers posted to Fallujah. One of them was Sergeant Ryan Warden, who gave up a career as a model to re-enlist as a Marine Corps sniper. The squad occupied a row of houses on the city's northern edge. "If the enemy is taking to the rooftops, you want to be on high ground, too," said Crane.

The marine snipers set up their rifles in small holes knocked out of walls with sledge hammers. Others hunkered down at the corners of windows, where they had drawn the curtains and positioned bookcases and other furniture to block light that might reveal their silhouettes. Iraqi gunmen were often hit in the early morning and early evening, as they traveled to and from the points where they attacked US forces. But some were more professional and had been seen doing combat dive rolls across streets or hidden behind civilians to try to avoid being hit.

One marine sniper dealt imaginatively with a distant gunman who grasped a child as a shield as he fired from the corner of a building.

"I shot three to four feet away from him, on the face of the building," he explained, "which made the kid run away and the man come out to inspect the impact. That is when my team member shot the armed individual in the chest."

Also in Fallujah was Sergeant Herbert Hancock, chief scout-sniper with the 1st Battalion, 23rd Marine Regiment, 31st Marine Expeditionary Unit and a full-time Texas SWAT police sniper, and his spotter, 22-year-old Corporal Geoffrey Flowers.

Hancock, 35, stepped off from the northern edge of the Fallujah peninsula on November 11, 2004, day one of the offensive. They were sent with a squad to secure a little island, but intense enemy fire near the bridgeheads blunted their advance. Insurgents filled the city, moving in behind their positions with indirect mortar and sniper fire.

"The insurgents started figuring out what was going on and started hitting us from behind, hitting our supply lines," said Hancock. "Originally we set up near a bridge, and the next day we got a call on our radio that our company command post was receiving sniper fire. We worked our way back down the peninsula, trying to find the sniper, but on the way down we encountered machine gun fire and what sounded like grenade launchers or mortars from across the river."

Elsewhere in Iraq, snipers were inhibited by the rules of engagement. Now they had a freer hand.

"In Fallujah, we really didn't have that problem," said Hancock, "because it seemed like everybody was shooting at us. If they fired at us, we just dropped them."

With a fire team pinned down nearby, Hancock and Flowers sought out the source of the enemy fire. Then they called in indirect fire to suppress that position and reduced it enough so they could also move forward and take cover in a house.

"We got in the house and started to observe the area from which the insurgents were firing at us," said Hancock. "They hit us good for about 20 minutes and were really hammering us. Our indirect fire hit them and must have been effective because they didn't shoot anymore after that."

The sniper team continued down the peninsula to link up with the Bravo Company's command post. Then they set up on a tall building and began shooting across the river at some suspected enemy spotters in vehicles.

"There were certain vehicles in areas where the mortars would hit," said Hancock. "They would show up and then stop and then the mortars would start hitting us, and then the vehicles would leave, so we figured out that they were spotters. We took out seven of those guys in one day."

But mortars and rockets still pounded the company's command post, so their commander told Hancock and Flowers to go find where the mortars were coming from and take them out. They moved south and linked up with the rear elements of the first platoon. Then they climbed up on a building and scanned across the Euphrates River. Through a spotting scope, they saw three to five insurgents manning a 120-mm mortar tube. They got the coordinates for their position and decided that they would engage them with the sniper rifle. When the next round came in, they saw two black-robed insurgents standing up looking right at them. Hancock laid his crosshairs on one man, shot, and he dropped.

Another got up on his knees looking to try to spot where the shot had come from. Hancock quickly reloaded and dropped him, too. Then mortars pounded the position.

Some 50 yards (45 meters) to the right, there were two other insurgents in a small house.

"There was some brush between them and the next nearest building about 400 yards [365 meters] south of where they were, and we were about 1,000 yards [915 meters] from them, so I guess they thought we could not spot them," said Flowers. "Some grunts were nearby with binoculars, but they could not see them, plus they are not trained in detailed observation the way we are. We know what to look for, such as target indicators and things that are not easy to see."

Hancock and Flowers then scanned several areas where they expected fire to come from, but the enemy mortars had fallen silent.

"After we had called in indirect fire and after all the adjustments from our mortars, I got the final eight-digit grid coordinates for the enemy mortar position, looked at our own position using GPS, and figured out the distance to the targets we dropped to be 1,050 yards [916 meters]," said Flowers. "This time we were killing terrorism from more than 1,000 yards."

Hancock was using an M40A3 with a Schneider Match Grade SS 73 barrel and a Unertl 10x sight with mil-dots and BDC scope, specially designed for Marine Corps. The shot was then credited as the longest kill-shot in Iraq.

In 2005, Marine Corporal Matt Orth made an even longer shot, taking out an insurgent at 1,256 yards (1,148 meters) with his M40A3. From Clearwater, Florida, he was deployed to Iraq with the 3rd Battalion of the 2nd Marine Regiment, supporting Company I at Camp Gannon on the outskirts of Husaybah, some 50 miles (80 kilometers) west of Baghdad. On April 11, Orth was holding a sniper position just outside Camp Gannon, when two suicide car bombers blew themselves up along the outer perimeter of the camp. Orth suffered a concussion and bruised ribs as a result of the blasts and eventually received a Purple Heart.

When he returned to duty after his injuries, he witnessed foreign fighters battling it out with local tribesmen in the city. He was then called over to the compound of the Iraqi National Guard with is spotter Sergeant C. J. Quinian.

"As soon as we got there, a guy was running out of an alley, shooting back into it. He then turned and started shooting at the ING compound," said 22-year-old Orth. "I took a shot and missed. Then I took a second shot and killed the insurgent."

This then became the longest kill shot in Iraq.

On September 27, 2005, Shadow Team Leader Staff Sergeant Jim Gilliland topped that, scoring the longest successful engagement in Iraq with a 7.62-mm rifle at 1,375 yards (1,257 meters)—three-quarters of a mile. Gilliland and his spotter, Sergeant Bryan Pruett, heard an enemy sniper had shot a fellow GI and focused their optics on a hospital a dozen blocks away. They saw the insurgent in a fourth-floor window. The target was only visible from the waist up, and the distance was so great that Gilliland had to set the scope on his M24 to maximum elevation. The powerful Leupold sight was only rated to 1,100 yards (1,000 meters). So, after adjusting for the wind, he aimed 12 feet (3.6 meters) high. The single shot hit the insurgent in the chest, killing him instantly.

"It was a one in a million shot," said Gilliland. "I could probably shoot a whole box of ammunition and never hit him again."

Later Gilliland learned that the soldier the insurgent had killed was 30-year-old Staff-Sergeant Jason Benford, a good friend.

Gilliland and his 10-man sniper detachment attached to Task Force 2/69 were credited with shooting at least 276 insurgents. Between 55 and 65 had been felled by Gilliland alone. One of his men, 22-year-old Specialist Aaron Arnold, of Medway, Ohio, chalked up a similar tally.

The team operated from a bombed-out observation post, code-named "Hotel" but nicknamed the "Ramadi Inn." It was scrawled with the slogans "kill them all," "kill like you mean it," and the words of Senator John McCain, "America is great not because of what she has done for herself but because of what she has done for others." This was the sniper team's answer to the graffiti in the streets around them, which boasted that Ramadi was "the graveyard of Americans."

Recalling his record-breaking shot, Staff Sergeant Gilliland said, "It was elating, but only afterwards. At the time, there was no high-fiving. You've got troops under fire, taking casualties and you're not thinking about anything other than finding a target and putting it down. Every shot is for the betterment of our cause."

Although they make up a highly effective killing machine, Gilliland worried about the burden he and his snipers had to bear.

"It's a very God-like role," he said. "They have the power of life and death that, if not held in check, can run out of control. Absolute power corrupts absolutely. Every shot has to be measured against the rules of engagement, positive identification, and proportionality."

The Shadow Team operated along the borderlines of the rules of engagement. They had to make a snap judgment as to whether a person in the crosshairs was an insurgent.

"Hunters give their animals respect," said Gilliland. "If you have no respect for what you do, you're not going to be very good or you're going to make a mistake. We try to give the benefit of the doubt. You've got to live with it. It's on your conscience. It's something you've got to carry away with you. And if you shoot somebody just walking down the street, then that's probably going to haunt you."

Despite Gilliland's record-breaking shot with the 7.62-mm round, it came nowhere near Sergeant Brian Kremer's Iraq War record with a Barrett M82A1 in March 2004. Using 12.7-mm Raufoss NM140 MP multipurpose ammunition, the US Ranger scored a kill from 2,515 yards (2,300 meters).

Although killing with a single long-range shot carries an enormous cachet within the sniper world, the Shadow Team was just as proud of their shooting all 10 members of a single IED group.

"The one-shot-one-kill thing is one of beauty, but killing all the bad dudes is even more attractive," said Gilliland. His motto was, "Move fast, shoot straight, and leave the rest to the counselors in 10 years." And he signed off his e-mails with "Silent souls make .308 holes."

Even a humble medic could turn the tables on an Iraqi sniper. New York National Guardsman PFC Stephen Tschiderer with E-Troop 101st Cavalry Division attached to the 3rd Battalion, 156th Infantry Regiment, was watching the traffic during a routine patrol in west Baghdad when he was shot in the chest by an insurgent sniper. Tschiderer was relaying information to the truck commander of his M114 Humvee when a sniper shot him from inside a silver van that was serving as a mobile sniper nest. The van was lined with mattresses to muffle the sound of the Russian Dragunov sniper rifle that was fired through a small hole. This was a technique they had copied from the Washington, D.C., Beltway sniper of 2002.

The impact of the 7.62-mm round knocked Tschiderer off his feet. The stopping force of his body-armor saved his life. "I knew I was hit, but I was uncertain of the damage or location of the hit," he said.

Dazed but not dead, the agile American jumped back onto his feet.

"The only thing that was going through my mind was, 'take cover and locate the sniper's position.'"

Tschiderer spotted the van parked across an intersection, some 80 yards (75 meters) away. When he alerted his team, they pursued the van and quickly disabled it. Two insurgents fled on foot, leaving a bloody trail. By the time the Iraqi police turned up to assist, a cordon-and-search operation was already under way. While the van's driver was detained, Tschiderer and the rest of the team followed the trail of blood. Locals directed them over a wall and into a yard where they found the wounded sniper. After cuffing the man who had tried to kill him, Tschiderer was giving the sniper emergency first aid.

"Treating the man who shot me didn't really sink in until afterwards," said Tschiderer. "At the time, I just did my job and didn't really think about it too much."

Searching the van, they found a video camera, which filmed the event. The insurgents plainly wanted to capture footage showing the death of an American. What they got was pictures of Tschiderer's lightning recovery and the American patrol's robust response to the insurgent's sniping.

Sergeant Timothy L. Kellner is thought to have clocked the largest number of confirmed kills in Iraq: 139 in all. But he did not make a song and dance about it, and on a mission, he was happy to let a colleague take the money shot.

In May 2006, Kellner was out on a surveillance mission in the Triangle of Death, to the southwest of Baghdad, with a four-man sniper patrol. It was an area riven by the division between Sunni and Shiite. When they were not killing each other, they spent their time killing coalition forces. It was an area full of bomb factories. The roads were too narrow to be patrolled in armored vehicles and were littered with IEDs, largely old 155-mm artillery shells that would kill or maim those lacking armored protection.

When the sniper team left the old power plant that the 1st Battalion of the 67th Armor, 4th Infantry Division, was using as a base, they carried with them a list of wanted insurgents and their mug shots. They were allowed to kill anyone on that list or anyone they found planting an IED. The main object of this mission was a man named Rasool Bandre Aass Fayhen Al Janabi. The only picture they had of him was a grainy printout. However, they did have a good picture of his associate, leading insurgent Abu Omar.

The intelligence section thought they knew where Rasool lived, and Charlie Company planned to target his house. The sniper team was being sent in to see what sort of resistance they might meet. To reach the house, the snipers had to cover 6 miles (10 kilometers) on foot. In the Triangle of Death, this was best done at night. Despite the heat, they wore ghillie suits for concealment when they reached their objective.

The area was full of date palms that presented them with cover, but there were roads to cross. In the darkness, they had to watch out for IEDs. This was all the more difficult as, in that area, the enemy used devices triggered by pressure plates. Despite the danger of being silhouetted, the sniper team crossed the roads slowly, with each man following in the footsteps of the one before.

At one point they saw a man smoking a cigarette outside his house. The point man on the patrol, Sergeant Ben Redus, dropped his backpack and pulled out his 12-inch Bowie knife, but then the man finished his cigarette and went back inside. He had not seen them.

They faced further danger of being spotted when they had to cross small bridges over the canals, but mostly they hugged the embankment. Otherwise, they crossed the canal on water pipes, which is no mean feat when you are carrying a 60-pound (27-kilogram) backpack and 40 pounds (18 kilograms) of other gear. Kellner particularly disliked this and once fell in a ditch. The others had difficulty suppressing their laughter. The fear was that the noise he had made in the fall had compromised the mission. They went on.

Following the paths local people used, they arrived near the target house. They set up behind a large drainage ditch, where a levee and reeds gave them cover. Sergeant Redus and PFC Chris Lochner were 440 yards (400 meters) from the house and kept it under surveillance. Redus had a 40x spotting scope. On this mission, Kellner acted as the radio man, while the fourth man, Sergeant John Nebzydoski, kept up security in the rear.

Soon after sunrise, a man came out of the house. It looked like Rasool, but they could not be certain. Consequently, they could not shoot him. They saw him stroll over to a nearby house, returning after a few minutes. Later, he delivered a small box there.

Hours passed. Then a man came out of the second house. Redus immediately identified him as Abu Omar. He walked over to the first man's house. Then the two of them walked out into the fields where the children played while the women were working. The men sat and talked. Abu Omar had his elbows propped on his knees.

The men agreed that, while they could not be certain about the man who looked like Rasool, they had positively identified Abu Omar. Kellner gave Lochner the okay to set up the shot. He raised his M24. The range was 367 yards (336 meters), and there was a gentle breeze of between three and five miles per hour (five and eight kilometers per hour). He dialed in the distance and reconfirmed the windage. Rebus could see Abu Omar had a detonation cord and blasting caps in his hand. Kellner then gave the order to fire.

The sound of the suppressed M24 fire was only heard by the snipers, and they could see the trace—the turbulence created by the shock wave of the bullet as it sped through the air at supersonic speeds. It hit Abu Omar dead center in the middle of the back.

They saw his shirt flap, but nothing happened. He did not crumple up or fall over. The elbows propped on his knees kept him upright. And the man who looked like Rasool kept on talking to him as if nothing had happened, though the snipers could see the blood slowly spreading out across the back of his shirt.

PFC Lochner prepared to take a second shot, but one of the children ran up to Abu Omar to say something. When Abu Omar did not reply, the child shook him. He toppled over dead. The children and the women screamed. Rasool stood there in disbelief.

By then, Kellner had called the quick reaction force (QRF) to come in and extract them. Meanwhile, a truck turned up. Abu Omar's body was slung on the back. It was just about to pull away when Sergeant Nebzydoski put a round from the M14 into the vehicle. Not knowing where there next shot was coming from, the men on board got out with their hands up. When QRF arrived, they arrested the suspects, including the man they confirmed was Rasool.

The insurgents were well aware of the danger US snipers presented. They made a mass attack on a sniper team from the 1st Cavalry Division led by Lieutenant Eric Johnson near the Baghdad airport on the night of April 18, 2004. Despite three gunshot wounds, Johnson and his men survived. Two months later, insurgents overran the sniper team from 2/4 Marines in Ramadi, killing all four of them. Later in Ramadi, an eight-man marine sniper element was crossing a street at 0230 when a bomb detonated, killing two and seriously wounding several others. Then in August 2005, six snipers of Headquarters and Service Company of the 3rd Battalion, 25th Marine Regiment, 4th Marine Division—a reserve company out of Brook Park, Ohio—were ambushed in Haditha, 140 miles (225 kilometers) northwest of Baghdad. Five members of the unit were killed. One was missing and was reported to have been seen alive but wounded and being driven through the streets of Haditha.

A few days later, a video was posted on the Internet which showed the insurgents rushing the marines. The Ansar al-Sunna group's website posted still photographs showing a bloody, badly wounded body wearing marine camouflage trousers, and two hooded gunmen standing in front of a display of captured gear and weapons, including two M40A4 sniper rifles. The insurgents said they had slit the throats of some of the marines. Masked gunmen had shown up in the Haditha public market that afternoon displaying helmets, flak jackets, and other equipment they said was taken from the bodies of the dead marines. They also handed out fliers that said, "They were on a mountain near the town so we went up, surrounded them, and asked them to surrender. They did not surrender, so we killed them."

The bodies of five of the marines were found in one place, and the body of the sixth was discovered later a few miles away. The US response was to send in 1,000 marines in Operation Quick Strike, which killed 40 insurgents and captured others—sadly, at the cost of another 15 American lives.

Then on August 27, 2007, near Samarra, a four-man sniper team from the 82nd Airborne Division suddenly found its rooftop outpost mass-assaulted by 40 foreign al Qaeda fighters. Outnumbered 10 to 1, the paratroopers held their ground in a 10-minute fight for survival in close quarters. Two paratroopers died, but a year later, Sergeant Chris Corriveau, from Lewiston, Maine, and Sergeant Eric Moser, of Tomball, Texas, received Distinguished Service Crosses—America's second-highest decoration for bravery—from President George W. Bush at a ceremony at Fort Bragg, North Carolina. Together, the sniper team had killed an estimated 15 enemy and wounded others.

However, progress was being made. The latest generation of body armor and Kevlar helmets could withstand the bullets from full-power 7.62x54-mm R rounds. Soldiers and marines now walked away with just painful bruises from what would have been a lethal wound. GIs perfected the "Baghdad shuffle," knowing that enemy snipers preferred taking potshots at stationary targets. US bases were ringed by concrete barriers and antisniper fencing, and the cupolas of armored vehicles were surrounded by bulletproof glass.

Technology also came into play. A sniper bullet-detection system called Boomerang was mounted in Humvees. It used acoustic sensors linked to a computer that separated the signature of a passing bullet from the background noise and tracked the related muzzle blast. The computer would then announce, for instance, "Rifle shot, 457 meters, four o'clock." This tipped the odds in favor of the countersniper.

Both the Army and Marine Corps boosted their sniper schools, using veteran snipers as instructors. Thousands of M14 rifles were brought out of storage, accurized, given new scopes, and issued to designated marksmen at platoon level, while a squad-level-designated marksman would be given an accurized M16 and optical sight. Iraq-bound snipers attended short shooting clinics, while those in-country were be given countersniper training. The country-wide sniper hunt was on.

In 2007, there had been almost 300 sniper attacks on the US Army, with 30 incidents in October, alone. The following year, the countersniper program had cut that by two-thirds. Then Jane's Defense magazine reported that sniping reports for 2009 had "all but disappeared."

In April 2007, Sergeant 1st Class Brandon McGuire, a platoon sergeant with 3rd Battalion, 509th Infantry Regiment from Olathe, Kansas, and his spotter were at the Forward Operating Base Iskandaryia, Iraq. They were observing a stretch of road that had recently been cleared of IEDs. The area had also seen a lot of mortar activity, and several US soldiers had been killed or severely wounded along that stretch of road by IEDs and mortars. Their hide was an abandoned shed. They had been sitting there for three days.

That morning the sky was clear. Soon after dawn, they noticed a man in Arab clothing walking back and forth along a series of canals. When he thought no one was looking, he crouched down, began digging into a bank of the canal, and unearthed a mortar tube. To McGuire, this made him a target. Nevertheless, he had to call the battalion's Tactical Operations Center and ask for permission to engage him. It was granted.

However, there was a crosswind of 8 to 10 knots (9 to 11 miles per hour). They could not wait for the wind to drop, as a sandstorm was heading their way. But here McGuire got lucky. There were kids flying a kite not far from their target, and McGuire was able to use the kites to help estimate the wind speed.

However, the man was now walking, moving up and down as he passed over the canals. Occasionally he disappeared completely.

"We watched for almost two hours before the target presented himself in such a way that I was able to get a clear shot," said McGuire.

By then he was 1,432 yards (1,310 meters) away, and McGuire did not think he would hit his target with the first shot. His plan was to get his first shot close enough for the spotter to see where it hit, then make an adjustment and hit the man with his second shot. Even this was going to be difficult; with the sandstorm now imminent, a swirl of dust would obscure their vision for a couple of seconds.

McGuire checked his breathing and then squeezed the trigger of his Barrett .50-caliber Sniper Weapon System. The swirl of dust kicked up. After it cleared, McGuire readied himself for a second shot, but he could not see the target.

"Where is he?" he asked his spotter.

"Holy shit, I think you got him," came the reply.

This hardly seemed possible. But confirmation came from the local elders who turned up at the forward operating base (FOB) and said that one of a mortar team had been killed, but they did not know who had done it. They did not even know that snipers were operating the area.

"No one knew who shot him," McGuire said. "It hurt them bad because they didn't know who was targeting them. It took a mental toll on them."

McGuire and his spotter had used such stealth that the kids flying the kites did not even notice. After a couple of seconds of disbelief, McGuire and his spotter went back to work scanning the area for targets.

The congratulations only came when he got back to his unit, who began calling the 1,310-meter kill the "million-dollar shot."

"For us, it was great," McGuire said. "We'd had so many soldiers killed and who had lost legs. After the shot, the daily mortar attacks and IEDs ceased in that area… Everyone was congratulating me," he said. "But to me, it seemed like another day in Iraq."

Michael Raab was 27 and had quit the Marine Corps four years earlier when the Iraq was invaded in March 2003. Still, he felt the urge to get involved. He was still thinking about it when President George W. Bush declared "Mission Accomplished." The moment seemed to have passed, but then he found that former buddies from the service were re-enlisting. Gradually they convinced him to do the same, and, in April 2004, he signed the papers, hoping to get into a Surveillance and Target Acquisition platoon with his friends who had been snipers. Even though he had not been trained as a scout-sniper, he got in.

At Camp Pendleton in California, Raab was taught to speak Arabic, while his buddies were out on the firing range familiarizing themselves with the M40A3. By the beginning of October, he found himself in the middle of the Triangle of Death. His team's first major operation was to be into the town of Sadr al Yusufiyah to support Fox Company, who intended to round up insurgents there. The town lay on a vital enemy supply route to Fallujah, where the battle was now under way. They were given only a few hours notice of the operation so that Iraqis working on the base would have no time to warn the inhabitants.

They headed out at night in a convoy of Humvees and trucks. The drivers kept the headlights turned off and navigated their way down the backroads using night-vision goggles. The scout-sniper team in the back kept low, since they were going into an area known to be littered with IEDs. As they approached Yusufiyah, they pulled off the road to allow the rest of Fox Company, led by the mobile security team, to go ahead.

They dismounted in a village called Mullah Fayyad, which was separated from Yusufiyah by a canal. By then it was growing light. The marines had set up a checkpoint. The sniper team waited there. When an approaching truck refused to stop, one of the snipers put a round into it. The bullet had hit the front of the truck half an inch to the left of the headlight, passed through the engine compartment, on through the bulkhead, and hit the driver in the leg, making a small entry wound but taking a large chunk of flesh out of his calf.

The scout-sniper team then moved up into Yusufiyah with the convoy. It was still early morning, but still it seemed unnaturally quiet. Then they heard a .50-caliber Browning heavy machine gun open up, followed by a burst of fire from an AK-47. Next, bullets came flying over their heads. Off to the right, they could see the top of a white truck behind some tall grass. It moved off, then stopped again, and bullets hit the side of the team's truck.

Raab put his gun to his shoulder. His team leader shouted at him, telling him not to fire. They had not positively established that the gunfire had some from the white truck, so it was against the rules of engagement to open fire on it. But Raab had made up his mind and pulled the trigger on his squad automatic weapon (SAW). The rest of the squad opened up, too. The AK-47 fell silent, though in the distance they could hear the mobile security team engaging other insurgents firing on them from the rooftops.

The white truck had come to a halt. One man was dead, another injured. A helicopter was called in to medevac him out. Another Iraqi claimed the dead man was his father and demanded compensation. No weapon was found, but a member of the mobile security force said that there was a place on the canal where it looked like someone had thrown something in. A black car had run into the back of the truck. There were six people in it, including a woman holding a baby. The car was peppered with bullet holes but, miraculously, no one had been injured.

The scout-sniper team moved on into the market area of Yusufiyah. Though there had been a firefight only a few minutes earlier, there were people on the streets. Even a woman who had been hanging out her washing before the bullets had started flying—and had then ducked inside for safety—resumed putting the laundry on the line. But there were no children around, and most of the people in the streets were middle-aged men. Raab suspected they had been the ones who had been firing on the marines earlier. But now they had no weapons with them, so they had to be considered noncombatants.

As Fox Company began patrolling the streets, the scout-sniper team was told to give them cover. But before they could take up position, there was a cry of "Incoming!" and mortars landed around them. They took cover in what remained of the old Ba'ath Party building. In the distance, they could hear the firefights as insurgents harassed the marine patrols.

The scout-sniper team was sent down the road to a school building. They were to set up there and keep a look out for where the mortars were coming from. From the roof, they directed coun-termortar fire, though they were itching to get out and deal with the enemy mortar teams themselves. That, after all, was their job.

After three days, they were pulled back, first to the Ba'ath Party building to get something to eat, but RPG fire began to pummel the building, so they were ordered up to a rooftop in the Iraqi National Guard compound. The scout-snipers were told to return precision fire with their M40A3s. This frustrated Raab. He loosed off a burst from his SAW at a man with an RPG who kept on popping out of a door and firing at them. Raab was immediately ordered to stop. Meanwhile, the rest of the scout-sniper team was firing "rapid bolt"— as fast as you can with a bolt-action rifle.

Around 150 yards (135 meters) away, they could see snipers behind the fronds of palm trees on a rooftop. They were even wearing what appeared to be ghillie suits. Then the scout-sniper team came under sniper fire themselves. In response, Raab fired another burst at a man trying to cross the road and cut him down. By then, there were two snipers firing at them. They exchanged shots for an hour before one of the enemy snipers was put out of action. The other one was still moving around the rooftop. To counter him, the snipers stopped working individually and split into sniper-spotter teams. As one took his shot, he was showered with bits of concrete from a ledge just two feet away. Another shot at the enemy sniper missed, and the spotter, in frustration, opened up with the M16 whose ACOG sight he was using to spot with, narrowly missing his partner's head.

A forward air controller (FAC) came up on the roof and a marine scout-sniper pointed out where the enemy sniper was. The mobile security team was ordered back and the FAC called in an air strike. Meanwhile, the FAC crew began taking potshots at the enemy sniper as well.

As the F-18 aircraft came screaming in, they had to abort their bombing run, as the mobile security team was still too close. As the planes circled, the scout-snipers kept firing to make the enemy sniper keep his head down so that he could not fire at the aircraft. The F-18s came in again. This time the mobile security team was well back, and the aircraft loosed off their cannon. After a second strafing run, the FAC called off the F-18, and the scout-sniper team went to finish off their meal. They were then pulled out of Yusufiyah and chastised for using so many rounds and scoring so many misses.

A few days later, the scout-snipers returned to the rooftop in the Iraqi National Guard compound and were given a chance to redeem themselves. They were ordered to take up position on the top of the tower at the water-treatment plant. While it gave the best field of fire in the town, the scout-snipers were not pleased, as it gave little protection from enemy fire. The manager of the plant was not happy either. He had already been so intimidated by the insurgents who had threatened him for allowing the Americans near his plant that he had sent his family to Baghdad. The manager himself had to stay; otherwise the town would have not water. But neither the scout-snipers nor the plant manager had any say in the matter.

First the plant had to be searched by the mobile security team for booby traps or any insurgents lurking inside. Then the scout-sniper team took up position on the rooftop. From there, they could see a nearby village that was known to harbor "foreign fighters." After little more than an hour, they began mortaring the plant. Using the spotter scope, they were able to tell that the mortar crew was no more than a few hundred meters away. But the fire base was hidden behind some houses and trees. As they could not get a shot on them, they called in mortar fire from Fox Company. Things fell quiet. Then they saw a car driving away from the position of the mortar sight. It had been seen driving toward it minutes before the mortar fire started, but under the rules of engagement they were not allowed to make contact.

They saw the car pull into the driveway of a house 220 yards (200 meters) away. Although they would like to have gone there and kicked the door, all the scout-snipers could do was pass the information to Fox Company, who might get around to raiding the house when they had the time. Once they had radioed their report, they were told to go up the tower and look for more mortar sites, but they disobeyed the order and kept watch from the roof instead.

Their next mission was to set up an observation post in a palm grove near the village said to be home to the foreign fighters. From there they were to watch a warehouse, thought to be a meeting point for the insurgents.

It was raining when they set off at 0100 hours. Since their footprints would show on the wet ground, they had to risk infiltrating down the road. They reached the palm grove without incident and set up the observation post on the edge of a canal where there was enough brush to hide them. But it was less than ideal as they had to conceal themselves among the greenery while wearing desert-colored camouflage.

One of the team fell in the canal while relieving himself and risked drowning under the weight of his body armor until his buddies fished him out. The situation was serious, but they could not help laughing. By noon nothing had happened. They grew bored, so they packed up had headed for the foreign fighters' village in the hope of provoking some action. Nothing came of it and they left after a couple of hours.

They were grateful when they were told to set up their next observation post indoors, in a three-story house on the outskirts of Mullah Fayyad. But the scout-sniper team was becoming annoyed that they were not being assigned the tasks they had been trained for. Next they were sent to set up an observation post to watch the home of a suspected bomb maker. But from the place they were to set up the OP, his house would be out of range. Next they were sent to guard a bridge, then it was back to the tower in the water-treatment plant. Again they managed to avoid going up it.

The insurgents made an attempt to overrun Yusufiyah. Many Americans were killed and wounded, but so were many more insurgents. One of the scout-sniper team got hit by a piece of shrapnel and had to be medevaced out. And still, despite their complaints, the scout-snipers were not deployed in their designated role. The only good news they got was that tower in the water-treatment tower was blown up by US combat engineers. It had been used as an target by enemy mortars.

Eventually, they were transferred to Golf Company and moved their area of operation. In February 2005, they were sent out into the desert, where they hardly expected to see any insurgents. Nevertheless, they dug in between two sand dunes, near a berm that overlooked a road. After just half a day, the lookout spotted someone digging up the road.

They grabbed their weapons and lined up on top of the berm. There were six men in all, digging a hole, ready to plant a 155-mm artillery shell they had on the back of a truck in it. The two men with M40A3s took aim. Rapid fire took three of the targets out. The other three men ran back to their vehicles. Raab estimated the distance at 550 yards (500 meters), then fired a burst from the M240G machine gun he was now carrying. Through the EOTech holographic gun sight, he could see that the rounds fell 165 yards (150 meters) short and he called up a correction at 715 yards (650 meters). An M40A3 took out another man. The whole team was now firing on the fleeing vehicles. Just as the truck was moving out of range, Raab managed to train M240G fire on it. He could see tracer bullets bouncing around inside the cab. That day, three injured Iraqis turned up in a local hospital. One had a hole in his chest and phosphorous burns from the tracer rounds. The other two had numerous bullet wounds. They were not expected to live.

Iraq

On the night of June 9, 2004, a four-man sniper team from C Company, 3rd Battalion, 153rd Infantry spotted insurgents firing a 60-mm mortar into an American installation. The snipers killed two of the three gunners and recovered the mortar, its ammunition, and a loaded RPG-7 launcher. Likewise, in 2005, US Army Specialist Ryan Cannon with the 82nd Airborne Division in Iraq could barely make out an insurgent mortarman in darkness, some 500 yards away, about to drop a round in his tube. The Iraqi paused to puff on a cigarette—just enough glow to illuminate him—and bang! Another mortar attack stopped.

In a classic case, a 1st Cavalry Division sniper, 25-year-old Staff Sergeant Jeff Young from Killeen, Texas, exploited the sun's shifting rays to pinpoint a hidden Iraqi sniper. "We got lucky when the sun was going down," he told Stars and Stripes. "It hit his scope at the right angle, and we got a glare in our direction so we engaged it."

Attesting to their effectiveness, enemy forces have sometimes targeted US snipers. On April 18, 2004, a sniper team from the 1st Cavalry Division led by Lieutenant Eric Johnson was mass-attacked at night near the Baghdad airport. Despite three gunshot wounds, Johnson and his men survived.

Two months later on June 21, 2004, in Ramadi, 20 miles west of Baghdad, two dozen insurgents overran a marine sniper team, shooting all four repeatedly in the head. Then they videotaped the bodies of the men from 2nd Battalion, 4th Marines, 1st Marine Division for propaganda distribution. Later, again in Ramadi, an eight-man marine sniper element was crossing a street at 0230 when a bomb detonated, killing two and seriously wounding several others.

When Operation Iraqi Freedom began, Sergeant Joshua Hamblin was part of the 3rd Battalion, 7th Marines. As his unit moved north out of Kuwait into Iraq in their Humvees, he was to act as a scout, carrying an M16 for his own protection. But he was also a sniper with an M40A3, then the very latest scoped sniper rifle, in a case beside him.

As they raced across the desert, Sergeant Hamblin's services were frequently called on. His job was to take out Iraqi roadblocks. He would do this from a range of 600 to 700 yards (550 to 640 meters), well beyond the range of an AK-47, which is a mere 330 to 440 yards (400 to 400 meters). It was, he said, like shooting ducks at a carnival.

As they approached Baghdad, the snipers were attached, or "punched out," to various companies in the battalion. When the company stopped for a rest, the snipers would occupy high ground to watch for enemy activity. Otherwise the scout-snipers would move out ahead and watch for suspicious activity. They saw few Iraqi soldiers, but there were plenty of young males of military age with short haircuts in civilian clothing. Plainly, these guys had discarded their uniforms and were trying to blend into the population, but under the rules of engagement, the marines were to ignore anyone who was not armed and did not try to attack the coalition forces. But if they saw an Iraqi who was armed, they were to take him down. Any Iraqi carrying an AK-47 was a target, and Hamblin said he never missed.

Once an area was occupied, the snipers had to support Special Operations raids that were looking for Ba'ath party members and former members of Saddam Hussein's regime. Sniper teams were on hand to protect them as they did building entries.

At the time, they were still afraid that Saddam might have chemical or biological weapons. So in the desert heat, weighed down with Kevlar vests and helmets, plus guns and ammunition, they were shrouded in heavy chemical suits and could hardly breathe. They even had to wear these when they slept.

"But worst of all was the lack of rest and the filthy conditions," said Hamblim. "There was no water for bathing, so whenever we found water or a broken pipe, we took time to wash down."

But they only had time to soak their heads and clothes, and keep moving. As for a commode, the best they could find was a hole in the sand.

The snipers, especially, found themselves deprived of sleep and were lucky to get two hours of rest before they were punched out to work another mission. It was not unusual to go two days or more without sleep, and they ran on willpower and sheer physical discipline.

When they approached the al Qaeda training camp at Salmon Pak, they were told to expect Iraqi resistance. Instead they found burned-out ruins. The camp, which was equipped with the fuselage of an airliner for training hijackers, had been bombed and strafed for several days. Abandoned military vehicles littered the street and, again, there were lots of young men with short haircuts.

As they headed up the Tigris River valley, the desert gave way to lush vegetation, so at last they had the protection of camouflage. But the summer was drawing on, and the heat made wearing their chemical suits unbearable. They began taking more breaks just to air themselves out. When they took off their suits, they would be drenched underneath.

"It was as miserable as having your own personal sauna bath that you wore—and couldn't get rid of," said Hamblin.

A week after leaving Salmon Pak, the word came that they could jettison their chemical suits.

"This was the most welcome news we had had in a long time," Hamblin said. "Finally we could work in our desert utilities and fight like normal marines. It felt like the weather had cooled by several degrees, and was a major turning point in the war for us."

As the 3/7 neared Baghdad, they began running into more minefields. In the distance, they could hear a lot of shooting going on and the heavy-weight pounding of artillery. More resistance was expected as they approached the Al Rashid Military Complex. There were breaches in the perimeter wire, and more mines scattered around. The buildings had been shelled or bombed, but there were no enemy soldiers there. However, there was a chance they would return, and the marines set up their defenses against a counterattack.

Hamblin and his partner, Sergeant Owen Mulder, were assigned an area of responsibility overseeing a business and residential area and set up a sniper observation post on a one-story house on the northeast side of the complex. From this position, they could observe anything approaching the complex from that direction. The house had a flat roof with a low wall around it which gave them some protection. They could shoot without being seen or targeted from around 440 yards (400 meters) out to about 820 yards (750 meters).

There were two companies stationed in the complex, one on each flank. They were about 165 yards (150 meters) away within the area covered by Hamblin and Mulder. Hamblin's M40A3 was fitted with a AN/PVS-10 day and night sight—which came in handy as they worked the position around the clock—while Mulder had an M40A1 sniper rifle with the standard-issue Unertl 10x scope. But he also had night-vision goggles. Night vision gave them an enormous advantage.

Around two hours after dark, they spotted a pickup truck approaching. It stopped some 440 yards (400 meters) short of the military complex. Men began jumping off the back of the truck. Each was carrying an AK-47.

"I got targets," Hamblin said to Mulder.

The driver got out and walked around the back. Like the others, he was wearing Western clothing but also had a military-style belt and harness. Someone in the back of the truck handed him ammunition or a grenade. Hamblin decided to take a shot. He lined the driver up in his sight and squeezed the trigger. He fell dead. Mulder aimed at another Iraqi and he went down, too. But instead of then running for cover, the Iraqis decided to recover the bodies of their fallen comrades.

They lined up targets one after another, like in a shooting gallery. Their pulses raced. It was hard not to get excited. More men appeared. They tried to drag the bodies away but fell victim themselves. Despite the rush of adrenaline, Hamblin and Mulder managed to remain professionally detached thanks to discipline and training. Again and again, they spotted a target, sighted in, squeezed the trigger, watched the man fall, worked the bolt, and moved onto another target.

Eventually, the Iraqis got ahead of the snipers. They managed to get the bodies of their dead and pull the truck around the corner, out of sight. Then it fell quiet. No bodies were left in the street. All that was left were pools of blood, scraps of clothing, and a few shreds of flesh.

Hamblin looked at his watch. It was an hour before sunrise. By then the Iraqis had realized that they were no match for the Americans in the dark. Night-vision equipment gave the coalition forces an unbeatable advantage. The Iraqis hoped that daylight would turn the odds in their favor, but they were wrong. A poorly led gang of men with AK-47s is no match for a disciplined and well-equipped sniper team.

Soon after dawn, they saw two men walking across the street, seemingly oblivious to what had happened there just an hour before. One of them was carrying an AK-47, which made him a legitimate target. Both snipers had seen them. Hamblin told Mulder that he was going to take out the one with the gun.

The range was about 450 yards (410 meters). As the man was walking across their field of vision, Hamblin aimed just in front of him. The man fell. He did not die immediately, but lay there twitching. Gradually, a huge pool of blood formed under the body as the life drained out of him.

His partner did not hang around to take care of his buddy or drag his body away. He ran off as fast as his legs would carry him.

After about 10 minutes, a truck nosed cautiously out of one of the side streets. It sat there for a few minutes with the engine running while the driver assessed the situation. Then it disappeared again. Fifteen minutes later the same truck came back. Again it sat half hidden while the driver checked to see whether it was safe to proceed. Deciding it was, the driver pulled out into the main street. There were seven or eight men on the back of the truck. A second pickup followed with a similar number of men on the back. They were armed.

The trucks stopped next to the dead body in the street. The men jumped down from the truck, seemingly unaware that they were in danger of suffering the same fate as their dead colleague sprawled on the road. They appeared angry, ready to get back at whoever had killed him, but there was no one in sight.

Without a word, the two snipers went to work. Hamblin took one truck, Mulder the other. Again they picked the Iraqis off one after the other. The men were too shocked or confused to try to escape. Soon 13 lay dead.

The one survivor pulled the dead driver out of one of the trucks, jumped behind the wheel, and began to drive off. The two snipers began firing at him. One of their bullets must have hit the gas tank. Suddenly, the truck exploded in a ball of flames, just like in the movies.

"I thought that cars and trucks blowing up when you shot at them was just Hollywood," said Hamblin, "but this one did exactly that."

The truck kept moving under its own momentum, so the snipers both put a shot through the driver's side of the cab. Two 175-grain boat-tail hollow points blasted through the thin sheet metal of the cab and killed the driver as the truck coasted on around the corner where the truck continued burning, just out of sight, for nearly an hour.

Bodies now littered the streets. There was one abandoned truck and another on fire. It looked like a major battle had been fought there, but it was the work of just two well-trained snipers. They had not even fired a full box of ammo yet, and the day had only just begun.

Later in the morning, Hamblin was scanning the street through his scope when he saw an Iraqi soldier come around the corner and begin walking toward the base. He was in uniform and was wearing a helmet and vest and carrying a sidearm. It was as if he thought the Iraqi military still occupied the base and he was turning up to work as normal. There was a row of lamp posts in the street. As he passed each post, Hamblin fixed the scope on him, watching as the range lessened.

An old man came out of a house and began gesturing at him, as if trying to tell him to get out of there. But the soldier took no notice and kept on coming. To Hamblin and Mulder, it looked like some bizarre comedy scene was being played out before their eyes.

Hamblin watched the soldier shrug his shoulders one last time. It was plain that he was going to take no notice of the old man and was going to keep on walking, come what may. So Hamblin squeezed the trigger. It was a perfect shot. Hamblin could see the vapor trail of the bullet as it flew straight toward the target. It hit him in the center of the chest. To Hamblin it appeared like it was happening in slow motion. He could see the dust fly off the man's shirt. On his face there was an expression of pure shock.

He looked down at the bullet hole in his chest as if surprised. Then he slumped forward and fell to the ground. Only then did he realize the danger he was in. He tried to crawl out of the kill zone, but it was too late for him. He only got a few feet, then lay very still. He was dead.

The local civilians were very interested in what was happening. Watching the action seemed to amuse them. After each deadly episode, they would come out, look around, and laugh and smile. Then they would look over toward the base and wave at the marines. It was like they were spectators at a sporting event.

By then there were a least 15 bodies laying out and two shot-up pickup trucks, one still smoldering. It could have been the set of a movie, but it was real. And the people lined up on the side of the street to inspect the carnage like they were at the market.

The action continued when a white pickup truck came careening out of a side street and speeding down the road toward the snipers. On the back was a man dressed in black with a black ski mask, and he was holding an AK-47. He was plainly a fedayeen and was hell bent on evening the score—or committing "suicide by marine," as Hamblin put it.

As the truck came flying down the road, the insurgent, holding on for dear life, looked up at the snipers on the roof. At the same time, Hamblin raised his head. For a fraction of a second, their eyes met. Then Hamblin's eye went back down to his scope. It was hard to maintain his aim on the target as the pickup truck bounced along the road. Hamblin aimed high and slightly ahead, then took the shot. The bullet hit him squarely and he went down in the back of the truck. Before he had a chance to take a second shot and take out the driver, the vehicle had turned away and raced around a corner out of sight, with the body of the dead fedayeen bouncing about in the back.

As they maintained surveillance, they noticed that a large number of vehicles were moving in and out of the area. This seemed suspicious. Most were light-colored Toyota pickup trucks. Hamblin and Mulder noticed that the trucks were coming into the neighborhood carrying stuff covered by tarps in the back, but they were coming out empty. Plainly they were doing a supply run, stocking a local strongpoint with weapons and ammo. They had to put a stop to this.

Under the rules of engagement you could shoot at a vehicle carrying weapons, taking its tires out or otherwise disabling it. The obvious candidate was a red Toyota sedan that had made four trips in and out of the stronghold. Mulder shot the driver, while Hamblin put a bullet in the back of the trunk. Again the car exploded as if it were in a movie. The trunk turned into a ball of flame as the car coasted around the corner. A few minutes later, it turned into a fireworks display. The trunk had been full of RPGs that began to cook off. As the grenades came screaming out of the vehicles and crashing into nearby buildings and parked cars, it sounded like a small war was going on.

As Hamblin and Mulder surveyed the scene of devastation below them, they realized that throughout the entire action, they had not been on the receiving end of any return fire. The two snipers were in total control of the situation and there was nothing the enemy could do about it. There was no opportunity for them to locate the snipers and set up to take them on without getting killed first. The two marines had cover of the entire area. They had longer-range weapons, and crazed fanatics with little training in marksmanship were no match for the skill and discipline of Marine Corps snipers.

While Hamblin and Mulder were in control of what was in front of them, they had no control over what was happening on their flanks. Regular Marine Corps units were engaging well-armed Iraqis. Bullets were flying. Some flew right over the snipers' heads and there was danger that they might become collateral damage. One of the snipers from the Marine Corps Scout-Sniper Platoon had already been injured. Marine Sergeant Aaron Wintterle was manning a vehicle checkpoint with one of the line companies when an Iraqi suicide vehicle approached. Wintterle had trained his Barrett .50 SASR on the vehicle when it exploded. A piece of shrapnel hit him in the face and broke his jaw. Immediately, his partner, Lance Corporal Jacob Heal, a new guy with the platoon who was still in training, grabbed the .50 Barrett SASR. He spotted an Iraqi who had been complicit in the suicide attack running back down the road. Heal took aim and blew out his chest.

As the day drew on, rounds came in from the sides. RPG explosions were as close as 55 yards (50 meters). But this was a distraction. Hamblin and Mulder's job was to secure the front. Every time they spotted an armed man, they took him out. They also saw armed trucks and fired on them, too.

They ran a simple system. Whoever spotted the target first called the shot. One would take the driver, the other any passenger at the same time.

"This was the great thing about having two sniper rifles there, since we could fire on two targets at the same time," said Hamblin.

In some cases, they were up against some serious weaponry, though nothing they could not handle.

"It was really weird to spot a pickup with a .50-caliber mounted in the back, then shoot the driver and gunner, then watch the truck just keep going like it's driven by a ghost," Hamblin said.

Hamblin and Mulder were up on the roof for three days straight. This followed three days of moving through Salmon Pak. Then they got four hours' sleep before returning to the roof for another three days. They were running on pure adrenaline, taking it in turns—one hour on, one hour off—to watch for the enemy. News of their deadly exploits spread. Any Iraqi venturing to their area would pull off his white T-shirt and wave it like a flag of truce until he got safely out of the killing zone. Then he would put it back on again.

The body count continued to climb. From that one position, Hamblin killed 17, Mulder 15. But soon no one else wanted to die for Saddam Hussein. While Hamblin and Mulder were at the Al Rashid Military Complex, effective resistance collapsed. The two snipers moved on into Baghdad proper with 3/7. As they pushed toward the city center, they could see vehicles on side streets that had been taken out the day before. Some were still smoldering, with rounds gently cooking off. They also ran into sporadic firing, both small arms and RPGs, but they swept this aside and pressed on toward their final destination, the Olympic Stadium. By then, thousands of cheering Iraqis had taken to the streets to welcome them. But even when they took up positions in the Olympic Stadium, they took incoming rounds, making it clear from the beginning that it would take years to pacify Baghdad.

For two weeks they continued their mission of surveillance and target acquisition missions before they pulled out to a permanent base camp. But Hamblin and Mulder would never again find such a target-rich environment as that at the Al Rashid gate.

In Iraq, the British established an outpost at Cimic House in Al Amarah, 150 miles (240 kilometers) north of Basra. Cimic stood for Civil and Military Cooperation, the British Army's term for reconstruction projects. It sat in the fork of the river between the Tigris and one of its tributaries, making it an easy place to defend. The compound there was 110 x 220 yards (100 x 200 meters). The main road passed its eastern boundary, which was a defended by a reinforced wall six feet high. The front gates were two sheet metal doors. To reach them from the road, vehicles had to weave their way through a series of 50-meter chicanes, a precaution against suicide bombers.

Sergeant Dan Mills was commander of the sniper platoon of the 1st Battalion, Princess of Wales's Royal Regiment (PWRR) when Y Company took over there in April 2004, a year after the country had fallen to coalition forces. The snipers set up on the flat roof of Cimic house. It had a three-foot wall around it, which gave them some cover, and a 360-degree view over the city. It was, Sergeant Mills said, an "ideal location—a sniper's Shangri-la."

Having formerly been the official residence of the governor of Maysan province, it was well appointed, with a garden and a swimming pool. And the snipers, considering themselves elite, banned anyone else from visiting the roof. Their only complaint was that the base was dry; there was no alcohol.

The snipers were to be the first line of defense. Their sangars— sand-bagged firing positions—in front and back gave them good arcs of fire, and the enemy would not be able to make it across the rivers easily without being shot. At the northern end of the compound were a water-treatment plant and a water tower that also provided good firing positions. The only weak point was the governor's two-story office, known as the Pink Palace. It was on the other side of the road from the main gates. That, too, was to be held.

However, at Al Amarad, the snipers found that they also had to go out on patrol. On their first foray into the city, they were attacked. Two men were badly wounded. The rest were rescued by a Warrior armored personnel carrier that carried them safely back to Cimic House.

Although the Coalition Provisional Authority did not want them to build up the defenses at Cimic House, the PWRR ignored that and built 10-foot antisniper screens around the compound with barbed wire along to the top to discourage suicide bombers. They removed the old Soviet weapons that littered the roof to make it look more Iraqi friendly and deployed NATO weapons instead. And that night they repositioned and rebuilt the sangars. The sniper team then set about learning every inch of the city's skyline and used laser range finders to draw up range cards so they could tell roughly how far away any target was.

During the day, they kept at least two sniper pairs on the roof, but others from the platoon liked to hang out up there as well, and they would lay out their kits beside them. The snipers were equipped with Accuracy International's L96A1, a bold-action sniper rifle with a stated range of 875 yards (800 meters). In practice, it was accurate enough to kill from up to 985 yards (900 meters) and give harassing fire up to 1,200 yards (1,100 meters). It took standard 7.62-mm ammunition, though snipers used Green Spot—that is, the first fifty thousand rounds from a new mold that are marked with a green spot that are reserved for the snipers; after that, the rounds get little dents or nicks that slightly affect the flight and are used only by infantry soldiers. The snipers carried German-made Schmidt & Bender sights that gave a magnification from 3 up to 12 times. At night, a Simrad night sight was clipped on top of it. Its large front aperture collected ambient light, converting it into shades of green. Spotters carried standard binoculars, larger range finders, Sofie thermal imagers, and World War II–vintage periscopes of World War II. The snipers were also protected by a couple of L7 General Purpose Machine Guns (GPMGs). The L7's 25-inch (63 centimeter) barrel gave it a range of 2,000 yards (1,800 meters), though by angling the barrel skyward, they could get the bullets to drop up to one-and-three-quarters miles (three kilometers).

The snipers were again inhibited by the rules of engagement. They were only allowed to engage those deemed to be clear threats. Meanwhile, the base came under mortar fire. The British responded by sending out teams at night to arrest the top men of the Office of the Martyr Sadr (OMS), the local branch of

Muqtada al-Sadr's Mahdi Army. This only made things worse. It was seen as an attack on the authority of Muqtada al-Sadr, and soon the whole city bristled with guns. They sealed off the city with the PWRR inside it, then the OMS demanded their prisoners back. Otherwise they would execute the hostages they held, which included a number of senior policemen. The snipers began amassing ammunition.

Then the news came that a man out on patrol had been hit by a round from a Dragunov. The OMS had a sniper. The British snipers on the roof of Cimic House began to give the patrol covering fire, engaging any muzzle flash they could see. The Cimic House came under fire, and the snipers spread out so that there was a pair on each of the four walls, as well as two in an elevated position above the stairwell and one in a newly reinforced sangar. They came under fire in a drive-by by a red Toyota that emptied two AK-47 magazines at them. They were also being mortared. At the same time, they were still trying to support the patrol. Eventually, some Warrior APCs got to them and they were extracted.

Then a badly damaged Warrior shuddered to a halt outside the main gate. It was driven by Private Johnson Beharry. The back was full of casualties, and the snipers kept the heads of the OMS down while they were unloaded. After being wounded twice in Iraq, Beharry won the Victoria Cross—Britain's highest decoration for valor—becoming the only living person to hold it.

Teenagers were soon swarming over Beharry's disabled Warrior. There was classified radio equipment in it. One of the snipers asked for permission to fire a warning shot to scare them off, but it was feared that if he hit the metalwork, the ricochet might injure someone. Instead, he put a shot through the glass of the driver's viewing optics, which scared off the scavengers. As darkness fell, they had to take out the Warrior's lights, which had been left off in the scramble to safety but were overloading the snipers' vision.

Through night-vision goggles at 275 yards (250 meters), one sniper took out the two headlights, three identification lights, and two indicators with one shot each. But there was nothing they could do when an American convoy on its way back to Kuwait was hit on the other side of town.

Mortar fire kept coming in, but by the time the snipers had plotted where they were coming from and loosed off a few shots, the enemy had moved on. But in the early morning, they spotted a heat signature through a Sofie thermal imager. By then, most of the snipers were sleeping and only four were left on duty. Through their Simrad night sights they could see a truck moving up with its lights off. Men with AK-47s slung over their shoulders got out and began unloading an 82-mm mortar. They were 600 yards (550 meters) away and in direct line of sight, plainly believing that they could not be seen in the darkness.

There were too many of them to be taken down by sniper fire. So they put down their L96s and picked up machine guns. One of them dropped an illumination round in the 52-mm mortar tube. When the OMS mortar team found themselves bathed in light, the snipers opened up with automatic fire. Sergeant Mills found his GPMG jammed, so he threw it aside and picked up a Minimi light machine gun. Two 82-mm rounds fell harmlessly in the river, but the men who had fired them were cut down. Three men dropped the rounds they were carrying and fled. One stopped after about 55 yards (50 meters) and turned and fired. This made him a legitimate target. He, too, was cut down. As more illumination rounds went, they could see the other two disappear into a hut 110 yards (100 meters) farther on. From what the snipers could see, there was no other way out.

A few minutes later, the two men came out again and made a run for a car. They reached it and opened the front doors. Then they made the mistake of raising their AKs and loosing off a few shots in the direction of Cimic House. This invited machine gun fire that tore the car to pieces. There were more men in the hut. They appeared in the doorway, armed. More bursts of machine gun fire were loosed and they suffered a similar fate. The rest of the mortar crew trapped in the hut had to play a waiting game. But they were up against snipers who were used to waiting days to get the right shot. Occasionally, they would put a round through the window to remind the OMS they were still there, and they shot up the mortar tube in case anyone else thought of using it. But this did not stop incoming mortars. More than 500 were fired at Cimic House in the first 10 days of May. The snipers replied by taking potshots at any OMS who showed himself.

On May 8, the British planned a major offensive to take back control of Al Amarad. It was to be supported by two US AC130 Spectre gunships. The snipers' role was to go out into the town and position themselves to take out any reinforcements that the OMS may call up from their stronghold in the Aj Dayya estate. They left the compound and infiltrated the town down back alleys. From backyards, they would scale selected houses and position themselves on the roofs, giving them a good view across the Tigris to the estate.

As the armored column entered the city, the OMS opened up with RPGs and small-arms fire. The tanks responded with fire from their chain guns, while infantrymen dismounted from their APCs and the AC130s circled above. On the Aj Dayya estate, armed men jumped into cars to join the fight. The snipers simply put bullets in the cars' tires. Then they radioed in the coordinates of a line of truck-mounted mortar tubes the OMS had set up for the gunships to deal with. Even though they were supposed to be covert, one of the snipers, Chris Mulrine, who was half-American, could not resist jumping to his feet and whooping when he saw the Spectres take out the mortars.

Then the British column stormed the OMS headquarters, killing more in a furious firefight. Inside they found a huge cache of weapons. Although the battle was won, the snipers stayed on the roof for the rest of the day in case a counterattack came from the Aj Dayya estate. But they were made to feel welcome. The owner of the house had heard the sniper whooping and came up to offer them some Arabic coffee. His father had lived in Britain and had served in the Royal Air Force. He let them use the bathroom and watch TV in the air-conditioned living room.

That night the British moved in to take over the town with little resistance. However, a muzzle flash was spotted at the window of a school house. In reply, a tank put a shell through it. The body of an OMS sniper was found in the ruins. With him he had a Dragunov sniper rifle.

Although the British had won a major battle against the OMS, now foreign fighters trained in Iran began to arrive in the city. When the decision was made to send out patrols in lightly armored Snatch Land Rovers again, the snipers returned to the roof of Cimic House to give them any covering fire they could, and they made a wager on how many minutes it would take before one of them was hit. The highest bet was 31 minutes, the lowest 11. The patrol was hit after just eight minutes.

Trouble brewed when the Coalition Provisional Authority's US bodyguards tried to prevent Y Company from using their showers. The British snipers ignored this. But when the confrontation came between one of them and the biggest of the bodyguards, it turned out that the American was an ex-US Marine Corps sniper. Instead of fighting, they ended up discussing the relative merits of various sniper rifles. Being a sniper transcended any national differences. Two other bodyguards had also been snipers. Consequently, they were invited up to the roof of Cimic House. While the Americans were intrigued by the standard British SA80 rifle, they brought with them a collection of captured weapons including a Dragunov sniper rifle and an AK-47 fitted with US telescopic sights. They managed to take out an OMS man who regularly loosed off an RPG. The reserved Brits did not go for the air-pumping and high-fiving that followed. However, they were impressed by the footage they were shown of the American snipers in action. In return for allowing them to shoot from the roof, the Americans ordered US equipment for the British snipers.

Mortars still rained down and the snipers went out on patrols that inevitably ended in firefights. They were then told that they were not to engage the enemy without permission. They decided to ignore this, as it was a sniper's job to engage any legitimate target they came across. This caused difficulties with their officers. But then it came down the chain of command that the rules of engagement had been changed. The snipers were then allowed to take out enemy spotters who were directing RPG and mortar fire, even if they were unarmed.

When mortar rounds next started falling, they spotted an Iraqi with binoculars and a radio who was plainly relaying where they were landing. He was 660 yards (600 meters) away. He got a round through the ribcage. After that, the OMS spotters were a little more cautious, and more of their mortars missed their target. So they simply fired more mortars, taking the scatter-gun approach.

The sniper platoon was out on patrol with two training ser-geants when they came under fire from two Dushkas, or DShK M1938s—World War II–vintage Soviet-made heavy antiaircraft machine guns that fire 12.7 x 108-mm rounds. The one to the left was on top of a house adjoining a mosque around 220 yards (200 meters) away. The one on the rooftop to the right was closer but had to fire at a more difficult angle.

As the patrol ran for cover, one of the snipers stopped in the middle of the road, took aim with his SA80, and before the OMS gunner could swing the heavy Dushka toward him, took the shooter out. AK-47s opened up, but they were quickly silenced with shots at their muzzle flashes. The second Dushka was taken out with a grenade. In the exchange, Sergeant Mills was hit, but the bullet had passed through the thick shoulder strap of his new US-issue rucksack, slowing it before it penetrated his body armor. He found the bullet in his shirt. It had left only a huge bruise. The training sergeants did not ask to come out on patrol again.

On their next patrol, they managed to creep up on an OMS sentry at the city hospital and have a chat. He told them that they had killed six and wounded eleven in the engagement. He also said that the commander of the British patrol had been killed, but he hadn't. Sergeant Mills knew because he had been right there with them.

They felt they were getting on top of the situation when they managed to capture a three-man mortar team who were relaxing after they came back from the firing line. Under interrogation they gave the names and addresses of their commanders. But before they could be arrested, Muqtada al-Sadr called a cease-fire. Soon after, power was transferred to a provisional Iraqi government.

But that was not the end of the trouble in Al Amarah. After a month of relative peace when they fired just a few mortars a week, the Mahdi Army took over all the police stations in the city, ousting the official police force, who were seen as being pro-Coalition. Patrols came under heavy fire again, and the snipers returned to their rooftop post. Sadr had put $200 on the head of each coalition soldier, and the whole town was now against them. The OMS now had their own snipers on the rooftops. Meanwhile, heavy barrages of mortars rained down again. A final convoy of Warriors, packed with food and ammunition, made it through. It also dropped off body bags. Things were looking bad.

Some OMS men simply charged the compound. They were easy to pick off. Others hid behind old women and children. They presented more of a problem. The gunmen liked to take their human shields from refugee huts some 660 yards (600 meters) to the north. A sniper pair saw a 40-year-old man carrying an AK-47 into one of the mud huts. Then they saw a muzzle flash from the window, so it was clear he was a legitimate target. One lined up his sights on the door, the other on the window. After 30 seconds, when they were both ready, he put a round through the top corner of the window where he could see the mud wall at the back, so there was no danger of hitting anyone. But it spooked the gunman, and he came running out of the door holding a 12-year-old girl in front of him. The other sniper let him get about a meter from the door, then squeezed the trigger. The round hit the man in the neck. He stumbled. The girl struggled free. She was covered in his blood, but unharmed. The man made an attempt to staunch the blood, but within a minute he was dead.

Cimic House was again under siege, though patrols went out at night to harass the OMS's mortar positions. The snipers covered them from the roof, even saving their new commanding officer who had unwisely gone out on patrol. He then gave permission for them to take down a tree that was blocking their view to the south.

By then the houses nearest the compound had been evacuated. The OMS who had been stupid enough to rush the compound had now been culled. Those who followed hugged cover. Attacking in waves of around 30, they used diversionary tactics to get close enough to fire accurate shots at the rooftop.

They called in air support. But coalition planes could not drop bombs or even fire their cannon in such a densely populated area. However, low-flying jets made the OMS keep their heads down. They soon got used to it, though, and the snipers on the rooftop had to work overtime. They were the outpost's only effective defense, and the OMS knew it, targeting them with high-caliber mortar rounds.

Sergeant Mills was hit on the helmet by an enemy sniper round. They scanned the landscape below, but he was professional enough not to risk a second one.

To relieve Cimic House, the British sent in another armored column. By then, OMS was so strong that they would not be able to retake the town as before. Instead, they would attack the Aj Dayya estate in the hope of sapping the enemy's manpower. And this time, the sniper platoon was to stay on their rooftop in case there was a counterattack on Cimic House.

The column soon ran into serious trouble. In a 23-hour action in the city, it did little more than give the defenders of Cimic House respite. When it withdrew, they knew that it was unlikely they would see a supply column again.

The situation now grew desperate. News came in of British casualties all over southern Iraq. Worse, American forces that had moved against Muqtada al-Sadr in Nafar had suffered heavy casualties. In the fighting, they had damaged the mosque there. This was likely to inflame every Muslim in Al Amarah. The interpreters and all the other Iraqi employees of Cimic House moved out.

The rooftop came under renewed sniper fire. It was so intense that the British snipers gave up the usual drill of moving after every couple of shots. If they were lucky, they would get a couple of hours sleep during a lull; if not they would get a couple of minutes.

By mid-August, mortar rounds were coming in at over 100 a day, and they could no longer risk sending patrols out into the streets to attack the mortar crews. It began to take its toll. The satellite dish was put out of action, robbing them of TV and calls home. Next, the electricity and water went off. No one could wash, though there was bottled water to drink. There was no sanitation, and food supplies began to dwindle. As the temperature rose toward 140°F, the place stank.

Two more snipers turned up. It was said that they were from the Royal Marines, but it was clear from the look of one of them that he was not. Plainly he was with Special Forces. He was carrying a large bag with him, and in it was a .50-caliber Barrett. It was clear why this sniper team had been brought in. The L96 had a range of 1,100 yards (1,000 meters), but the major concentration of the OMS was at 1,320 yards (1,200 meters), and their headquarters was at 1,860 yards (1,700 meters). The Barrett would bring them within range.

That afternoon they saw an OMS commander who was standing on a rooftop, orchestrating an attack from the north. He was over 1,750 yards (1,600 meters) away. A round from the Barrett hit the AK-47 he had slung across his chest. It exploded and the man was blown off the roof.

The incoming sniper pair used the Barrett for 12 hours, then turned in. But they left the gun with the PWRR snipers so they could use it. Mills and Mulrine tried it out. They found that there were three types of rounds: There were regular brass ball rounds; others had flash tips painted in red and yellow that exploded in a ball of fire, so you could see where you had hit at great distances; and then there were the gray ones, which were armor piercing. Mills and Mulrine put a score of these through an abandoned car. In the morning, the incoming specialist sniper told them not to use the gray-tipped rounds, as they were very expensive, but it was too late.

The Barrett kept the enemy gunmen away, but they could do nothing about the mortars, and crews set up on the far side of buildings and lobbed them over. One injured the chef and destroyed the kitchen, and they were growing short of ammunition.

Two 82-mm mortar rounds landed on the roof, but the snipers were protected behind sandbags, though one of their L96s was put out of action by shrapnel. The mortars had come from a small park in front of the OMS headquarters, but the Barrett could do nothing about them because there was a building in the way. The sniper carrying had influence, though. He had a direct connection to headquarters and called in an air strike. What's more, he was on first-name terms with the airborne air controller.

When the 82-mm mortar began to fire that night, the entire sniper platoon was on the roof to watch as two F-16s came in. They confirmed that there were no civilians in the streets nearby, and one of the F-16s dropped a 500-pound laser-guided bomb. It hit the park, destroying the mortar and killing its crew. A huge cheer went up from Cimic House.

But the next morning, the mortars started up as usual. The Barrett and its crew were ordered back to Baghdad. Intelligence warned of an imminent attack, and the entire sniper platoon was assembled on the roof. A crowd gathered below, and they were addressed by a man with a bullhorn. The snipers saw gunmen using the cover of the crowd to take up position. A single RPG was aimed at the rooftop. This was the signal for the rest to open fire. But they remained under cover, and at 550 yards (500 meters) they were out of range of most weapons. The snipers took out some of them, but three-quarters of an hour later they began to retreat. But then, as they were celebrating this minor victory, the order came for the PWRR to withdraw from Cimic House.

Everything they could not carry had to be left behind. Papers were burned and the building was wired for detonation. But as they had not lost a man to enemy fire, the men did not want to leave. Their feelings were conveyed to headquarters, and they were allowed to stay for the time being.

That night was curiously quiet, but the mortars started up the next morning. They continued throughout the night and through to the next. But at dawn they stopped. Then at noon, the mortars began again, accompanied by sniper fire. This was so intense that all the British snipers could do was keep their heads down.

Enemy reinforcements arrived by bus, and they attacked in force from all sides. Sniper rifles were abandoned for machine guns. It was clear that they meant to overrun Cimic House. They could not expect another armored column to ride to the rescue, and Spectre gunships were vulnerable to rocket attack and could not risk flying during the day. They were on their own.

The Recce Platoon joined the snipers on the roof and began taking on the enemy. They cut them down, but the enemy numbers continued to grow. As ammunition ran low, they got permission to use high-explosive rounds in the mortar they had previously used to fire illumination rounds.

The snipers had not been trained to fire a mortar. The first shot was 110 yards (100 meters) too long and 55 yards (50 meters) too wide. The second was 55 yards too short. The third was right on target. They shot off three more rounds, killing or dispersing a large group.

A Chinese rocket was aimed at Cimic House's back gate, and it was taken out by one of the Warrior's chain guns. A sniper spotted two gunmen trying to climb over the gate formerly used by Cimic House's civilian employees. He took off the first man, which alerted the men in the compound, who took out the second. But these were minor diversions. Elsewhere the attack continued. Then another sniper spotted an opportunity. Right in front of the attacking gunmen was a pile of jagged shale. One mortar round in the middle of it turned the stones into shrapnel. A few more sent the Mahdi Army running, and the men on the rooftop cut them down as they fled.

Then they heard more mortars coming in. But there were no explosions. When the smoke cleared, only the dead and the dying were left outside the compound. The rest had disappeared. They had won.

Headquarters ordered a resupply and the Royal Welch Fusiliers were sent in to replace them. While they waited for them to arrive, OMS snipers started up again. After they left, a cease-fire was signed and Cimic House—or what was left of it—was handed over to the Iraqis.

CHAPTER SIXTEEN

Afghanistan

Sergeant Stan Crowder was an infantryman in the 2nd Battalion of the 187th Infantry Regiment —the "Rakkasans." During 9/11, he was stationed at Fort Campbell, Kentucky, the home of the 101st Airborne Division—the Screaming Eagles—who, like the rest of the military, were mobilized immediately.

Crowder was a trained sniper. He was one of the few non–Green Berets to be allowed to take the Special Operations Target Interdiction Course—the Special Forces' Sniper School—at Fort Campbell. By mid-January, Sergeant Crowder was on his way to Kandahar in southern Afghanistan. From there he was posted to Khowst on the border of Pakistan's notorious Tribal Areas, where he was to undertake sniping missions with the Green Berets. On arrival there, they were to make a running landing from the Chinook. But there was a mix-up at the landing zone—the pilot was blinded by the dust kicked up by another helicopter and crashed.

Crowder was injured, and his right eye was rescued at a hospital in Uzbekistan, and he was sent to Germany to recuperate. He was then due to return to Kentucky but was eager to get back in the fight. When he heard that two military transports were heading back to Afghanistan from nearby Ramstein Air Base, he managed to talk his way on board, though he turned up in Kandahar with nothing but what he had on his back. He arrived just in time to join Operation Anaconda, an American-led operation to sweep the Taliban and al Qaeda out of the Shahi-Kot Valley.

Crowder was to be a spotter for Staff Sergeant Jason Carracino. Their mission was to support a rifle platoon. They were supposed to have landed at night, but the sun was up by the time they reached the landing zone, and when they made the 10-foot jump from the helicopter, they were already under fire. Carracino was still unpacking his M24 when Crowder spotted an Afghani with an AK-47 less than 165 yards (150 meters) away. Crowder dropped to a kneeling position and leveled his M4. The wind was gusting and difficult to judge. Crowder shot and hit the man, but he did not go down. He put the red dot on his chest a second time. Again he fired; again the target did not fall. So he aimed higher, right in the middle of the man's face. This time when he squeezed the trigger, the bullet hit the target at the base of the neck, downing the man for good. Carracino had been so busy checking his M24 that he did not even know Crowder had made his first kill.

The sniper team held back about 110 yards (100 meters) behind the rifle platoon. That way they would take out anyone who tried to close in on them and, if the opportunity presented itself, peel off and go hunting on their own. However, the rifle platoon was almost constantly under fire as they moved up to their blocking position, so the snipers had to stay on as security.

The al Qaeda–Taliban (AQT) had well-prepared positions. Their small-arms and mortar fire was also surprisingly accurate because they had made a of series markers with piles of rocks so they could accurately estimate the range. In some places, they had chiseled out the rock to take the base plate of a mortar. The tube could simply be slotted in and would be automatically on target.

The enemy had other heavy weapons. Rounds of Dushka chased the platoon sergeant to cover when he inexplicably stripped off his helmet and body armor to take a drink in a stream. An RPG landed at a corporal's feet. It did not go off, but sprayed him with shrapnel when it broke up.

When the rifle platoon reached its blocking position in a mountain pass, the sniper team got a request from a team of machine gunners in a post above. They were being shot at by an enemy sniper on a ridgeline some 990 yards (900 meters) away. However, he had only failed to hit his target because at that height the wind became even more erratic, gusting 15 to 20 miles per hour.

Carracino and Crowder climbed up to the machine gunners position and set up on the ridge. They scanned the ridgeline opposite but saw no one. They figured if the guy was a professional sniper, he would not risk being silhouetted on the top of the ridge but would hide himself in the rocks below. For two hours, they searched the ridge for the sniper. Eventually, they concluded that he must have gone. Just then, a bullet came whizzing overhead. The sniper was no longer shooting at the machine gunners. He was targeting them.

But that one shot had been a mistake. Even in the bright sunshine, Crowder had spotted the muzzle flash. He searched the area with the spotter scope. Soon he spotted the head and shoulder of a man with a gun who was partially obscured by a pile of rocks. Slowly he vectored Carracino in on him. The enemy sniper was directly in front of them at a slight elevation. Carracino confirmed that he could see him and was dialing in the range and taking aim. The problem now was the wind.

Crowder asked the machine gunners to give them a burst so they could follow the tracer. It was being blown all over the place, but Crowder worked out that if Carracino fired a little to the left in the slight calm between the heavy gusts, he should be right on him.

The first shot missed the enemy sniper's shoulder by just 3 inches (7.6 centimeters). Crowder gave Carracino a slight correction to the left. The second round hit the sniper in the stomach and he disappeared. Crowder was worried. The shot would have killed the man, but not right away. He might still be in condition to fire back.

While the machine gunners were congratulating the snipers on their shooting, Carracino and Crowder kept their eyes on the enemy sniper's position. After a few minutes, the wounded man pulled himself to his feet. He was weak but still armed and dangerous. Carracino shot again. The bullet ricocheted off the rocks in front of the gunman. A fourth shot hit him in the chest and he went down for good.

The range, they worked out, was 816 yards (746 meters). With a 7.62-mm round, that was very good shooting at that altitude.

Canadian snipers came into their own in Afghanistan. A team of five snipers from the 3rd Battalion of the Princess Patricia's Canadian Light Infantry (PPCLI) fought alongside the US Army's "Rakkasan" Brigade of the 187th Infantry Regiment for nine days during Operation Anaconda. After weeks of precision air attacks, it was the first big ground offensive in the war on terror.

In the early hours of March 3, 2002, the Canadian snipers under Master Corporal Graham "Rags" Ragsdale assembled on Bagram Airfield. Born in Kincarding, Ontario, in 1969, he joined the Canadian Forces after graduating from secondary school and became a paratrooper with 2 Commando of the now-disbanded Canadian Airborne Regiment, Special Service Force. There he gained qualifications in reconnaissance, communications, mountain operations, and sniping. After leaving the military to attend university, he rejoined and was posted to 3 PPCLI where he gained the mortarman, leadership, jumpmaster, freefall parachute instructor, unarmed combat instructor, British pathfinder, and sniper instructor qualifications. In 2000, he completed a tour of duty in former Yugoslavia with NATO's Stabilization Force (SFOR).

Then he was given the command role of battalion master sniper in charge of the sniper group and was deployed to Afghanistan.

His men were graduates of the Canadian Army's grueling sniper course that awards passing grades to only three or four out of a dozen recruits. After spending a month doing guard duty at Kandahar Airfield, they were raring to go. They had been specifically requested to join this US-led mission, the first to use conventional troops rather than Special Forces.

"We were in the right place at the right time and lucky enough to do it," said Master Corporal Arron Perry.

Born in Moncton, New Brunswick, Perry joined the army reserves at the age of 17. By the time he landed in Afghanistan, he was 30 and had served one tour in Croatia and two more in Bosnia. Before he became a sniper, he had served as a paratrooper and an instructor in unarmed combat. A massive man, he was a tireless weightlifter and moonlighted as a nightclub bouncer in downtown Edmonton. His superiors found him intimidating, and he had little regard for authority. Just weeks before deploying, his regimental sergeant major complained—in writing—that Perry had "an attitude problem… [that] has gone unchecked for a long period of time."

In Afghanistan, he was one of a team of three men who carried a McMillan TAC-50 tactical rifle. Perry was the principal shooter. Ragsdale was his spotter, while Corporal Dennis Easton provided security, standing guard behind them and being the eyes in the back of their heads.

The sharpshooter with the second team of snipers was 26-year-old Corporal Rob Furlong. He had been in training to be a sniper since he was a child on the East Coast. He and his friends would lay out a rotting fish and try shooting the flies it attracted out of the air with their pellet guns. Although naturally right-handed, Furlong taught himself to fire left-handed. When he took his sniper course in 2001, he did all his target shooting left-handed and even came to prefer shooting that way.

His spotter on Operation Anaconda was Master Corporal Tim McMeekin, a tall, solidly built soldier from Manitoba who had been seconded into the unit immediately before they deployed to Afghanistan. An American, Sergeant Zevon Durham, had been brought in as security.

Each three-man team had one bold-action TAC-50 sniper rifle, five-round magazines, one 203-mm grenade launcher, and three rifles—standard Canadian C7s, a variant of the M16 made by Diemaco/Colt Canada. With all this heavy equipment to carry, the snipers operated with flak jackets or helmets.

The Chinook carrying Perry, Ragsdale, and Easton took off first, heading for the mountains of western Afghanistan. They landed before dawn, but the landing zone had not been well chosen. Within minutes, enemy fighters opened up with small-arms and mortars. Perry, with his rifle on his back, ran for higher ground.

"Anyone who says they are not scared is crazy," he said. "But it was great."

In that first hour, Perry fired at target after target, some as far away as 1,650 yards (1,500 meters). The three of them, along with US Special Forces, rescued a company of the US 101st Airborne Division who had been pinned down by enemy fire.

"His shots were incredible," said Sergeant Major Mark Nielsen of the 101st Airborne. "'One shot, one kill.' If I had to send him a sweatshirt, that's what it would say."

The Chinook carrying Furlong, McMeekin, and Perry was a few minutes behind, and as their chopper approached the landing zone, the enemy opened fire. The pilot immediately turned the Chinook around and headed back to Bagram, leaving the others at the center of a hornet's nest on the ground. They returned a few hours later in force. By then the enemy had disappeared.

But it did not mean they had gone away. As dusk fell, mortars began raining down, and muzzle flashes lit up all around their position. Furlong hit the deck, but McMeekin kept his head up, grabbed the rifle, and started to engage targets.

"The guy was an absolute machine," said Furlong.

At the night drew on, they got an al Qaeda machine gun in their sights. Crawling up to a good position, they set up their TAC-50. It was a hugely powerful weapon.

"Firing it feels like someone slashing you on the back of the hockey helmet with a hockey stick," said Furlong.

When he hit his first target, an enemy gunman at a distance of 1,860 yards (1,700 meters), he said all that ran through his mind was finding his next target.

"All I thought of was September 11 and all those people who didn't have a chance, and the American reporter who was taken hostage, murdered, and his wife getting the videotape of the execution; that is my justification."

Ragsdale said that, when they first landed in the combat zone, "our spider senses were tingling … we didn't know what to expect." But the Canadians soon took control of the situation. The following morning, after coming under machine gun fire, Ragsdale managed to ease his gun barrel between two rocks and quickly located an enemy sniper hiding behind a small piece of corrugated steel that was propped up between two trees. He estimated the distance to be 1,860 yards (1,700 meters) and fired one shot through the metal, killing the man instantly.

Ragsdale remembered thinking afterward, "That's one less bullet that's gonna be coming at us, one less person we have to think about."

For the next nine days, the Canadian snipers became an all-star unit of sorts, shuttling from hill to hill, sometimes by foot, sometimes by four-wheeler, as they were needed. Their bullets destroyed enemy lookouts and protected American troops as they moved through the valley. Then, when all hell broke loose, they moved in to annihilate the source of fire. And along the way, they began breaking records.

First it was Perry hitting an enemy forward observer from 2,526 yards (2,310 meters), beating the previous record of 2,500 yards (2,286 meters) set by US Marine sniper Carlos Hathcock in Vietnam in 1967. The Canadian sniper was at an altitude of 8,500 feet (2,590 meters) and the target, across a valley, was at 9,000 feet (2,745 meters). This gave him the advantage. A bullet will travel farther and faster at high altitudes because the air is thinner.

The record lasted only one day. The following afternoon, Furlong saw three men lugging weapons up to an al Qaeda mortar nest high in the mountains. McMeekin spotted the same trio though his Vector, a binocular-like device that uses a laser to pinpoint a target thousands of meters away. In a low whisper they discussed tactics and agreed that they should take out the biggest threat first. In this case it was the man in the middle. He was carrying an RPK machine gun. According to McMeekin's Vector, he was 2,657 yards (2,430 meters) away—that's just over one-and-a-half miles. It took four long seconds for Furlong's bullet to reach its target.

Furlong adjusted the elevation knob on his scope, raising the barrel of the gun with each turn. The farther away the target, the higher the barrel needs to point. This was routine. Furlong had practiced this a thousand times back at the base in Edmonton, though no one had been taught to shoot this far. Adjustments had to be made for the wind. If it is blowing to the left, the sniper aims slightly right. Again, the effect is less at high altitudes where the air is thinner. A sniper and his spotter will discuss these factors like a golfer and his caddie lining up a long putt.

"You can teach a certain amount of it," said Furlong. "But there is a large percentage that you must have naturally. A good shooter is born. You can't teach someone to be a good shot if they don't naturally have it."

Furlong stared through the scope with his left finger tickling the trigger. Behind him, McMeekin gazed through his Vector, re-confirming the precise distance one last time.

"Stand by," Furlong said. Then he squeezed the trigger.

The first shot missed, but did not alert the target. He reloaded. A second round missed too, but not by much. It pierced the man's backpack. Still he went on about his business.

"They had no fear," Furlong said. "They didn't run. I guess they've just been engaged so many times."

Furlong knew exactly why that second shot missed. He had squeezed the trigger slightly to one side instead of following a perfectly straight line. Even a fraction of a millimeter can make a huge difference over that distance—in this case, the difference between a man's backpack and his heart. This time, after he had reloaded and lined up his rifle for a third try, he took a moment to check that his grip was flawless.

"Stand by," Furlong said again. Another loud pop echoed through the valley and a .50-caliber shell—which is rocket-shaped and almost as long as a beer bottle—sliced through the Afghan sky. Four seconds later, it hit the man square in the torso and ripped apart his insides.

Between them, the Canadian snipers chalked up 20 kills. The US commanders who they were with nominated all five for Bronze Stars. The Canadian commander in Afghanistan, Lieutenant Colonel Pat Stogran, was on the runway at Bagram to congratulate them when they got back. But all they wanted were showers and a phone call home. They had had neither since they had left home over a month before. The days of crawling and shooting, and long hours waiting in cover left the Canadian snipers exhausted.

"You don't realize what you've done to your body and how tired you are till it's all done. I think we slept 14 or 15 hours when we got back," said Furlong. His clothes were so dirty that he threw them in the garbage.

"They had been on for so long they kinda stood up on their own," he said.

Lieutenant Justin Overbaugh, of the American scout platoon to which the Canadian snipers were attached, said it was a pleasure to work with them.

"Their professionalism was amazing," he said. "The Canadians were a very large asset to the mission. I would have loved to have 12 Canadian sniper teams out there. I'd have no problems fighting alongside of them again."

He said the Canadian snipers' equipment was far superior to the Americans'. Their rifles had longer range than the US weapons and better high-tech sights.

Ragsdale's sniper teams then went out on Operation Harpoon with 500 Canadian and 100 American troops. It was the largest Canadian offensive since the Korean War. Again they were praised, this time by the authorities in Ottawa.

"The sniper teams suppressed enemy mortars and heavy machine gun positions with deadly accuracy," said Vice Admiral Greg Maddison after Operation Harpoon ended. "Their skills are credited with likely having saved many allied lives."

However, when they returned from the field after five days, an officer pulled them aside, warning them that Perry was under investigation for allegedly desecrating an enemy corpse. It was said that he had cut off a dead man's finger, put a cigarette in the corpse's mouth, and stuck a sign on his lifeless chest that said "Fuck Terrorism." It was also alleged that he had defecated on a second body.

While the allegations were only leveled at Perry, they tarnished the whole outfit.

"Five days earlier I got off the plane and was met by the colonel who said, 'You guys are outstanding,'" Furlong said. "And then five days later you're told you're under investigation, so everything that happens before goes to shit. You can build a hundred bridges and rob a bank, but you'll never be known as a bridge builder."

Lieutenant Colonel Stogran called in the National Investigation Service (NIS), the major crimes unit of the Military Police. Under heavily armed guard, investigators went to the Shahi-kot Valley to exhume the corpse at the center of the case. They took photographs, made notes, and collected DNA. They also found the sign that said "Fuck Terrorism."

Ragsdale was stripped of his command. Perry's tent was searched and a knife seized. Then a Canadian chaplain claimed that Perry swore at him in a threatening manner and had him arrested for "conduct unbecoming." Three weeks after returning as a hero from the Shahi-kot Valley, Perry was on a plane back to Canada in disgrace. He was bitter.

"From day one, we're taught to trust," he says. "Loyalty, loyalty, loyalty. Then all of a sudden, you're abandoned and dropped."

Two days after Perry left camp, an American general arrived at Kandahar Airfield to distribute Bronze Stars. With him he had five medals reserved for the snipers. They remained unawarded. The night before the awards ceremony, Canadian military officials in Ottawa asked the US to put the decorations on hold while the investigation was going on.

"They represented Canada's best," said Sergeant Major Nielsen. "It's a grave mistake to allow something like that to go unrecognized."

No more missions came their way either. American troops could not understand it. But those who had been on Operation Anaconda would visit to express their commiserations. They would also bring cans of tuna or packs of instant noodles to supplement the Canadians' standard army rations.

Nevertheless, news of Furlong's record-breaking shot leaked out. He agreed to give a few interviews, provided his name was not mentioned. Meanwhile, back in Canada, Perry was the star of his own media circus. He denied all the charges leveled at him and insisted that he had done nothing wrong on in the Shahi-kot Valley. It was a case of battlefield humor gone wrong. He had tossed another soldier a Tootsie Roll sealed in a plastic bag, saying that it was a severed finger from one of the bodies. It seems that another soldier overheard this and misinterpreted it. As for the cigarette and the "Fuck Terrorism" sign, Perry says hundreds of people, officers included, walked by that corpse, but nobody felt the need to do anything about it.

"I know for a fact that I didn't do it," he says of the sign. "And to the best of my knowledge, no one from the Canadian sniper detachment did it." However, he did admit that he supported the sign's sentiment.

When Furlong returned to Canada, he was harassed by NIS investigators. It was clear that they had a single agenda—to get rid of Perry, who had a reputation for insubordination. Suspended on full pay, he was not allowed even to visit the base and returned to working as a doorman. After 10 months, the NIS finally admitted that they did not have enough evidence against Perry to press charges. They did not discover who had printed the sign, no finger was found, and the DNA from the corpse did not match any found on Perry's knife.

The five snipers were then awarded the honor of being mentioned in dispatches, and the American ambassador to Canada pinned on their Bronze Stars at a ceremony in Edmonton. But this was no happy ending. Furlong and Perry left the army, while Ragsdale fell into depression over his demotion and was diagnosed as suffering from posttraumatic stress disorder.

While the investigation dragged on, news of the 2,657-yard (2,430-meter) kill circulated on the Internet, though it was mistakenly attributed to Perry.

"I hope the record stands forever," wrote one American blogger.

But then in November 2009, 35-year-old Corporal Craig Harrison of the British Household Cavalry recorded a confirmed sniper kill of 2,707 yards (2,475 meters) when he took out two Taliban machine gunners south of Musa Qala in Helmand Province, Afghanistan. This was nearly 1,000 yards (914 meters) beyond the effective range of his British-built Accuracy International L115A3 Long Range Rifle, which was chambered in .338 Lapua Magnum. The British Army's most powerful sniper weapon, it is designed to be effective at up to 1,640 yards (1,500 meters) and is supposedly only capable of "harassing fire" beyond that range.

Tom Irwin, a director of Accuracy International, said, "It is still fairly accurate beyond 1,500 meters, but at that distance luck plays as much of a part as anything."

"Conditions were perfect, no wind, mild weather, clear visibility," Harrison said. He was also helped by the thin air. Musa Qala is 1,140 yards (1,043 meters) above sea level.

Corporal Harrison dropped the two Taliban machine gunners with successive shots when he and his colleagues were in open-topped Jackal 4x4 vehicles providing cover for an Afghan national army patrol south of Musa Qala in November 2009. When the Afghan soldiers and Harrison's troop commander came under enemy fire, the sniper, whose vehicle was farther back on a ridge, trained his sights on a Taliban compound in the distance.

"We saw two insurgents running through a courtyard, one in a black dishdasha, one in green," said Harrison. "They came forward carrying a PKM machine gun, set it up, and opened fire on the commander's wagon. I rested the bipod of my weapon on a compound wall and aimed for the gunner firing the machine gun. The driver of my Jackal, Trooper Cliff O'Farrell, spotted for me, providing all the information needed for the shot, which was at the extreme range of the weapon."

He made nine practice shots to get the range. But his first shot on target was a kill shot.

"The first round hit a machine gunner in the stomach and killed him outright. He went straight down and didn't move," he said. "The second insurgent grabbed the weapon and turned as my second shot hit him in the side. He went down, too. They were both dead." A third shot disabled the gun. "It was just unlucky for the Taliban that conditions were so good and we could see them so clearly."

At such an extreme range it took the 8.89-mm bullets almost three seconds to reach their target after leaving the barrel at nearly three times the speed of sound. The distance to Harrison's targets was measured by a GPS system to be 2,707 yards (2,475 meters).

In a remarkable tour of duty, Harrison cheated death a few weeks later when a Taliban bullet pierced his helmet but was deflected away from his skull. During the incident, his vehicle was hit 36 times by Taliban fire.

"One round hit my helmet behind the right ear and came out of the top," he said. "Two more rounds went through the strap across my chest. We were all very, very lucky not to get hurt."

He later broke both arms when his army vehicle was hit by a roadside bomb. Harrison was sent back to the UK for treatment, but insisted on returning to the front line after making a full recovery.

"I was lucky that my physical fitness levels were very high before my arms were fractured, and after six weeks in plaster I was still in pretty good shape," he said. "It hasn't affected my ability as a sniper."

Corporal Harrison discovered that he had set a new record only on his return to UK barracks six months later. The shot earned him the nickname the "Silent Assassin." In all, he killed twelve Taliban and wounded seven others.

Australian sniper Benjamin Roberts-Smith also distinguished himself in Afghanistan. First, he was awarded the Medal for Gallantry for an incident that took place in Oruzgan Province in central Afghanistan. As a Lance Corporal with Australia's SAS Regiment,

Roberts-Smith was employed as a patrol scout and sniper. On May 31, 2006, he was sent with a patrol to establish an observation post near the Chora Pass. Three days later, the post had become the focus of attention for the Anti-Coalition Militia force. They made repeated attempts to locate and surround the position. When they tried to outflank the observation post, Roberts-Smith and his partner moved out of their relatively secure position in order to locate and neutralize the militia and regain the initiative.

With the Militia halted on one flank, two more militiamen tried to attack the observation post from the other side. Roberts-Smith again moved out to neutralize them. He then realized that the forward edge of the observation post was not secure and made the decision to split the team, taking up an exposed position forward of the patrol so he could effectively employ his sniper weapon. Isolated in this precarious position, he saw a group of 16 militiamen advancing across open ground toward the observation post. Roberts-Smith then used his sniper rifle to stop their advance, even though he received very accurate small-arms fire from another group of militia to his flank. For 20 minutes, Roberts-Smith held this position without support, securing the position for his patrol and robbing the enemy of the initiative. He was eventually reinforced by his sniper partner, and together they continued to hold off the militia's advance for another 20 minutes until offensive air support arrived.

If that was not enough, four years later, he won the Victoria Cross, the highest award for gallantry in the British Commonwealth. On June 11, 2010, a troop of the Special Operations Task Group conducted a helicopter assault into the village of Tizak, Kandahar Province, to capture or kill a senior Taliban commander. But as soon as they got their feet on the ground, they came under machine gun and RPG fire from the high ground around them. Two Australians were wounded, and the rest of the troop was pinned down by fire from three machine guns in a fortified position on the high ground to the south of the village. Under the cover of close air support, suppressive small-arms, and machine gun fire, Roberts-Smith and his patrol maneuvered to within 77 yards (70 meters) of the enemy to neutralize the their machine gun positions and regain the initiative.

The patrol drew very heavy and sustained fire from the enemy position. Nevertheless Roberts-Smith and his patrol members fought their way forward until, at a range of just 44 yards (40 meters), the weight of fire prevented further progress. Roberts-Smith noticed an insurgent about to throw a grenade at his patrol, took him on, and killed him at point-blank range. With the members of his patrol still pinned down by the three enemy machine guns, he exposed his own position in order to draw fire away from his patrol, allowing them to bring fire to bear against the enemy. His actions enabled his patrol commander to throw a grenade and silence one of the machine guns. Seizing the initiative, Roberts-Smith stormed the enemy position with a total disregard for his own safety and killed the two remaining machine gunners.

"He just tore into the enemy," said one of Roberts-Smith's friends. "He is the epitome of the Spartan soldier. It was only a matter of time before he would demonstrate his true ability."

This act of valor enabled his patrol to break into the enemy position and to lift the weight of fire from the remainder of the troop, who had been pinned down by the machine guns. Seizing the fortified gun position, Roberts-Smith then took the initiative again and continued to assault the enemy. With another patrol member, he engaged and killed one more. His action enabled his troop to go on and clear the Taliban from the village of Tizak. After this victory, the rest of the Taliban in Shah Wali Kot District retreated from the area.

Meanwhile, two US Army Special Forces snipers were victorious in what may well be the most remarkable gunfight in US military history. Faced with a mass attack from the Taliban one night, the two Green Berets took on the enemy with night vision–equipped semi-automatic rifles fitted with suppressors that silenced their weapons and eliminated muzzle flashes. Although one American was killed in the shootout, they reportedly killed 75 Taliban with just 77 rounds.

Further Reading

Cabell, Craig, and Robert Brown. *Snipers: Profiles of the World's Deadliest Killers*. London: John Blake, 2005.

Cavallaro, Gina and Matt Larsen. *Sniper: American Single-Shot Warriors in Iraq and Afghanistan*. Guilford, CT: Lyons Press, 2010.

Coughlin, Jack, Casey Kuhlman, and Donald A. Davis. *Shooter: The Autobiography of a Top-Ranked Marine Sniper*. New York: St. Martin's Griffin, 2006.

Culbertson, John J. *13 Cent Killers: The 5th Marine Snipers in Vietnam*. New York: Presidio, 2003.

Culbertson, John J. *A Sniper in the Arizona: 2nd Battalion, 5th Marines in the Arizona Territory, 1967*. New York: Presidio, 1999.

Dougan, Andy. *Through the Crosshairs: A History of Snipers*. Cambridge, MA: Da Capo, 2006.

Gilbert, Adrian. *Sniper One on One: The World of Combat Sniping*. London: Sidgwick and Jackson, 1994.

Haskew, Michael E. *The Sniper at War: From the American Revolutionary War to the Present Day*. Staplehurst, UK: Spellmount, 2004.

Henderson, Charles. *Marine Sniper: 93 Confirmed Kills*. New York: Berkley Trade, 2001.

Henderson, Charles. *Silent Warrior: The Marine Sniper's Vietnam Story Continues*. New York: Berkley, 2003.

Kugler, Ed. *Dead Center: A Marine Sniper's Two-Year Odyssey in the Vietnam War*. New York: Ballantine, 1999.

Lanning, Michael Lee. *Inside the Crosshairs: Snipers in Vietnam*. New York: Ballantine, 1998.

LeBleu, Joe. *Long Rifle: A Sniper's Story in Iraq and Afghanistan*. Guilford, CT: Lyons Press, 2008.

Lilin, Nicolai. *Free Fall: A Sniper's Story from Chechnya*. Edinburgh, UK: Canongate, 2011.

Pegler, Martin. *Sniper: A History of the US Marksman*. Oxford, UK: Osprey, 2007.

Raab, J. Michael. *Every Day is Monday: U.S. Marine Snipers in Iraq*. Scout Writer, 2009.

Roberts, Craig, and Charles W. Sasser. *Crosshairs on the Kill Zone: American Combat Snipers, Vietnam Through Operation Iraqi Freedom*. New York: Pocket Star, 2004.

Roberts, Craig, and Charles W. Sasser. *One Shot One Kill: American Combat Snipers, World War II, Korea, Vietnam, Beirut*. New York: Pocket Books, 1990.

Roberts, Craig, and Charles W. Sasser. *The Walking Dead: A Marine's Story of Vietnam*. London: Grafton, 1989.

Senich, Peter R. *The Long-Range War: Sniping in Vietnam*. Boulder, CO: Paladin, 1994.

Stronge, Charles. *Kill Shot: The Deadliest Snipers of All Time*. Berkeley, CA: Ulysses, 2011.

Ward, Joseph T. *Dear Mom: A Sniper's Vietnam*. New York: Ballantine, 1991.

Wasdin, Howard E., and Stephen Templin. *SEAL Team Six: Memoirs of an Elite Navy SEAL Sniper*. New York: St. Martin's, 2011.

Other Ulysses Press Books

Warrior Elite: 31 Heroic Special-Ops Missions from the Raid on Son Tay to the Killing of Osama bin Laden

Nigel Cawthorne, $14.95

They are the strongest, best-trained, and most powerfully equipped soldiers in the world. The select few who overcome near-impossible odds. The special-ops forces. Presenting real-life stories that read like fictional thrillers, *Warrior Elite* recounts over two dozen of modern warfare's most riveting, dangerous, and infamous missions.

Canine Commandos: The Heroism, Devotion, and Sacrifice of Dogs in War

Nigel Cawthorne, $14.95

From the battlefields of WWI to the present day mountains of Afghanistan, dogs have been loyal companions and trusted compatriots to soldiers throughout history. Now the most exciting, heartwarming, and heroic stories are compiled in this incredible collection.

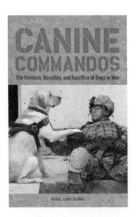

Kill Shot: The 15 Deadliest Snipers of All Time

Charles Stronge, $16.95

Profiling the 15 best military snipers of all time, this full-color book presents the most exciting real-life stories of excellence in duty during wartime. From mile-long hits in Afghanistan to confirmed kills deep in the jungle of Vietnam, *Kill Shot* gives all the details of the most amazing shooters.

Against Their Will: An Encyclopedia of Sadistic Kidnappers and their Innocent Victims

Nigel Cawthorne, $14.95

Delving into the minds of twisted criminals who hold young women in endless captivity and telling every excruciating detail of the brave survivors' stories, *Against Their Will* is the first comprehensive compendium to describe the most disturbing kidnappings of all time.

Serial Killers and Mass Murderers: Profiles of the World's Most Barbaric Criminals

Nigel Cawthorne, $14.95

In one chilling chapter after another, this book profiles a terrifying succession of homicidal maniacs. A fascinating investigation of the dark side, it takes readers inside the minds of the people who committed the world's most notorious and horrendous crimes.

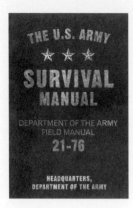

U.S. Army Survival Manual: Department of the Army Field Manual 21-76

Headquarters, Department of the Army, $13.95

Drawing on centuries of rigorous training and treacherous field testing, this field guide covers every imaginable scenario, from finding drinking water in the desert, stalking game in the arctic, and building a fire in the jungle to recognize signs of land when lost at sea.

To order these books call 800-377-2542 or 510-601-8301, fax 510-601-8307, e-mail ulysses@ulyssespress.com, or write to Ulysses Press, P.O. Box 3440, Berkeley, CA 94703. All retail orders are shipped free of charge. California residents must include sales tax. Allow two to three weeks for delivery.

About the Author

Nigel Cawthorne is known for his best-selling Sex Lives series, including *Sex Lives of the Kings and Queens of England* and *Sex Lives of the Roman Emperors*; the books are available in 23 languages. He is also the author of *Serial Killers and Mass Murderers* (Ulysses Press), *Warrior Elite* (Ulysses Press), *Strange Laws of Old England*, *Curious Cures of Old England*, and more than 60 other books.